Shifting Dynamics of Contention in the Digital Age

STUDIES IN MOBILE COMMUNICATION

Studies in Mobile Communication focuses on the social consequences of mobile communication in society.

Series Editors

Rich Ling, *Nanyang Technological University, Singapore*
Gerard Goggin, *University of Sydney, Australia*
Leopoldina Fortunati, *Università di Udine, Italy*

Haunting Hands: Mobile Practices and Loss
Kathleen M. Cumiskey and Larissa Hjorth

A Village Goes Mobile: Telephony, Mediation, and Social Change in Rural India
Sirpa Tenhunen

Negotiating Control: Organizations and Mobile Communication
Keri K. Stephens

Cultural Economies of Locative Media
Rowan Wilken

Transcendent Parenting: Raising Children in the Mobile Age
Sun Sun Lim

Shifting Dynamics of Contention in the Digital Age: Mobile Communication and Politics in China
Jun Liu

SHIFTING DYNAMICS OF CONTENTION IN THE DIGITAL AGE

Mobile Communication and Politics in China

Jun Liu

OXFORD
UNIVERSITY PRESS

OXFORD
UNIVERSITY PRESS

Oxford University Press is a department of the University of Oxford. It furthers
the University's objective of excellence in research, scholarship, and education
by publishing worldwide. Oxford is a registered trade mark of Oxford University
Press in the UK and certain other countries.

Published in the United States of America by Oxford University Press
198 Madison Avenue, New York, NY 10016, United States of America.

CIP data is on file at the Library of Congress
ISBN 978-0-19-088727-8 (pbk.)
ISBN 978-0-19-088726-1 (hbk.)

9 8 7 6 5 4 3 2 1

Paperback printed by Marquis, Canada
Hardback printed by Bridgeport National Bindery, Inc., United States of America

To Hui, Zhixi, and Zhixian

CONTENTS

ILLUSTRATIONS

FIGURES

TABLES

PREFACE

The idea of writing a monograph on mobile communication in contemporary China can be traced back to my thesis project, while I was a graduate
student in Xiamen University, on socio-political changes introduced by mobile technologies in the Chinese society in 2006. I chose mobile communication as my research interest, which was motivated by the enjoyment
and inspiration I got from reading Rich Ling's *The Mobile Connection: The
Cell Phone's Impact on Society* and Paul Levinson's *Cellphone: The Story of the
World's Most Mobile Medium*. As to my choice of the specific idea involving
mobile technology and contentious politics, it has its origin in the unexpected, "defiant" role of mobile phones that has been exemplified in a protest in Xiamen one year later in 2007, when public discontent about the local
government's decision to establish a petrochemical factory swelled into a
massive campaign initiated through the tool of *mobile-phone text messages*.
Text messages were not only used to demonstrate public anger but also
helped organize several gatherings of residents, totaling over 20,000, to
protest the decision. The phenomenon aroused my interest and made me
wonder what the political implications of mobile technology would be in
a country with the world's largest—and fastest-growing—mobile phone
users. Whether mobile-phone-facilitated movements could change the current authoritarian regime, whether they could advance people's capacities
of fighting for justice when faced with authorities, and enhance the overall
political participation of the citizenry?

These issues captivated me, taking me on a journey first to Copenhagen,
then to Stanford, then back to Copenhagen, and to Oxford. This project has
grown stronger in the course of the journey. Through it all, the often controversial role of (mobile) technology in political contention is becoming
clearer. In general, I hope the book will make the following four distinct
contributions, two theoretical and two empirical. I briefly present them as
follows.

The principal theoretical goal of this book is to advance a theoretical framework that integrates the current state of discussion on the Information and Communication Technologies (ICTs) and political contention across sociology and communication. The first two chapters contain reviews and discussions on the subject. The second theoretical goal concerns the politics of ICTs, and mobile technology in particular, in the authoritarian China. I hope to advance a theoretical model to interpret the embedding of mobile communication in China, which should take into consideration the specific contextual factors such as social network, media ecology, and repertoire of contention, among others. Along with the second theoretical goal is the empirical focus of the work. I want to give a comprehensive empirical analysis of contentious politics, mediated by mobile communication that has yet appeared in literature. Last but not least, along with the first theoretical goal, is the comparative and empirical perspective of the book. I justify and validate the broader application and implication of the theoretical framework in this book by having contentious cases from the United States, Egypt, and China in the last chapter. I hope this book will flesh out and deepen our understanding of technology-mediated political contention and, most importantly, human beings and their communications in and behind the technology.

No academic journey is ever possible if it was taken alone. I would like to first express my gratitude to four people who have significantly helped shape the content of this work. I have been very fortunate to have had Klaus Bruhn Jensen as an intellectual mentor and supportive colleague. I cannot thank him enough for his shrewd insights and unstinted encouragement over the past ten years. Rich Ling and his preeminent work on mobile communication offered me eye-opening suggestions one could have ever hoped for. Doug McAdam provided nuanced comments that drove me to focus on the strengthening of my argument substantially. Finally, a special debt of gratitude to Ralph Schroeder, who read an early version of the manuscript and inspired me to get to the dynamics of "subterranean sphere" cultivated by mobile communication.

In addition to these four, I want to thank Alexandra Segerberg and Rasmus Kleis Nielsen for their thought-provoking and conducive critiques of my efforts, which significantly added to the improvement of this work. Sid Tarrow and Peter van Aelst gave me concrete and insightful comments on the communication-centered theoretical framework. Ralph L. Rosnow offered comments on the discussion of rumors spread through mobile phones. Thanks to Rich Ling (again), Gerard Goggin, and Leopoldina Fortunati as the editors-in-chief, *Studies in Mobile Communication*, and the anonymous reviewers who gave me sharp yet impartial feedback. I want to thank all the interviewees, without whom I would have never accomplished this project. My thanks also go to Sarah Humphreville, Bronwyn Geyer, Hallie Stebbins, and Hannah Doyle and the people at the Oxford University Press. And thanks to Jingnan Zhou for her valuable linguistic suggestions. Any existing shortcomings of the book remain my responsibility alone.

I gratefully acknowledge all my friends and colleagues in the Department of Communication at the University of Copenhagen, including, but not limited to, Maja Horst, Stine Lomborg, Rasmus Helles, Jacob Ørmen, Andreas Lindegaard Gregersen, Taina Bucher, and Anne Mette Thorhauge, for creating the most supportive, motivating, and productive academic environment I've ever been associated with. I feel lucky to have been working with them, and I am constantly inspired by their thoughts.

This project was generously supported by funds provided by the Carlsberg Foundation (CF14-0385), Ragna Rask-Nielsen Grundforskningsfond, and the S. C. Van Fonden (1267, 1503). Chapter 3 integrates part of my articles "Digital Media, Cycle of Contention, and Sustainability of Environmental Activism" (*Mass Communication & Society*, 2016, 19(5), 604–625) and "Making Sense of Uses of Information and Communication Technologies as Contentious Repertoire" (*European Journal of Sociology/Archives Européennes de Sociologie*, in press), Chapter 4 incorporates part of my article "Mobile Phones, Social Ties, and Collective Action Mobilization in China" (*Acta Sociologica*, 2017, 60(3), 213–227).

Finally, I dedicate this book to my family from the very bottom of my heart. To my parents for their enduring support, trust, and encouragement. To Hui Zhao, my kids Zhixi Liu (who was born while this book was being written) and Zhixian Liu for making it all worthwhile. They are what keeps me from succumbing to feelings of inadequacy and ineptitude.

CHAPTER 1

Introduction

Movements in Communication

Society not only continues to exist . . . **by** communication, but it may fairly be said to exist . . . **in** communication. (Dewey, 2004, p. 4, emphasis in original)

THE DANGER OF "INVOLUTION"

The Zapatista movement,[1] "People Power II,"[2] the Nosamo movement,[3] the political turbulence in the Middle East since December 2010 (Howard & Hussain, 2013; Lynch, 2012), the Occupy Wall Street movement (Gleason, 2013; Nielsen, 2013), and the "Indignados" movement (Anduiza, Cristancho, & Sabucedo, 2014; Monterde & Postill, 2014) are among the many waves of political contention that swept across the globe over the past decades. These instances of political contention have stimulated a series of studies on Information and Communication Technologies (ICTs)

---

1. An indigenous uprising formed to disrupt the state and create a space for democracy, Mexico's Zapatista movement, commencing in 1994, has been considered as one of the first to exploit the internet to support a local struggle (Russell, 2005).
2. "People Power II" was a four-day political protest in the Philippines in 2001, in which both Short Message Service (SMS) and internet communication (e.g., online forums and email discussion groups) dramatically contributed to the swift organization of rallies that overthrew then President Joseph Estrada (Qiu, 2008a).
3. "A textbook example for the power of IT" (Hachigian & Wu, 2003, p. 68), the Nosamo movement in South Korea entailed internet-based organizations and text messaging that brought thousands of former President Roh Moo-hyun's supporters to campaign rallies in 2000.

and contentious collective action—such as revolutions, riots, protests, and demonstrations—to thrive appreciably as an exciting, relevant but highly fragmented and debated field (e.g., Bennett & Segerberg, 2012, 2013; Bimber, Flanagin, & Stohl, 2005; Cammaerts, Mattoni, & McCurdy, 2013; Castells, 2012; Diani, 2000; Downing, 2008; Earl & Kimport, 2011; Gladwell, 2010; Van Stekelenburg, Roggeband, & Klandermans, 2013; for general discussions, see Earl, Hunt, & Garrett, 2014; Garrett, 2006; Rodríguez, Ferron, & Shamas, 2014). On the one hand, interest in this field endures, and interrogation of and deliberations about the role of ICTs in political activism and social movements proliferate. On the other hand, the existing literature from a wide range of disciplines such as sociology, political science, and communication studies still rarely achieves a consistent framework for the analysis of how ICTs may transform the arena of contentious collective action. Notably, confined within disciplinary boundaries, very little of the existing research is able to cross different disciplines to initiate reciprocal dialogue.[4] As Garrett (2006, p. 203) convincingly summarized in a review of literature on ICTs and protests 14 years ago, "[f]ew works are commonly cited across the field, and most are known only within the confines of their discipline [of sociology, political science, or communication]." In a recent discussion, Earl and Garrett (2017, p. 480) maintained that the field "would be as problematic as social movement scholars continuing to ignore political communication research." Likewise, taking scholarship on digital media and youth engagement as an example, Maher and Earl (2017, p. 59) identify a similar issue, i.e., studies are hampered by "an astounding neglect for existing social movements research." With "greater self-absorption, isolationism, internal development, and parochialism . . . at the expense of conceptual innovation, bold experiment[ation], and open change," such an introversive tendency, or what Lee (2016, pp. 657–658) helpfully describes as "an involutionary process," risks the danger of intellectual isolation and hinders a comprehensive understanding of ICTs and contentious collective action from a transdisciplinary perspective.

This book joins an ongoing effort to improve the interdisciplinary understanding of ICTs and contentious collective action (e.g., Anduiza, Jensen, & Jorba, 2012; Bennett & Segerberg, 2012, 2013; Bimber, Flanagin, & Stohl, 2012; Bimber et al., 2005; Earl & Kimport, 2011; Papacharissi, 2015). To bridge dispersed knowledge and stimulate cross-field learning, it outlines a *communication-centered* framework that articulates the intricate relationship between technology, communication, and contention. Further, it prods us

4. But, see, Cammaerts, 2012; Della Porta, 2011; Earl et al., 2014; Garrett, 2006.

to engage more critically with existing theories on digital-communication technologies and movements. More specifically, the present study suggests communication as a key process that distributes political opportunities, maneuvers mobilizing structures, shapes cultural framing, articulates contested meanings, and facilitates relational dynamics among these interrelated factors in contentious collection action (McAdam, McCarthy, & Zald, 1996a; McAdam, Tarrow, & Tilly, 2001). By contentious collective action, or contentious politics (Tilly & Tarrow, 2006), I follow Tarrow's definition, i.e., nonroutine forms of collective action that bring "ordinary people into confrontation with opponents, elites, or authorities" in diverse forms—"brief or sustained, institutionalized or disruptive, humdrum or dramatic" (2011, pp. 7–8; also see McAdam, Tarrow, & Tilly, 2009). This inclusive definition allows us to observe a broad spectrum of contentious activities in society. It is necessary to bear in mind that this book is by no means a polemic against theoretical and methodological pluralism in the study of contentious politics, e.g., the political process model (McAdam, 1982), the network approach (Diani & McAdam, 2003), or the cultural approach (e.g., Baumgarten, Daphi, & Ullrich, 2014; Goodwin, Jasper, & Polletta, 2009; Johnston & Klandermans, 1995). Rather, with an eye to the critical significance of the communication dimension of contentious collective action, as I will present shortly, this book casts new analytic light on areas and aspects of the dynamics of contention and movements that other conceptual schemes or perspectives have glossed over and, most importantly, which enables us to forward cross-disciplinary dialogue and learning about the topic.

In addition to the theoretical endeavor, this book focuses on mobile communication technology,[5] one of the most common examples of ICTs nowadays in the world (e.g., Castells, Fernandez-Ardevol, Qiu, & Sey, 2007; Ling, 2004, 2008), as the example and offers an empirical analysis of its influence on political contention. More specifically, by employing the theoretical framework in the discussion of mobile communication and contentious collective action in contemporary China,[6] the book presents

5. I use the terms "the mobile phone," "mobile communication technology," "mobile handset," "the mobile," "mobile tech," and "mobile device" in this book interchangeably to refer to mobile-based devices. This does not usually include tablet devices like the iPad.

6. The term "China" in this book refers to "the Chinese mainland" unless otherwise specified. Throughout this book, I use *pinyin*, China's official phonetic system, to romanize Chinese names, save in a few instances (such as Chin-Chuan Lee) where the older Wade-Giles system is better known. Chinese names appear with the family name preceding the given name, except for a few Chinese authors who use the Western style of putting the family name last.

a nuanced portrayal of an emerging dynamics of contention—both its strengths and limitations—through the embedding of mobile communication into Chinese society and politics, despite the presence of increasingly repressive control of digital-communication technologies by the authorities (e.g., King, Pan, & Roberts, 2013b, 2014). Mobile communication in this book subsequently refers to the articulation, interaction, and collaboration that have been carried out using mobile-based technologies, both feature phones and smart phones. Finally, at the end of this book, we further explore the application of the theoretical framework in a comparative study with examples from other parts of the world, including the Freedom Summer of 1964 in the United States and the Egyptian Uprising in 2011, in order to offer a brief generalization of changes ICTs have introduced to contentious collective action. By consolidating and synthesizing relevant concepts and theories from different disciplines and by applying the framework to some concrete examples, the book fertilizes the field of ICTs and contentious collective action.

The Introduction takes up four topics. It first lays out a general, communication-based perspective on the scholarship of contentious politics and social movements to illustrate that communication, a long-existing but *implicit* focus within current scholarship, has always been a key issue in political contention. Such a sketch from the sociology of movements regarding the ways communication can be found central to the dynamics of contention in literature further aims to overcome the deficiency that, as Pfau identifies it (2008, p. 599), "communication scholars often lack a general knowledge about . . . facets of communication [other] than their own specialty or of allied disciplines." Second, to convincingly pinpoint the changes and transformations that are afforded by ICTs, if any, to contentious collective action in the digital age, I take the view that research should be *explicitly* focused on communication as an intermediary between ICTs and contentious collective action. That is to say, the analysis should center on communication in political contention *before* moving to an interrogation of whether (specific) communication that generates contention is introduced, shaped, and influenced by ICTs. This focus helps overcome precarious technological determinism and media centrism (e.g., Ampuja, 2012) and encourages further dialogue among media and communication scholars, political scientists, and sociologists by emphasizing human beings—more precisely, their communicative practices and networks—as the political agent in contention. Third, I expound the embedding of mobile communication in contemporary Chinese society and politics. The growth in mobile phone subscriptions in China has been exponential over the past three decades since the mobile phone was first made available at the end of the 1980s, and it continues to rise. What may happen to contentious collective actions after mobile technologies have become a structured and integral part of everyday life in contemporary China? At the end of this Introduction, I present a chapter-by-chapter outline of the book, moving from the theoretical framework to empirical evidence and analyses about mobile communication and contentious collective action in contemporary China and, further, those contentious actions that employ ICTs in the broader world.

MOVEMENTS IN COMMUNICATION: A COMMUNICATION PERSPECTIVE

This section examines "communication" in the literature of social movements and collective action. By engaging in this examination, I want to both disentangle the relevance of communication for this project and delimit the term "communication" itself in terms of the extant literature, allowing it to become more defensible for further interdisciplinary dialogue. The discussion largely follows the seminal, comparative framework that consists of political opportunities, mobilizing structures, framing processes, and their interactions (McAdam et al., 1996a; McAdam et al., 2001) to survey key literatures on movements and actions.[7] Acknowledging the criticism and deficiencies of the framework,[8] I also integrate knowledge from other perspectives and approaches, such as New Social Movement (NSM) scholarship based in European post-1960s movements. I close by proposing my thoughts on interpreting contentious collective action as one that exists within the process of communication, in which the relational parts of contention, including political opportunities, mobilizing structures, framing processes, strategic choices (Jasper, 2004), and repertoires of contention (Tilly, 1995; McAdam et al., 2001) are enacted and interrelated.

Despite the lack of explicit emphasis on communication (but see Bennett & Segerberg, 2015; Castells, 2009a; Della Porta, 2011), the literature on the emergence, development, and influence of contentious collective action can be readily interpreted with an implicit acknowledgement of the relevance of the dynamics of communication. Contentious collective

---

7. For a similar discussion, see Garrett, 2006. Nevertheless, a significant difference between Garrett's work and my framework will be elaborated in Chapter 2.

8. For instance, structural bias at the expense of overlooking cultural variables (Goodwin & Jasper, 1999) and the missing "actor" in the framework (Mische, 2003, p. 91).

action can be read as consisting of diversified forms of organized social or political acts carried out by a group of people with common interests to address their material or cultural demands, as well as a coordination of their efforts (e.g., Goodwin & Jasper, 2004; Jasper, 1998; Melucci, 1989, 1996; Olson, 1975; Tilly, 2004). From the standpoint of communication, contentious collective action entails both the internal, interactive dynamics among two or more people and the external, communicative mechanism between particular organizations as well as that between organizations and their circumstances. In essence, communication prevails in the perception and expansion of political opportunities, the activation of mobilizing structures, and cognitive and affective mobilization through interactive-framing processes. I will explicate each point in the following.

Tracing the classic framework of movements and actions (McAdam et al., 1996a), the internal, interactive dynamics incorporate mobilizing structures, or *"those collective vehicles, informal as well as formal, through which people mobilize and engage in collective action"* (McAdam, McCarthy, & Zald, 1996b, p. 3, emphasis in original). Here, (interpersonal) persuasive communication (Klandermans, 2013) acts as an essential organizational vehicle of collective action by delivering trust and reciprocity (McAdam, 1986; McAdam & Paulsen, 1993; Polletta, 2012), leveraging network resources (Diani & McAdam, 2003), establishing shared awareness and identity (Friedman & McAdam, 1992; Melucci, 1996), and engendering control and coercion during movement actions (Jasper, 1998; Snow, Zurcher, & Ekland-Olson, 1980). "The various interactive and communicative processes that affect frame alignment" (Snow, Rochford, Worden, & Benford, 1986, p. 464) occupy the central place in micromobilization, or network mechanism in social movements. Similarly, Oliver, Marwell, and Teixeira (1985, p. 547) attribute mobilization to "the possibilities for organizing, communicating, and coordinating" and consequently identify organization and communication costs as two central issues in fostering mass action. In short, communication plays an indispensable role for microsocial models of mobilization (Marwell, Oliver, & Prahl, 1988), as it activates existing social ties as the facilitators of these actions.

Apart from mobilizing structures, political opportunities afford the collective a structural potential for action (McAdam et al., 1996b, p. 5). Despite political opportunities being exogenous institutional changes that enhance or hinder prospects for movements beyond the collective (Eisinger, 1973; Goldstone, 1991, p. 408; McAdam, 1996, pp. 25–26; Tarrow, 1996), discussions necessitate the mechanism of assessment and the perceptual elements of opportunity by which activists are made cognizant of changes in the structure of political opportunities. As McAdam, Tilly, and Tarrow remark, "[n]o opportunity, however objectively open, will invite mobilization *unless* it is a) visible to potential challengers and b) perceived as an opportunity" (2001, p. 43, emphasis added). To put it another way, "structures of opportunity and threat are objective factors that *may or may not be perceived* by challengers" (McAdam et al., 2009, p. 264, emphasis added). Without denying the relevance of structural change, the argument evidently stresses the communicatively constructed dimension of political opportunities within which individuals become politically aware and active. More specifically, it deals with the issues that—*by which mechanism and to what extent—the broader set of political structural changes has been communicated to be visible and reliable for encouragement for movements.* These thereby account for the collective perception of political opportunities and constraints that decidedly affect the mobilization of opinion, the emergence and development of movements, and the ways in which insurgents mount claims and organize (e.g., McAdam et al., 2009, p. 264; Tarrow, 1996). In practice, without the subjective perception of political structural changes established via communication, groups hoping to pose a challenge may not engage in contention despite simultaneous, favorable structural conditions (Kurzman, 1996, p. 154). Zdravomyslova's study (1996) on Russian *glasnost* reforms and democratization, for instance, observes the suspended emergence of protests one year after Gorbachev's announcement of *perestroika* as changes in the structural aspect of politics were opened up because "it takes time for people to realize new opportunities for political action" (p. 123). In line with this argument, studies have differentiated the "signal" model from the "structural" model, with the former tackling the perceptual elements of opportunity as "effects of signals sent by the political system" (Meyer & Minkoff, 2004, p. 1464). Furthermore, the awareness of possible success, or what Kurzman underscores as "perceived opportunities," can far "outweigh" (Kurzman, 1996, p. 166) structural opportunities to affect the outcome of contention.[9] This is a view echoed by Meyer and Minkoff, as "*visible signals* of such changes in the political environment . . . may have greater symbolic than substantive import" (2004, p. 1467, emphasis in original). Taken together, the literature here identifies political opportunities as a dependent variable that is associated with dissemination and perception of information about structural changes in opportunity. Examining this issue helps us to understand the mechanism by which exogenous

9. For instance, Kurzman's discussion (1996) on the Iranian Revolution of 1979, in which people's perception of political opportunities drove revolutionary protests, independent of structural opportunities.

factors could be translated as invitations to action, *regardless* of changes in opportunity.

The other strand in the extant literature that regards political opportunities as a dependent variable representing communicatively constituted outcomes emerges from the consideration of the reciprocal relation of movements to structures of political opportunity, i.e., the movement-initiated change in the structure of political opportunities (McAdam, 1996, pp. 35–37; Meyer & Staggenborg, 1996, p. 1634–1635). Emphasis focuses on the crucial importance of diffusion processes, or Tarrow's coined phrase, the "diffusion of contention," by which the "word of successful—and learnable—collective actions" (1993b, p. 83) from early risers become available to subsequent challengers, either within movements or across contexts (e.g., transnational movements, see Tarrow, 1996, pp. 52–61). The question regarding how communication spreads word of contention has thus received greater attention in the discussion (e.g., Andrews & Biggs, 2006; Koopmans, 2004; Myers, 2000; Strang & Soule, 1998). Earlier literature tends to treat collective action as a kind of contagion that displays the irrational transmission of anti-social behavior (Tarde, 1903; Le Bon, 1897). In subsequent studies, attention has been focused on diffusion dynamics (e.g., McAdam & Rucht, 1993). The oft-noted role of channels of diffusion (Andrews & Biggs, 2006, p. 756; McAdam & Rucht, 1993, p. 69), including social networks (McAdam & Rucht, 1993; Walgrave & Wouters, 2014), social movement organizations (SMOs) or associational communication networks (McAdam, 1983; Minkoff, 1997; Wang & Soule, 2012), and mass media (Gamson & Wolfsfeld, 1993; Myers, 2000; Oliver & Maney, 2000; Oliver & Myers, 1999), in informing potential activists of similar struggles, connecting otherwise unconnected individuals via a shared response to events, shaping the public opinion and framing of contentious issues, and routinizing protests as institutionalized politics clearly indicate the importance of communication—such as media coverage of protest and tactical diffusion (Earl, 2010; Givan, Roberts, & Soule, 2010; McAdam & Rucht, 1993; Soule, 1997)—in expanding the possibility of institutional change by generating an indirect but essential effect on the political opportunity structure (e.g., McAdam, 1995; McAdam & Rucht, 1993; Tarrow, 1996). Recently, works on changes in digital communication technologies that facilitate the trend of political activism beyond borders echoes these discussions, noting, for instance, the impressive speed and reach of information diffusion online (e.g., Bennett, 2005; Della Porta & Mosca, 2005; Theocharis, Lowe, Van Deth, & García-Albacete, 2015). Yet, whether digital communication technologies like the internet and mobile phones are replacing mass media such as newspapers and television in the process of contention diffusion remains a question (Andrews & Biggs, 2006, p. 772).

Communication, in specific ways, facilitates the process of interpretation and framing that shapes, encourages, or constrains the development of movements. The literature dealing with framing specifically looks at movements as the production, maintenance, and contestation of beliefs, emotions, and meanings (e.g., Benford & Snow, 2000; Jasper, 2008; Johnston & Noakes, 2005; Snow & Benford, 1992; Snow et al., 1986). Being "an active, processual phenomenon that implies agency and contention at the level of reality construction" (Benford & Snow, 2000, p. 614), movement-framing processes are developed during ongoing interactions among movement actors. As Garrison points out, "[c]ollective action frames are not merely aggregations of individual attitudes and perceptions but also the outcome of *negotiating shared meaning*" (1992, p. 111, emphasis added). Communication—including social interaction and constructions of meaning, interpretation, and negotiation—therefore underpins and constructs collective action frames as interactive, discursive processes through which various core framing tasks emerge, contest, transform, or disappear, moving people to the streets.

Social movement and collective action theories also consider communication as a special resource—or "a strategic dilemma" (Della Porta & Mosca, 2005, p. 166)—for collective action. In resource mobilization theory (RMT), communication occupies a central role, as a key issue for movement organization is how effective it is at garnering resources—including media-spawned communication—for action and support both from within and from outside organizations (McCarthy & Zald, 1973, pp. 18–19; 1977, p. 1217; Zald & McCarthy, 1979, p. 3). The capacity to communicate with larger publics, to manipulate images and perceptions of movements, and to share information across social and temporal divides has been counted as "a political asset" (Bennett, 2005, p. 222). Moreover, studies on media and movements specifically explore the ways social movements are symbolically communicated and are deliberately constructed to be salient in communicating text through frames (e.g., Entman, 1993; Gamson & Wolfsfeld, 1993; Johnston & Noakes, 2005).

The importance of communication to collective action and social movements has also been elaborated further by NSM scholarship with a social constructivist approach. NSM scholarship sees social movements as the articulation and diffusion of contested meanings and identities and their relationships to culture, ideology, and politics (e.g., Buechler, 2000; Laraña, 1994; Melucci, 1996; Touraine, 1988). Among them, a processual approach to social movements has been advanced with greater emphasis on the role of everyday processes of communication, including interacting, networking (e.g., "submerged networks" [Melucci, 1985, p. 801]), experiencing, and constructing (alternative) meaning(s), identity, and solidarity, all of which contribute to "the creation of a collective subject of action" (Melucci, 1996, p. 84) in social movements. The diffusion of ideas and values, and subsequent meaning construction, as Van Stekelenburg and Klandermans stress, arises as "a movement's primary function" (2009, p. 31).

The point of this section is not to sketch a full-blown theory of the relevance of communication in movements but rather, by scrutinizing relevant literatures, to tease out and consequently call attention to the fact that communication, in various forms, permeates the emergence, evolution, and development of contentious politics. Communication is present and pervasive in *every* phase and *every* aspect of actions and movements. Social movements and collective action consist of a variety of communicative practices and networks. With various emphases, scholarship on social movements and contention has delved into the central role of communication, but often implicitly, to understand how collective actions emerge, interact, coalesce, and evolve. As McAdam, Tilly, and Tarrow (2001, p. 22) remark in their seminal work, *Dynamics of Contention*, "[w]e treat social interaction, social ties, communication, and conversation . . . as active sites of creation and change. We have come to think of interpersonal networks, interpersonal communication, and various forms of continuous negotiation—including the negotiation of identities—as figuring centrally in the dynamics of contention." In this regard, far beyond "a finished product" (Kavada, 2016, p. 9), contentious collective action can be dissected as an open-ended, interactive process (McAdam et al., 2001, p. 22)[10] that entails a series of communications, both formal and informal, between a plurality of individuals with common purposes or shared identities and the state, elites, or opponents of political or cultural actions (Diani, 1992, p. 13). To be clear, *elements of contention, rather than being fixed or static in advance, are reflexively constituted and iteratively enacted within acts, processes, and networks of communication.* Viewing contention as a communicative process turns particular attention to the *interactive* nature of movements and actions, the *processual* quality of long- and short-term factors that need to be examined in order to understand the trajectories of movements beyond

---

10. This book follows McAdam, Tilly, and Tarrow (2001) and considers collective action as the *processes* of political struggle.

"moments of madness" (Zolberg, 1972), and the relational mechanism in which elements of movements concatenate and impact one another. To adapt Dewey's (2004, p. 4) eminent statement, contentious collective action not only continues to exist *by* communication, but it may fairly be said to also exist *in* communication.[11] Taking a "communication-constituting-contention"[12] perspective to consider contentious collective action thereby casts analytic light on areas and aspects of the dynamics of movements and contentions that other conceptual schemes or perspectives may have glossed over or ignored (e.g., movement as networks; Diani & McAdam, 2003). This issue becomes particularly prominent after the adoption of ICTs in protests and movements—and consequently the debate over this issue—springing up around the globe.

BRIDGING ICTS AND CONTENTIOUS COLLECTIVE ACTION: COMMUNICATION AS INTERMEDIARY

With the increasing ubiquity of ICTs around the globe and their widespread use in contention, ICT-mediated communication has become one of the focuses of interrogation in current scholarship on contentious collective action. Nevertheless, whether—and to what extent—ICTs (are likely to) affect and transform collective action remains a highly divergent topic (e.g., Diani, 2000; Earl, Kimport, Prieto, Rush, & Reynoso, 2010). Some scholars demonstrate that ICTs, including mobile phones, emails, blogs, social media, and social networking sites, have brought changes to both the nature (e.g., Bennett & Segerberg, 2012, 2013; Earl & Kimport, 2011; Shirky, 2008)[13] and repertoires of contention (e.g., Earl & Kimport, 2011; Juris, 2008; Lievrouw, 2011; Postmes & Brunsting, 2002; Rheingold, 2002). Others reserve their attitude toward the issue (Tilly, 2004, p. 104; also see, e.g., Morozov, 2011; Tarrow, 1998), contending that "activists adopt new technologies when those technologies serve their purposes. But purposes override techniques" (Tilly, 2010, p. 42). Wolfsfeld, Segev, and

11. This is not to say, as Earl and Garrett (2017, p. 489) criticize, that social movements should be recast as fundamentally communicative acts.

12. The term here is different from "the communicative constitution of collective action" (Olufowote, 2006), in which collective action refers to coalitions within organizations.

13. See, for instance, Earl and Kimport as they champion the new "Theory 2.0" (2011, p. 14, pp. 27–29) in sociological interpretations of social movements because ICT as "a new 'digital repertoire of contention' . . . reflects . . . fundamental theoretical shifts" (Earl et al., 2014, p. 365; also see Earl, 2010).

Sheafer (2013, p. 119, emphasis added) further assert that there is "a *negative* correlation between the level of communication technology available in a particular country and the level of protest . . . the greater the level of the internet and social media penetration, the lower the level of protest."

Without doubt, as studies show, ICTs offer people the chance to act out in much more sophisticated and powerful ways than ever before (e.g., Castells, 2012; Della Porta & Mosca, 2005). But the question remains contested whether ICTs simply reinforce existing forms of movements or, instead, they open up new avenues for driving people into contention (Polletta, Chen, Gardner, & Motes, 2013). Arguing the fact that "weak ties" on social media are insufficient for "high-risk activism" (McAdam, 1986), Gladwell asks "[w]hat evidence is there that social revolutions in the pre-internet era suffered from a lack of cutting-edge communications and organizational tools?" (Gladwell & Shirky, 2011, p. 153, also see Gladwell, 2010) Similarly, Earl et al. (2014, p. 363) wonder if "existing theories designed to explain protest prior to the pervasive use of ICTs [can] be readily adapted to explain online activism and [thereby explain] how technologies relate to protest."

Scholarship from media and communication studies has made intellectually vibrant and empirically rich contributions to the debate by underlining the relevance of ICTs in social movements (e.g., Bennett, 2003; Bennett, Breunig, & Givens, 2008; Bennett & Segerberg, 2012, 2015; Cammaerts, Mattoni, & McCurdy, 2013; Mattoni, 2016; Mattoni & Treré, 2014; Poell, 2014). While, undoubtedly, current scholarship yields vital insights on the role of ICTs in movements, it also has two significant limitations that particularly hinder reflective dialogue with other disciplines.

First, with an overarching and legitimate focus on media, scholarship from the disciplines of media and communication largely remains dominated by, using Gerbaudo's (2014, p. 266) term, "technological analysis of social movements." To be clear, even though being fully aware of and therefore trying to avoid technological determinism, current scholarship maintains a strong, and in some case, exclusive, preference on media technologies in contentious collective action with a general disinterest in a host of broader topics, such as the historicity of contention, a complex understanding of communication, the frameworks of the political economy of ICTs, and established knowledge within the field (e.g., Liu, 2016; Rodríguez et al., 2014). Discussions that take for granted the juxtaposition of media (technologies) and political contention, such as "email" and "social movements" (Kavada, 2010; Wall, 2007), "social media" and "collective action" (Margetts, John, Hale, & Yasseri, 2015; Segerberg & Bennett, 2011), and "social media" and "revolution" (Eltantawy & Wiest, 2011), tend to "see technology not only as an independent variable from which all the other variables (organizational practices, objectives and tactics) depend, but also as the only thing that can unite otherwise egotistical individuals" (Gerbaudo, 2014, p. 266). This tendency, or "the technological-fascination bias," as Mattoni and Treré (2014, p. 255, emphasis in original) correctly observe, treat the use of media technologies as "movement in *itself*," thus oversimplifying "the complexity of social movement practices in the use of technologies and . . . overestimate[ing] the role played by the media [technologies]" (see also Rodríguez et al., 2014, p. 153). Here, existing scholarship with a focus on media technologies exemplifies the similar problem as McAdam and Boudet (2012, p. 2) identify in movement scholarship: "a starkly Ptolemaic view of social movements," i.e., "a view of contention that is broadly analogous to the Ptolemaic system, with movements substituting for the Earth as the center of the political universe." What is different in this case is simply replacing "movements" with terms such as "media technologies," "ICTs," or "digital media,"[14] which inevitably brings its own risk of exaggerating the causal potency of ICTs while obscuring the role of other elements in political contention, such as "the richly contextual human relations that surround media use" and the complexity of communication processes in movements (Rodríguez et al., 2014, pp. 152–154).

Second, and related to the first point, is the lack of comparison and integration of interrogations in *both* face-to-face and tech-mediated communications[15] in contention. It is essential to recognize that, even among existing studies, quite a few have acknowledged the relevant role of face-to-face communication, compared to ICT-mediated communication (Kavada, 2010, pp. 361–363; Lim, 2012, p;. 242–243; Tufekci & Wilson, 2012, p. 370). Nevertheless, scholarship that investigates tech-mediated communication rarely considers and *compares* the role of face-to-face communication versus what is technologically mediated in order to pinpoint the change—or even the "revolution"—that has been introduced by ICTs. This, to a certain extent, may be due to the deep-rooted intellectual

14. This can be seen in a large number of discussions on alternative media, activist media, participatory media, community media, radical media, social movement media, and grassroots media.

15. In a general sense, the term "tech-mediated communication" here refers to *both* mass-mediated communication and digitally mediated networked communication. This is in line with Snow, Zurcher, Ekland-Olson's discussion (1980, p. 790): "By face-to-face communication, we refer to all information, whether it be verbal or nonverbal, that is imparted when two or more individuals or groups are physically present. In contrast, mediated communication refers to information dissemination through institutionalized mass communication mechanisms, such as radio and television, or through institutionalized, but individualized and privatized, communication mechanisms such as the mail and telephone."

separation of interpersonal and mass communication (Reardon & Rogers, 1988) in the field of communication studies, despite some efforts to bridge such separation by advocating human bodies as "media of the first degree" that parallels with technologies as "media of the second degree" and meta-technologies as "media of the third degree" (Jensen, 2010). Furthermore, the lack of consideration of face-to-face communication risks the danger of misinterpreting agency in contention by having an exclusive focus on tech-mediated communication. On top of that, this greatly impedes possible conversation about and comparison between the work with a specific focus on media (technologies) and those in other disciplines, such as sociology and political science, in which media (technologies) are often not an essential focus (e.g., Diani & McAdam, 2003; Jasper, 2004, 2008; McAdam, 1982; McAdam et al., 1996a; McAdam et al., 2001; Tarrow, 2011; Tilly & Tarrow, 2006). This leads, again, to the inevitable critique of (media) technological determinism and the unfortunate disarticulation and even incommensurability (Kuhn, 1963) of knowledge in the field.

To overcome the limitations, especially the criticism about media centrism (e.g., Deacon & Stanyer, 2014) or technological determinism, i.e., to draw a possible causal link between the use of ICTs and the emergence of collective action, and to bridge the gap between media/communication studies and sociology and political science, I suggest instead we take communication as an intermediary between ICTs and contentious collective action in the interrogation of political contention in the digital age (Figure 1.1). As illustrated in Figure 1.1, contentious politics can be understood as being shaped or facilitated either by face-to-face or tech-mediated communication (including ICT-mediated communication), or both. To cheer for ICTs as a "liberation technology" (Diamond, 2010; Diamond & Plattner, 2012) hence necessitates a juxtaposition of all forms of communication that exist in political contention and their possible contributions to political contention. Meanwhile, the use of ICTs has been seen as improving both quality and quantity of communication in society, by allowing increasing access to information, by diversifying channels of participation, and by

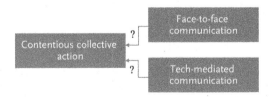

Figure 1.1 A simplified illustration: Contentious collective action shaped and influenced by face-to-face, tech-mediated communication, or both?

blurring the boundaries between public and private, to mention a few (e.g., Bimber et al., 2005; Castells, 2009; Rainie & Wellman, 2012). The transformation of the dynamics of communication, a key process within social movements but now *partially* mediated by ICTs, consequently may afford potential changes in collective action. Toward this end, to understand the influence of ICTs on collective action entails a careful interrogation of changes in communication practices and networks under the influence of technologies that underlie and structure the emergence, development, and diffusion of collective action in the digital age.

Assessing communication as an intermediary to discern the role of ICTs in collective action, again, albeit without explicit elaboration, is well-acknowledged in existing scholarship. Studies on ICTs and political protests have recognized that the emerging (mass) communication system supported by ICTs, which integrates on- and offline personal networks, was found overwhelmingly to be the main source for information about political protests (e.g., Postmes & Brunsting, 2002, p. 294; Tufekci & Wilson, 2012, p. 367). Studies of ICTs as parts of an organizational repertoire probe network-based forms of "connective action" taking shape around practices of interpersonal communication, sharing, expressing, and listening even without traditional organizations (Bennett & Segerberg, 2012a; Shirky, 2008). In this process, as Bennett and Segerberg elucidate, "communication . . . [as] . . . a prominent part of organizational structure" (2012, p. 739) invites individuals to speak up and share personal stories, further encouraging the engagement and diffusion of movements to other parts of the world for assimilative actions. Expressive affordances[16] of ICT-mediated communication also construct resonance within publics, enable people to feel the meaning of the movement for themselves, make movements affectively driven, and transform the mechanism of online political movements (Papacharissi, 2015). For movements across boundaries, ICTs support transnational websites, with communications, again, occupying a key element in the assessment of the political capacity of technologically mediated movement networks for spreading the word (e.g., Ayres, 1999; Bennett, 2005, p. 211).

ICTs do not only infuse communicative practices and networks for movements. As self-organizing communication technologies, they have also introduced new types of communication structures and new forms of communication for contentious collective action, such as

---

16. For a reflective discussion on affordance in literature on ICTs and contentious politics, see Chapter 3.

what Castells calls "mass self-communication" (2009, p. 55; also see Enjolras, Steen-Johnsen, & Wollebæk, 2013, p. 891). This horizontal form of communication embodies the power of self-generated, self-directed, self-selected, and many-to-many forms of communication, offering to restructure communication networks and flows that allow "social movements and rebellious individuals to build their autonomy and confront the institutions of society in their own terms and around their own projects" (Castells, 2007, p. 249). Meanwhile, while the hybrid communication system (Chadwick, 2013) connects (contentious) politics and citizens to each other, allowing them to interact with each other, and affect one another in new ways, tech-mediated communication also redefines the locus of politics by engendering "changes to the category of the political itself" and facilitating "the politics of communication" (Zayani, 2015, p. 13). In short, communication not only shapes elements in contention but also opens up different worlds for contention.

A focus on communication while deliberating the relation between ICTs and collective action eschews optimism or pessimism about technology, as the dynamics of communication—and the control over it—serves as a more fundamental element for the success or failure of social movements. Abundant examples indicate that, although activists were well-equipped with ICTs, political repression and commercial control of technological infrastructure and internet networks, as well as suppression of communication flows within the networks (Morozov, 2011; Van Laer & Van Aelst, 2010, p. 1162), have sometimes led to depression and demobilization of movements by altering communicative structures (Youmans & York, 2012, p. 316). Again, ICTs themselves do not—and cannot—produce changes in collective action in a direct way, let alone dictate success or failure. Instead, the embeddedness of digital technology affords and underpins changes in communication practices and networks, which may restructure the dynamics of collective action (Pavan, 2014). In this sense, as many studies point out, ICTs should be perceived as *context* for action (Bimber, 2017; Bimber et al., 2012), or as *"an emerging technological environment"* for action in an era of digital ubiquity (Ganesh & Stohl, 2013, p. 428, emphasis in orginal; also see Papacharissi, 2015, p. 121), rather than a variable with (direct) impact on collective action. To this end, it is rather the transformational power of the new forms of tech-enabled *communication* and the consequent changing nature of groups and collectives.

In a broader sense beyond collective action and social movements, the prevalence and penetration of digital communication technologies around the globe and in everyday life have impinged upon the perception of time and location, which restructures spatiotemporal limits of communication practices and networks and establishes an always-on feeling in the connected environment (e.g., Bimber et al., 2012; Castells, 2009; Licoppe & Smoreda, 2005; Rainie & Wellman, 2012). These transformations further suggest that research should be sensible to recognizing the ways in which communicative practices and processes change, as they are reprogrammed by communication technologies, and their subsequent impacts on collective action. Conceptualizing communication as an intermediary between ICTs and contentious collective action, the question we should explore is: *Among various modes of communication, such as face-to-face or mass communications, which may shape and influence political contention, how do the (radical) changes in our ability to communicate with one another, introduced, underpinned, and afforded by ICTs, (re)structure and articulate interrelated elements of movements and actions?*

TAKING THE MOBILE PHONE FOR GRANTED IN EVERYDAY LIFE IN CHINA

Amid many ICTs that have become an integrated part of communicative practices and the everyday experience of modern life, the mobile phone is unquestionably the one thing that brings the most drastic alteration, given its increasing penetration and nearly universal, all-but-indispensable usage. The inventors of the handheld mobile phone in 1973 were probably not able to foresee the extreme popularity it would garner around the world only 47 years later. According to the statistics from the International Telecommunication Union (ITU), by the middle of 2016, mobile phone coverage has already reached near-ubiquitous levels, with a penetration rate of 95%, or more than 7 billion, of the global population (ITU, 2016). Among them, for many developed countries, the smartphone penetration rate is already close to the saturation point (e.g., for the UK, see Arthur, 2014). Meanwhile, in developing countries, like Tanzania, Uganda, and Kenya, mobile phones are also pervasive, with the number of mobile-broadband subscribers growing at double-digit rates to reach a penetration rate of around 40% (Pew Research Center, 2015). No longer a luxury device for communication, notably, mobile communication technology is losing its sense of external reality to become, instead, an "invisible means" (Katz, 2003b, p. 18). Its omnipresence has become part of the "taken-for-granted" (Ling, 2013) world of its user. Mobile communication establishes an "always-on" connection (Ling, 2004, 2008) to the internet and social networks, and this mode functions as "a new model of social communication" (Rheingold, 2002, p. xvi). In this process, to which Katz draws attention, the mobile phone entails "the use of communication tools not on a 'one to one' basis but rather in a context of group membership and social identity" (Katz, 2003b, p. 17).

It is nearly impossible to talk about the development of mobile phones without mentioning China (e.g., Wei, 2006). Mainland China now has one of the largest and most populous information-technology infrastructures in the world in terms of mobile network scale and customer base, serving most counties with seamless coverage in both urban and rural areas (China Mobile, 2007). The total number of mobile subscriptions has topped 1.3 billion, which boasts a penetration rate of 99% of the total population (China Internet Network Information Center [CNNIC]), 2014; Reuters, 2014), while the penetration rate of smartphones achieves 83% (Google, 2018). In the latest report by CNNIC (2018), China's total internet-user count is about 772 million users, or nearly 56% of the total population. The number of mobile internet users snowballs to an impressive 753 million. In other words, nowadays, the mobile communication network has become enormous: China's mobile internet is nearing total ubiquity among internet users, with 97.5% of China's internet users accessing the web via their mobiles.

Taking a general view above, mobile phone use has increased while use of other forms of ICTs has decreased, including desktop computers, laptops, and tablets. Reality, unsurprisingly, is much richer and more varied. Whole city blocks full of telecom stores have cropped up in Chinese cities as diverse as Harbin in the north and Haikou in the south. Urban metro stations, bus stops, and the walls of buildings and bridges have all become display sites for mobile advertising. Governmental agencies, radio and TV shows, internet portals, and advertising companies all vie for attention on and through mobile devices. For the younger generation, mobile handsets represent a fashion item and the symbol of the "thumb lifestyle" that allows them to connect to mobile messaging apps and access the internet at any moment. For rural-to-urban migrants, wireless connections are important vehicles for finding job information, flirting with lovers, or staying close with relatives in the distant countryside (e.g., Law & Chu, 2008; Law & Peng, 2006; Lin & Tong, 2008; Wallis, 2013). For working-class communities and senior citizens, mobile technologies meet their information-gathering and communication needs (Qiu, 2009; Wallis, 2013). For businesspeople and civil servants, mobile communication carries vital up-to-date information and innovations of the "mobile government"—that is, citizens using mobile devices to access electronic government services. For those who do not have the money to promote their services by traditional means, spray-painting mobile numbers on walls or sidewalks has become a new kind of guerrilla advertising. Mobile phones are described as "the last thing we look at before sleep each night, and the first thing we reach for upon waking." On average, Chinese adults are spending more than 2.5 hours per day using their mobile devices (about 75 hours a month!) (Clark, 2018). The study carried out by the Chinese Academy of Social Sciences (CASS) and Tencent, one of the largest social media platform operators, recognizes that 94% of the young population suffers from "nomophobia" (Valdesolo, 2015)—feelings of discomfort when they forgot their mobile phones at home; around 87% of them check their social networking apps, such as WeChat and QQ, on their mobile phones at least once every 15 minutes, and 80.5% have tried to refrain from frequently checking their phones but found it extremely difficult. These statistics exemplify that mobile communication is, no doubt, a structured part of contemporary Chinese society, as mobile phones seamlessly integrate themselves into the everyday lives of the Chinese people, including the politics.

What happens to contentious collective action, as an aspect of politics, after mobile communication technologies become a structured part of everyday life in China, where the number of "collective incidents" (群体性事件)—a euphemism used by the Chinese authorities to describe protests, group complaints, and so on—has surged dramatically over the past 25 years (Perry & Selden, 2010) and where ICTs have been increasingly adopted both for and against activism (e.g., King, Pan, & Roberts, 2013a; Yang, 2009; Zheng, 2008)?

In practice, ubiquitous mobile communication exerts a growing influence over people's social and political practices, with the increasing use of the mobile phone functioning as an efficient tool for aggregating and articulating citizen input or popular discontent during the process of public opinion formation and political participation. For instance, Chinese youth sent text messages and chain emails in 2005 to exhort citizens to boycott Japanese merchandise, and then took to the streets in more than 10 cities, giving logistical information on protest routes and even what slogans to chant.[17] In terms of local environmental activism,

---

17. The text message read: "If Chinese people didn't buy Japanese goods for one day, 1,000 Japanese companies would go bankrupt. If they didn't buy Japanese goods for six months, half the Japanese people would lose their jobs; if they didn't buy Japanese goods for a year, the Japanese economy would collapse. Send this on to other Chinese people and we won't need a war!" (Harney, Sanchanta, & Yeh, 2005).

the residents in Xiamen, Chengdu, Dalian, Ningbo, and Kunming, among others, shared information with the help of mobile communication about the alleged misdeeds of party officials, as well as the civic actions that were organized against them in 2007, 2008, 2011, 2012, and 2013 (e.g., YouTube, 2011; Yu, 2011; Zhu, 2007). Circulating and relaying mobile calls and text messages about long-standing complaints related to the increased operating costs and traffic fines that had been imposed on taxi companies, on top of government fees, thousands of taxi drivers went on strike in Chongqing and were soon followed by their peers in Wuhan, Haikou, Zhengzhou, Guangzhou, Fuzhou, Shenzhen, and Wenling, among other cities, between 2008 and 2013 (*China in Pictures*, 2009; Elegant, 2008; Yang, 2008). Wielding text messaging and camera functions, Chinese migrant workers, normally perceived as a less tech-savvy population, mobilized and videotaped a wide range of contentious activities including mass strikes and protests against greedy corporations and their local government allies in the emerging Chinese labor movement (e.g., Barboza & Bradsher, 2010; Liu, 2013; Weber, 2011; Xie & Zhao, 2007). One of the latest telephonic innovations for voice calls and WeChat enables thousands of army veterans across the country to self-organize "self-defense rights" demonstrations against long-running issues such as mistreatment, corruption, and poor job prospects in multiple Chinese cities (Buckley, 2018). Given the huge and still-growing mobile population and the similarly large and still-growing number of contentious collective action in China, what is surprising is that so little attention and systematic analysis has been devoted to mobile communication technologies and their influence on political contention.[18]

It is relevant to remind ourselves before starting our interrogation that, as Bimber (2017, p. 3) expressed the following concern, the expansion of the possibilities of action in the new (technological) context is *not* equal to increased political behavior or motivation for action. Putting it differently, people do not join a protest simply because they have mobile phones. Instead, the focus situates on what the Chinese find in the mobile communication, what they try to mold it in and make of it in political activism, how they can relate its contentious possibilities to themselves—in short, how we might observe a specific, mobile-enabled culture attempt to make itself at home in the transforming communicative and political environments in contemporary China.

18. However, see the analyses in Liu, 2013, 2015, 2017; Lee & Chan, 2018; Qiu, 2008b, 2009, 2017; Wallis, 2013; Weber, 2011; Wei, 2016.

ORGANIZATION OF THE BOOK: CHAPTER-BY-CHAPTER OUTLINE

This book consists of six chapters. To sum up the Introduction, it assessed and identified lacunae and challenges in the existing literature on ICTs and contentious collective action. Through a survey of relevant scholarship on social movements and contentious politics, I proposed to explicitly make communication a key element in a tripartite framework of contentious politics and social movements (McAdam, et al., 1996a; McAdam, et al., 2001) and, further, to regard communication as an intermediary between ICTs and contentious collective action. The introductory chapter further elucidated the embeddedness of mobile communication technologies within Chinese society and, thus it also has become a context for (political) action and can therefore impact contentious politics.

The lacunae in Chapter 1 motivates this study to develop a theoretical framework as a modest attempt to address the gap, which is detailed in Chapter 2: "Toward a Synthetic Framework." In line with existing scholarship that underlines the relevance of communication (e.g., Bennett & Segerberg, 2012, 2013; Castells, 2009; Kavada, 2016; Rinke & Röder, 2011), I join the effort by proposing a framework that integrates knowledge from the fields of communication, sociology, and political science and that centralizes and sensitizes (Blumer, 1954) communication—and further, the politics of communication—enabling an interrogation of contentious collective action and, not least, the possible influence of ICTs. Without scrutiny of the various forms of communication and metacommunication in contention, I specify, it would be hard to rationalize the relevance of digital communication technologies in contentious collective action. Issues of methodology are also discussed in Chapter 2.

Chapters 3 to 5 present a set of empirical analyses of the multiple dimensions of the embedding of mobile communication technologies into (contentious) politics in contemporary China. These chapters start with a general discussion on key terms in the sociology of movements—*repertoire of contention* in Chapter 3, *mobilization* in Chapter 4, and *rumor* in Chapter 5. Then they draw on the communication-centered framework to dissect the fine-grained mobile communication process and its influence on the relational mechanisms between political opportunities, mobilizing structures, and framing processes as contentious collective action unfold. At the end of each chapter, I expand the discussion beyond the case of China to shed a broader light on these issues. More importantly, following McAdam, McCarthy, and Zald (1996a) and transcending current literature that normally looks at one or two elements of the perspective, these three chapters scrutinize the three elements in an interrelated and relational dynamic. They also demonstrate how the embedding of mobile communication shapes daily practices beyond the overt contested and contentious moment and sustains covert disobedience by generating a new politics of communication—i.e., new categories of politics—as "everyday resistance" (Scott, 1985).

Chapter 3, "From Affordance to Repertoire of Contention," analyzes the political circumstances and opportunities under which mobile phones emerge as a part of the repertoire of contention. A precise picture of the role of ICTs—the mobile phone in this case—in contentious collective action should *not* just look at the use of specific communication technologies in contention. Instead, an investigation necessitates the perception of certain (functions of) communication technologies as repertoire of contention on the basis of affordances that structure the possibilities of the use of technology. Through fieldwork and in-depth interviews, I indicate that taking (certain functions of) mobile phones as the protest repertoire derives from a confluence of given social group's habitus of media use that manifests particular affordances (Gibson, 1977) and the learned experience of the contested means of the past in official mass communication. Perhaps more interesting in this process is the observation that communication and metacommunication of official media coverage of ICT-mediated political activism modularizes and legitimizes the use of mobile phones in protests, and hence shapes specific ways people have harnessed their mobile phones—a mundane, personal communication device—as a key repertoire for civil disobedience and political activism.

Chapter 4, "More Than Words: The Integrative Power of Mobile Tech as a 'Reciprocal Technology' for Micromobilization," probes mobile-mediated mobilization. Ingrained into everyday life, mobile communication has woven itself into contemporary social relationships and networking. Yet, what kinds of changes are made possible with the introduction of mobile communication into mobilization? This chapter argues for an understanding of the political significance of the social embeddedness of ICTs by showing how the mobile phone, as "a reciprocal technology" (Ling, 2013, p. 160), has been uniquely effective in committed collective action recruitment and mobilization. By taking *guanxi*-embedded, mobile-mediated mobilization in China as a case study, Chapter 4 illustrates that the pervasive culture of "*guanxi* networks" (or, the "Chineseness" of mobile phone use [Chu, 2012, p. 12])—the importance within Chinese culture of feelings of personal indebtedness to another person for a past favor, and the cultural obligation to reciprocate—establishes an essential reinforcement or expansion of the already present technological features of mobile communication. In this process, remarkably, it is the metacommunication of interpersonal, reciprocal relationships via mobile communication that acts as a key element of these networks that enhances the technological features of mobile devices for protest mobilization. The chapter, furthermore, sheds greater empirical and theoretical light on the influence of mobile communication on the process of micromobilization, as well as its political and social implications beyond the Chinese institutional and cultural context.

Chapter 5, "To Retweet Each and Every Rumor": 'Mobile Rumoring' as Contention," discusses the practice of rumor diffusion via mobile communication, or what I call "mobile rumoring," as "covert resistance" (Scott, 1985, 1990) against the hegemonic discourse of the authorities. What drives easy diffusion and proliferation of rumors via mobile phones and other ICTs, even in the face of intensified rumor control, surveillance, and punishment from the regime? As the answer unfolds, the Chinese state's strategies to suppress communication in the guise of so-called rumor unwittingly establishes the socio-cultural foundation for rumor proliferation, while, specifically, the official denunciation of rumor becomes a political opportunity that triggers the collective practice of rumor diffusion against the authorities. The call for rumor dissemination thus becomes both an action—a type of tactic, or covert resistance—and a frame to contest communication control and political manipulation by the authorities. Both contested identity and dissenting emotion join as counter-authority initiatives that represent the dynamic behind mobile rumoring in China today, redefining the practice of politics.

Whereas each can be read separately, these three chapters have been organized in a way that delivers a coherent presentation of empirical evidence and conclusions of the theoretical framework: How mobile communication contributes to the dynamic and relational mechanisms among political opportunities, mobilizing structures, and framing processes. These chapters also address the fact that if (mobile) communication technologies can enable or assist people who are seeking progressive social and political change in contemporary China, it will do so not as an inevitability, but rather, as a means of change alongside other forces (e.g., habitus and official media's "mouthpiece" role in Chapter 3, social relationships in Chapter 4, and shared experience and emotion in Chapter 5).

I close by offering my summary and reflections in Chapter 6, the conclusion, regarding the implications of the embedding of mobile communication into politics in contemporary China. The political relevance of mobile communication technologies relies not just on their capacity to provide affordable communication to human agency and generating new mediated visibility, but the relevance of these devices also relies on their capacity to carve out new opportunities for political action, to accumulate social resources as mobilizing structures against authoritarianism, and to shape people's perception of their (potential) political agency or political subjectivity. Further, mobile communication technologies facilitate a broader sense of the contentious communicative sphere as an organizational form articulating a societal, collective horizon of experience in social structures for the possible democratization of communication in contemporary China. Whereas mobile communication technologies entail new affordances to the Chinese people who are engaging in politics, the conclusion further broadens the scope of investigation to cases of political contention beyond China in order to illustrate how and to what extent the communication-centered framework may shed light beyond China to more precisely pin down the influence of ICTs on contentious collective action.

CHAPTER 2
Toward a Synthetic Framework

We treat social interaction, social ties, communication, and conversation . . . as active sites of creation and change. We have come to think of interpersonal networks, interpersonal communication, and various forms of continuous negotiation—including the negotiation of identities—as figuring centrally in the dynamics of contention. (McAdam, Tarrow, & Tilly, 2001, p. 22)

To encourage crossing disciplinary boundaries that regrettably make the field of ICTs and political contention fragmented and disconnected, as the Introduction defines it, contentious collective action can be appreciated, to an extent, as an activity constituted *in* and *through* communication. This by no means suggests that, as Earl and Garrett (2017, p. 489) put it, social movements are "fundamentally communicative acts." Instead, various communicative practices and networks prevail in collective action and articulate elements of political contention, as illustrated in the perception and expansion of political opportunities, the maintenance and activation of mobilizing structures and resources, the interactive and affective mobilization that occurs through framing processes, and the negotiation and diffusion of contested meanings and identities. A careful examination of communication in relation to classic frameworks of contentious politics (McAdam et al., 1996a; McAdam et al., 2001) therefore helps cast new light on the dynamics of contention, which advances interdisciplinary dialogue in the field.

This book is definitely not alone in noting the relevance of communication in political contention. The first part of this chapter hence begins with a review of extant scholarship on the issue, including some pieces that specifically emphasize communication in ICTs and political activism. The second part revolves around the communication-centered framework that I propose, which involves various forms of communication—i.e., interpersonal, mass, and networked communications (Jensen & Helles, 2011)—along with corresponding metacommunication (Ruesch & Bateson, 1951) that focuses on the (de)codification of contextually bounded social codes and values, especially in the application of digital communication technologies for communication and contention. This framework promises a multitude of dimensions, from micro-processes to meso-level analyses to macro-overviews, to explore and compare ICTs and contentious collective action in different spatiotemporal contexts. The third part of the chapter concludes with methodological notes of this study.

ICTS, COMMUNICATION, AND DYNAMICS OF CONTENTION

Although studies are increasingly recognizing the relevance of ICT-mediated communication in initiating, networking, coordinating, and transforming contentious collective action, as mentioned at the beginning of the Introduction, the absence of an integrated framework across different disciplines makes it difficult to articulate connections and commonalities between—and further, beyond—these disparate works. This situation also makes it difficult to facilitate dialogue between them (e.g., Earl & Garrett, 2017). In this regard, Garrett's (2006) work can be seen as the first attempt to achieve such a framework. Nevertheless, his review-based framework merely "situate(s)" (p. 204) existing scholarship within the classic framework of social movements that comprise political opportunities, mobilizing structures, and framing processes (McAdam et al., 1996a), instead of *establishing* a synthetic framework on the topic across disciplines. Full compliance with the framework of social movement studies has its merits. Nevertheless, it also risks losing the disciplinary direction, uniqueness, and advantage of communication studies[1] and cedes the field to a subspecialty of sociology or political science, or political sociology (Walder, 2009) more precisely. Part of this move, as Earl and Garrett (2017, p. 481, emphasis added) have already indicated, results in the gap that "there has not been a large focus on *explicitly* communicative process[es] within movements." In this respect, an interdisciplinary

---

1. Even though communication study itself stands at a crossroads (e.g., Craig, 1999; Pfau, 2008).

framework requires a synthesis of knowledge and contributions across different disciplines. In recent years, a few studies have taken the first step to digest, advocate, and combine multidisciplinary knowledge to explain digitally mediated contentious collective action (e.g., discussions on "mediation opportunity structure" [Cammaerts, 2012] and on political communication and social movement studies [Earl & Garrett, 2017]). Yet, a synthesis framework remains missing in the field.

Meanwhile, an emerging body of scholarship is starting to uphold and further exemplify the importance of communication in ICT-mediated contention. Among them, some examine changes in communication practices and networks brought by ICTs that shape or re-articulate elements of contentious collective action. For instance, Cammaerts (2012) presents the framework, called a "mediation opportunity structure," that integrates the political opportunity structure approach with the concept of "mediation" to highlight communication practices as not just symbolic and discursive but also instrumental and material to the realization of the movement's goal. Papacharissi (2015, p. 4) explores the form, texture, and shape of networked communication (the "discursive mediality" of Twitter [p. ix] in this case) that establishes affective attunement on the basis of mediated feelings of connectedness to drive publics "to tune in and emotionally align with the movement." Bennett and Segerberg (2012) advance the concept of "connective action" to stress self-motivated political action in the digital age under the influence of a technologically enabled personalized action frame and networks of personalized communication as flexible mobilizing structures. Likewise, Gerbaudo (2012, p. 139) treats ICT-mediated communication as the movement's organizational structure. Others take communication at the center to develop different theoretical frameworks and approaches for a renewed understanding of digitally mediated collective action. In a series of studies, Bimber, Flanagin, and Stohl (2005, 2012; Flanagin, Stohl, & Bimber, 2006) acknowledge "the emergent communicative dynamics of organizing" (Bimber et al., 2012, p. 173) in organization-based collective action. Rinke and Röder (2011) advocate a communication model that consists of the media ecology of protest, communication culture, and temporal-spatial unfolding to explain the case of the Egyptian revolution in 2011. Kavada (2016, p.9) advises a communication approach to consider collective action as "emerging in conversations and solidified in texts."[2]

---

2. There are other scholars who try to integrate emerging concepts in communication studies like "mediatization" into ICT-mediated collective action (e.g., Mattoni

Without denying the importance and merits in these pieces of scholarship, they are beset by at least two shortcomings. First, existing studies largely limit the scope of their examinations to one or two elements in the framework of social movements, be they political opportunities (Cammaerts, 2012), organizational structures (Bennett & Segerberg, 2012; Bimber et al., 2012; Bimber et al., 2005; Flanagin et al., 2006; Gerbaudo, 2012), framing processes (Bennett & Segerberg, 2012), or the affective/emotional perspective (Papacharissi, 2015). Yet, as McAdam, McCarthy, and Zald (1996b) underline in their original discussion of the framework, a fuller understanding of movements postulates the dynamic relations among political opportunities, mobilizing structures, and framing processes beyond one or another of these factors (also see McAdam et al., 2001). Admittedly, a comprehensive framework should instead address both elements of contention and the interactive, relational dynamics among them. An illustrative example is that, as Bennett and Segerberg (2012, p. 746) briefly recognize in their influential work, personalized messages traveled more easily in Spain and Greece than in France or Italy in connection with dissimilar structures of political opportunities in different countries. Unfortunately, they stop pushing their discussion forward without looking at the interactive dynamics among elements of contention. A fuller picture addressing such dynamics instead allows us to observe that, as part of the political structure, divergent media coverage and the diffusion of protests between the Italian newspapers and media in other countries exerted a decisive influence on contradictory interpretations and expectations—i.e., framing—of the protests, significantly hindering persuasive effects from personalized action frames on coalition building and mobilization on the ground (Zamponi, 2012, pp. 420–421).

Second, with the umbrella term "communication," existing studies leave out the richness and complexity of the meaning of the term. In other words, to what do they refer when using the term "communication" in their analyses? Does it mean the exchange of messages, the diffusion of information, the interpretation of media coverage, the negotiation of meanings, all of the above, or something else entirely? The ambiguity makes the term too vague and hence insufficiently robust to guide analysis. Without doubt, what cannot be ignored is the fact that communication is indeed "a richly meaningful term" (Craig, 1999, p. 120). Extant scholarship does clearly recognize this issue by, for instance, admitting that

& Treré, 2014). Nevertheless, the concept itself suffers from the critique of media-centrism or technological determinism (Deacon & Stanyer, 2014; Jensen, 2013).

ICT-mediated communication "involv[es] more than just exchanging information or messages" (Bennett & Segerberg, 2012, p. 753) or calling for "a
more detailed understanding of how protest and its mediation is received
and decoded in different ways by increasingly fragmented populations"
(Cammaerts, 2012, p. 131). Still, the concern raises questions for delimiting
the very key term "communication," as well as for specifying the relationship between communication and contentious elements to achieve a more
solid grounding for understanding communication in contention.

BRINGING COMMUNICATION TO THE FORE: A SYNTHETIC, COMPARATIVE FRAMEWORK

Conceptualizing and Sensitizing Communication in Contention

Before the presentation of the synthetic, communication-centered framework, how shall we demarcate "communication" in contention? Clearly,
the concept of communication we have discussed so far in the literature
of movements and political action encompasses Carey's (2008) views
of communication as transmission and ritual. To be sure, for one thing,
communication in contention embodies the exchange and transmission
of information over distance (Carey, 2008, p. 15), such as (interpersonal)
interactions in micromobilization (e.g., Snow, Worden, & Benford, 1986),
"*visible signals*" of changes in political opportunity structure (e.g., Meyer
& Minkoff, 2004, p. 1467, emphasis in original), media coverage and diffusion of protests (e.g., Meyer, 1993; Tarrow, 1993a), to name just few
examples from our earlier discussion. For another, beyond the exchange
of information per se, communication also involves the (de)codification,
interpretation, and contestation of meaning, such as the *symbolic* importance of favorable political opportunities for activism (Meyer & Minkoff,
2004, p. 1470) and the collective action frame as the manner in which
communication is interpreted, and the generation and diffusion of these
interpretations (Benford & Snow, 2000, p. 614; Garrison, 1992, p. 111). To
quote Castells's (2009, p. 54 emphasis added) specification:

> Communication is the sharing of meaning through the exchange of informa-
> tion. The process of communication is defined by the technology of commu-
> nication, the characteristics of the senders and receivers of information, their
> cultural codes of reference and protocols of communication, and the scope of
> the communication process. Meaning can only be understood in the context of
> *the social relationships* in which information and communication are processed.

In short, given the above discussion, the communication-centered framework in this book will delve into *both* the transmission and ritual dimensions of communication in contentious collective action, as will be illustrated with focuses on various forms of communication and metacommunication in the follow-up section. Apart from this, I am not aiming to provide a list of definitive variables for consideration in relation to communication. Rather, following Blumer's (1954) suggestion, I take "communication" as a sensitizing concept, that is, something that encourages research to be sensitive to (changes in) communicative practices, networks, and activities in articulating the elements in the framework of contentious collective action.

Communication and Metacommunication in the Articulation of the Dynamics of Contention

The proposal framework considers the complexity of the flows of communication in our everyday lives. One of its key purposes is to disentangle the different contributions of face-to-face, mass, and networked communication to contention in order to pinpoint and schematize the role of ICTs in political action. The framework suggests two dimensions to excavate its analytical power: First, different forms of communication—i.e., face-to-face, mass, and networked communication (Jensen & Helles, 2011, p. 519)—and, second, their corresponding metacommunication (Ruesch & Bateson, 1951). The general question is as follows: During periods of contentious collective action, *through which forms of communication and metacommunication have political opportunities been generated and disseminated? Further, which mobilizing structures have been aggregated and activated, which framing processes have established and struggled with, which identities have been articulated and contested, and what kinds of relational mechanisms among these interrelated factors have been (re)constructed and enunciated?* I will expatiate on elements in the framework as follows.

Various forms of communication. In analyzing communicative practices in contemporary society, Jensen and Helles (2011, p. 519) develop a matrix of six prototypical communicative practices (Table 2.1) "instantiated both in face-to-face interaction and in digital as well as analog media technologies." Vertically, the matrix distinguishes interpersonal, mass, and networked communication. Horizontally, the distinction deals with synchronous and asynchronous communication, i.e., whether an immediate contact and transfer of information takes place. Each cell then illustrates different media that support each type of communication. Note

Table 2.1 SIX COMMUNICATIVE PRACTICES

	Asynchronous	Synchronous
One-to-one	Email, text message	Voice, instant messenger
One-to-many	Books, newspapers, audio and video recordings, Web 1.0 / webpages, downloads	Broadcast radio and television
Many-to-many	Web 2.0 / wiki, blogs, social network sites	Online chatrooms

Source: Based on Jensen & Helles, 2011, p. 519.

that media in the matrix do not suggest only communication outlets or technical tools.[3] Instead, as Jensen explicates, media comprise (1) human bodies and their extensions in tools (as media of the first degree); (2) analog technologies (as media of the second degree) like books, newspapers, radio, and television—commonly known as "the mass media" that shape up as one-to-many media institutions and practices of communication; and (3) digital technologies (as media of the third degree) that integrate one-to-one, one-to-many, and many-to-many forms of communication (Jensen, 2010, pp. 64–71).

Following the matrix allows us to capture a nuanced multitude of dimensions of both mediated and face-to-face communication in the process of contentious collective action, from micro-processes (e.g., microstructural mobilization via interpersonal communication) to meso-level analyses (e.g., framing and SMOs) to macro-overviews (social construction of political opportunities). The matrix further reminds us, again, that social movements do not exist alone in digital communication technologies (Freelon, McIlwain, & Clark, 2018, p. 991). Rather, ICTs would be, at best, "an important component" (Freelon et al., 2018, p. 991).

Metacommunication. First coined by Bateson (1951), metacommunication provides clues as to how the information that has been communicated should be decoded between the communicators. Originally used mostly in the analysis of interpersonal interaction, metacommunication refers to "all exchanged cues and propositions about (a) codification and (b) [the] relationship between the communicators"

---

3. For a similar discussion, see Howard and Hussain's work on the term "digital media" in political contention, which includes not only the information infrastructure and tools and the content, but also "the people, organizations, and industries that produce and consume both the tools and the content" (Howard & Hussain, 2013, p. 13).

(Ruesch & Bateson, 1951, p. 209). That is to say, a complex process that involves not just a verbal exchange of information, which is normally regarded as "communication," human communication also encompasses a variety of exchanged cues and propositions, which, as Bateson suggests, shall be considered as metacommunication. In the process of exchanging information, for one thing, metacommunication provides clues as to how the information that has been communicated should be decoded. For another, metacommunication embodies a mutual relationship between communicators, which significantly influences how the information should be understood. These two forms of metacommunication overlap and intertwine in interpersonal communication practice. The point here is not that the exchanged information via interpersonal interaction is not important to study. Rather, the same information can be framed by different metacommunication codes and relationships, making the interpretation or perception of the information entirely different—even its opposite (e.g., Grof, 1981).

In essence, the concept of metacommunication calls for a shift from studying explicit exchanged information to studying the communication practice itself and the communicators' *relationship* in order to thoroughly understand human communication activity. The emphasis on communication practices as such is notably in line with Carey's ritual view of communication that underscores communication per se as a meaningful practice for human beings. I use the term "metacommunication" here in a broad sense beyond interpersonal interaction, or, like Jensen (2010) points out, as "an aspect of any communicative practice in any medium." Admittedly, Bateson (1951, p. 42) also delineates this issue by talking about metacommunication in mass communication as an example:

> Every citizen learns through the impact of mass communication how to interpret the meaning of messages not only by assessing the content, but above all by watching certain cues related to the manner of presentation. Punctuation, emphasis, attention-getting, assignment of roles, and the expression of emotion can all be seen as messages about communication, which guide the recipient in his understanding—his decodification and evaluation of the messages.

The foregoing elaboration exemplifies mass communication and entails metacommunication.

In short, metacommunication helps explain the nuances of codification and decodification in different communication practices in consideration of social relationships between the senders and receivers in a specific society. It further embodies, for instance, culture variability in communication (Gudykunst, 1997; Gudykunst & Lee, 2005)[4] and the influence of high-/low-context culture on meaning interpretation (Hall, 1976). Different forms of communication accordingly involve their corresponding metacommunication—which I will go into next.

For interpersonal communication, the relationship in metacommunication engenders implicit mutual awareness. From a Batesonian perspective, the very act of human communication carries an underlying but significant cultural valence as a determinant of both the interpretation/decodification of exchanged information and the follow-up actions: "*each participant [is made] aware of the perceptions of the other*" and that "this *mutual awareness* becomes a part determinant of all our action and interaction" (Ruesch & Bateson, 1951, p. 208, emphasis added). Such awareness is relevant because its quality and degree determines "the qualities and characteristics of metacommunication between persons" (Ruesch & Bateson, 1951, p. 209). Beyond the information exchange, the mutual awareness of the existence of and the relationship between the interlocutors thereby plays a key role in human interaction in the social world as it definitively shapes the metacommunication of interpersonal communication. Following this argument, we should consider the mutual awareness concerning the existence of each of the interlocutors and the relationship between them when investigating the process and effect of human communication, be it face-to-face or otherwise mediated.

For mass communication, Bateson's discussion above already emphasizes the influence from "certain cues" (1951, p. 42), largely media language as metacommunication, on the interpretation and evaluation of the message beyond its content, as news stories are molded and modified in specific ways to (try to) influence the audience. What is more important, I believe, is the inclusion of a consideration of the relationship between government, mass media, and its audience and, thus, the "reputation" of a media institution with its audience (Pan, 2016, p. 3) for a full picture of the relational meaning of mass communication to its audience. As Gamson and Wolfsfeld (1993, p. 120) explicate, "media systems vary both organizationally and ideologically. Media organizations vary in prestige." Disparate relationships between government, mass media, and its audience hence define the specific role of mass communication in a given society—"watchdog" or "mouthpiece"

---

4. National culture, according to Gudykunst and Lee (2005, p. 30), "influences communication . . . through the cultural norms" and "the ways individuals are socialized in their cultures."

(Whitten-Woodring & James, 2012), for instance—can further manipulate the audience's reading of a news story. The presence of news coverage of a social movement in the independent mass media, with its role as "watchdog" or "the Fourth Estate," posit Gamson and Wolfsfeld (1993), not only facilitates mobilization but also legitimizes the movement. Metacommunication also includes questions such as to what extent mass media's coverage is reliable and credible in the eye of its audience (which exemplifies the relationship between mass media and its audience and the codification of the news story [Pan, 2016, p. 3]). In the cases where mass media functions as an official "mouthpiece," or "throat and tongue" like China, mass communication commits itself to building a forced consensus as the basis of communist rule and legitimacy (Chang, Wang, & Chen, 1994). In short, to explore metacommunication in mass communication, we may explore the following questions: What kind of role does mass media play in a given context? What is the relationship between mass media and its audience? How does mass communication cover news stories and in which specific ways?

Given the basis of networked individuals (Rainie & Wellman, 2012), networked communication integrates metacommunication that emerges from interpersonal communication. Earlier scholars like Walther (1992, p. 79), for instance, recognize "affection and metacommunicative cues" such as special punctuational marks, intentional misspellings, and lexical surrogates in computer-mediated networked communication, that contextualize the message within the relationship and epitomize the relational communication among communicators (also see Parks & Floyd, 1996). Meanwhile, non-textual cues such as pictorial and graphic representations further become involved in metacommunication of, for instance, emotion in networked communication (e.g., "emoticons," see Dresner & Herring, 2010).

To summarize, metacommunication accentuates that the process of exchanging information embodies clues as to how the information that has been communicated should be decoded in terms of both the specific context that communication is raised from and the mutual relationship between the senders and receivers. Just like Castells (2009, p. 54 emphasis added) points out, "[m]eaning can only be understood in the context of *the social relationships* in which information and communication are processed." The emphasis on metacommunication allows us to overcome a reductionist approach in exploring ICTs and activism that, as several studies critique (e.g., Fenton & Barassi, 2011; Rodríguez, Ferron, & Shamas, 2014; Wolfsfeld, Segev, & Sheafer, 2013), oversimplifies or erases the deep and rich contextualization of social and political life in favor of the novelty of ICTs. Consideration of metacommunication—and therefore context—is a matter that further resonates with the cultural turn in social movement studies, which see political opportunities being embedded in and defined by cultural meanings and practices (e.g., context-specific emotions [Jasper, 1998, 2008] and repertoires as "the culturally encoded ways in which people interact in contentious politics" [McAdam et al., 2001, p. 16]). Here, in the communication-centered framework, taking metacommunication into consideration helps disclose—and thereby compare—distinct repertoires in different contexts, as activists may codify communicative practices symbolically and strategically, for instance, to unite and inspire political actors and action (e.g., Sreberny & Mohammadi, 1994; Tarrow, 2013). It also encourages the bridging of the classic dichotomy between transmission and ritual views of communication with a specific focus on the performative aspect of communication beyond the diffusion of information or message (for specific discussion, see Rodríguez, 2011).

Communication, metacommunication, and elements of contention. As McAdam et al. (2001, p. 22) affirm, "social interaction, social ties, communication and conversation [are] . . . active sites of creation and change." Then, how do communication and metacommunication, be they face-to-face, mass, networked, or some combination thereof, come to shape and articulate elements of contention (Figure 2.1)?

For political opportunities, as already discussed, communication in the broad sense shapes both the perception and expansion of changes of opportunity structure. Hence our first set of questions focuses on the *perception* of political opportunities, or the "signal" model (Meyer & Minkoff, 2004, p. 1464), which defines political opportunity structure as "*consistent—but not necessarily formal, permanent, or national—signals to social or political actors which either encourage or discourage them to . . . form social movements*" (Tarrow, 1996, p. 54, emphasis in original).

- RQ 1: What are the modes of communication and metacommunication through which activists are cognizant of changes in the political environment (which in turn reinforce the sense of political efficacy and encourage or discourage prospects for mobilization)? Are they interpersonal, mass, or networked forms of communication, or some combination thereof?
- RQ 2: How are the opportunities and constraints of political structures metacommunicated?

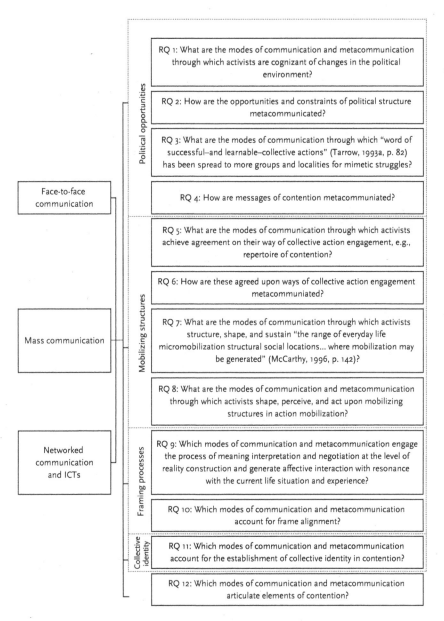

Figure 2.1 Communication and metacommunication in the articulation of dynamics of contention.

The exogenous "structural" (Meyer & Minkoff, 2004) aspects of the opportunity variables, following what scholars have previously identified (McAdam, 1996, p. 27, also see Meyer & Minkoff, 2004; Tarrow, 1996), include (1) the relative open or closed nature of the institutionalized political system; (2) the stability of the broad set of elite alignments that typically undergirds a polity; (3) the presence of elite allies; and (4) the state's capacity and propensity for repression.[5]

As Gamson and Meyer (1996, p. 276) advise, "[o]pportunities open the way for political action, but movements also make opportunities." The spread of contention occupies a key place in demonstrating the way in which movements can shape, create, or expand the opportunities for subsequent movements (Tarrow, 1993a, 1993b, 2010). As McAdam (1995, p. 2) reminds us, "the specific social processes that account for the spread of contention are by no means uniform." Therefore, our second set of questions regarding communication/metacommunication and political opportunities goes as follows:

- RQ 3: What are the modes of communication though which "word of successful—and learnable—collective actions" has been spread to more groups and localities for mimetic struggles and "be sustained far longer than the episodic and cathartic collective actions of the past"—are they interpersonal, mass, networked communication, or some combination thereof? (Tarrow, 1993a, p. 83)
- RQ 4: How are messages of contention—"the ideational, tactical, and organizational lessons of the early risers" metacommunicated? (McAdam, 1996, p. 33)

Mobilizing structures, or the organizational infrastructure of social movements, involve "those agreed upon ways of engaging in collective action," such as tactical and modular social movement repertoires and SMO forms, but they also embrace, more importantly, "a wide variety of social sites within people's daily rounds where informal and less formal ties between people can serve as solidarity and *communication facilitating structures* when and if they choose to go into dissent together" (McCarthy, 1996, p. 143, emphasis added; also see McAdam et al., 1996b, pp. 3–4). McCarthy's definition here is twofold in relation to communication and metacommunication. For one thing, we may explore the communicative mechanism through which activists navigate, learn, negotiate, and agree upon ways of participating in collective action.

---

5. The conceptualizations of political opportunities vary greatly and are thus beyond the scope of our discussion here. For more discussions, see Goldstone, 2004; Goodwin & Jasper, 1999; Koopmans, 1999; Meyer, 2004; Tarrow, 1996.

- RQ 5: What are the modes of communication though which activists achieve agreement on their modes of engaging in collective action, such as their repertoires of contention—are they interpersonal, mass, networked communication, or some combination thereof?
- RQ 6: How are these agreed upon ways of engaging in collective action metacommunicated?

For another, the definition unequivocally stresses the significant role of communication in both structuring and activating mobilizing structures, i.e., "collective vehicles"—"the meso-level groups, organizations, and informal networks" (McAdam et al., 1996b, p. 3)—and social relations (Goodwin & Jasper, 1999, p. 44) in everyday life as "the relational underpinning for most collective action" (McCarthy, 1996, p. 147). Such a view that situates mobilization of contentious moments into everyday contexts resonates with Melucci's emphasis on the relevance of everyday processes of communication and networking (what he coins as "submerged networks" (1985, p. 801) that underpin manifest contentious activity. Accordingly, we ask:

- RQ 7: What are the modes of communication though which activists structure, shape, and sustain "the range of everyday life micromobilization structural social locations . . . where mobilization may be generated: these include family units, friendship networks, voluntary associations, work units, and elements of the state structure itself"? (McCarthy, 1996, p. 142)

The availability of mobilizing structures, nevertheless, stands as a necessary, but not a sufficient condition for actual mobilization. Goodwin and Jasper (1999, p. 45) raise awareness about equally likely *demobilization* on the basis of social relations and SMOs (also see McAdam & Paulsen, 1993). Snow, Zurcher, and Ekland-Olson (1980, p. 795) contend that "the 'motives' for joining or continued participation are generally emergent and interactional rather than pre-structured . . . they arise out of a process of ongoing interaction." Because of that, the key issue concerns how mobilizing structures operate, rather than seeing mobilization as structurally given. Not surprisingly, the potential of the mobilizing structure has to be activated, so as to convince people to participate in the mobilizing action.

- RQ 8: What are the modes of communication and metacommunication though which activists shape, perceive, and act upon mobilizing structures in action mobilization?

Framing processes, then, denote interactive—or, in some studies, "interactional" (Snow et al., 1986)—discursive processes through which shared meanings have been negotiated, contested, modified, articulated, and established. Snow et al. (1986, p. 464) have labeled "the various interactive and communicative processes that affect frame alignment," i.e., the linkage between individual and SMO interpretive orientations, as micromobilization. We then ask:

- RQ 9: Which modes of communication and metacommunication engage the process of meaning interpretation and negotiation at the level of reality construction and generate affective interaction that resonate with the person's current life situation and experience?
- RQ 10: Which modes of communication and metacommunication account for frame alignment?

Communication also articulates collective identity, or "an individual's cognitive, moral, and emotional connection with a broader community" (Polletta & Jasper, 2001, p. 285). For this reason, we ask:

- RQ 11: Which modes of communication and metacommunication account for the establishment of collective identity in contentious collective action?

We should not forget that elements of political contention interact with each other, instead of remaining static or isolated. For instance, mobilization entails a process of diffusion in interpersonal network (Walgrave & Wouters, 2014). Protest diffusion generates "interpretative frames that not only inspire and justify collective action, but also give meaning to and legitimate the tactics that evolve" (Snow et al., 1986, p. 477). The strategic frame in turn affects its ability to mobilize members and supporters, gain support from other groups, and defuse opposition (Polletta & Jasper, 2001). Beyond forms of action, contentious repertoires "connect and belong to sets of actors" (Crossley, 2002, p. 49), and hence articulate into existence the collective identity of participants in contentious action (Polletta & Jasper, 2001, pp. 292–293). Consequently, we ask:

- RQ 12: Which modes of communication and metacommunication articulate different elements of contention and drive people to act collectively?

Cutting to the heart of the objections of the communication-centered framework promises to compare different forms of communication and their respective influences on elements of contention in order to pinpoint the change bought by ICTs. In answering such a question, four theoretical reasons point out the need to scrutinize a multiplicity of forms of communicative practices and their roles in contentious collective action.

First, research on ICTs and contentious collective action risk the danger of theoretical inaccuracy, or exaggerating the role of ICTs in contentious collective action if *only* the use of ICTs and tech-enabled communication in movements is considered. In practice, studies have reminded us that tech-enabled communication does not override unmediated, classical forms of social organizing and structuring, i.e., face-to-face communication (Kavada, 2010, pp. 361–363; Lim, 2012; Milkman, 2017; Tufekci & Wilson, 2012), nor the traditional and the mainstream, mass communication (e.g., Fenton & Barassi, 2011). For instance, during the Occupy Wall Street (OWS) movement, "participants' physical, face-to-face interactions continue to be crucial complements to virtual network building. Many OWS activists commented on the importance of Zuccotti Park and the other occupied spaces for their movement . . . in-person meeting and other direct interactions were essential for" the Dreamers, Black Lives Matter, and the anti-sexual violence movement (Milkman, 2017, p. 9). Moreover, there are (always) many non-activists with various ICT devices who do *not* participate, as well as activists without ICT devices. Taking into consideration both mediated and face-to-face communication allows research to pin down the transformation introduced by ICTs, if any, by comparing the impacts of mediated and unmediated communication on contentious collective action.

Second is the concern of "multiple embeddings" of communications similar to the argument on the role of social ties in movements (McAdam & Paulsen, 1993, p. 642). With a narrowly construed focus on communication in a single medium at a time, research may fail to acknowledge conceptually or treat empirically the fact that individuals are invariably embedded in multiple communicative flows and networks that may expose the individual to conflicting pressures toward contentious collective action. For instance, messages from social media (many-to-many communication) may advocate protest engagement, but a person's family members and colleagues (one-to-one communication) may reject participation. The Freelon et al. (2018, p. 1006) study on the Black Lives Matter movement acknowledges multiple communication channels, apart from digital media (i.e., Twitter in their study), in movements, such as "letters and phone calls from constituents [and] conversations with colleagues." Similarly, González-Bailón, Borge-Holthoefer, Rivero, and Moreno (2011, p. 6) in the examination of online recruitment remind us about "the relative weight that different sources of information have in shaping individual behavior."[6] Specifying the form(s) and dimension(s) of communication and metacommunication thus gives us a better grasp of the communication dynamics that induce people to become involved in collective action and in the end, provides us with a more complete explanation of the communicative processes involved in political movements and collective action.

Third, I follow the suggestion made by McAdam et al. (2001) about a relational, interactive model to better understand the dynamics of political contention. Therefore, the framework should consider how various communicative practices are enacted in different elements of contention and, more importantly, how they facilitate interactions among them. For instance, research would examine how one-to-many mass communication improves the perception of political opportunities in society and encourages one-to-one interpersonal mobilization or many-to-many networked communication. Addressing communication also overcomes earlier critiques about the missing "actor" in the framework in *Dynamics of Contention* (Mische, 2003, p. 91) or the neglect of human agency in political opportunities (Goodwin & Jasper, 1999) or framing (Benford, 1997, pp. 418–419), as it centers the human being as the actor and its communicative practices as a key element in political movements.

Fourth, metacommunication advances the understanding of ICTs as "*social* technology" (Bennett, 2005, p. 205, emphasis in original; also see "the symbolic character of technology in protest culture" in Gerbaudo, 2014, p. 266) beyond the instrumental use by revealing contextually bound social codes and values that are inscribed in the application of technology for communication and contention (e.g., online political satire in China, see Yang & Jiang, 2015). In this regard, to discern metacommunication allows us to delve into the articulation of social and political meanings and experiences within social movements as well as to compare contentious collective actions in different contexts—why some succeed but others fail, even with the same communication technology.

---

6. For similar discussions, see, for instance, González-Bailón et al. (2011, p.6) which acknowledge that unobserved exposure to information, except the one from Twitter, is "overestimating the influence effects of Twitter activity."

In short, as a middle-range theory (Merton, 1968), the communication-centered framework is able to transcend the limits of extant discipline-confined approaches to the field by conceptualizing the evolving relationship between (technologically mediated) communication and contentious collective action, and by integrating bodies of literatures that are isolated from different disciplines. For one thing, social movement scholars would do well to acknowledge insights in communication studies and expatiate on the relevance of communication in contentious collective action (e.g., Earl & Garrett, 2017). For another, communication scholars would benefit from integrating the sociology of movements, going beyond specific—sometimes, narrow-scope—examination of ICTs and contentious collective action by considering the broader dynamics of contention, comparing face-to-face, mass, and networked, or ICT-mediated communications, and pinpointing various kinds of communication that different technologies afford that shape contentious collective action. Before moving toward an inquiry of whether—and if so, how—mobile communication technology brings change to contentious politics in contemporary China, the next section will briefly discuss the methodological issue, with more information in the Appendix: Methodological Reflections.

METHODOLOGICAL NOTES

As mentioned in the Introduction, existing scholarship has barely touched on the subject of mobile communication and contentious collective action in China from a systematic perspective; the topic remains largely unexplored. Therefore, both the novelty and specific nature (i.e., political contention in China) of the topic call for an exploratory study in using a qualitative approach. To achieve the above goals, this book employs a case study design to investigate "a contemporary phenomenon within its real-life context" (Yin, 2009, p. 18), as this design allows for comparing differences within and between cases as well as generalizing commonalities across the cases.

The data collection for this book has been carried out over 10 years. I started to collect data on the use of mobile phones—largely to spread government-labeled "rumors"—during the outbreak of the severe acute respiratory syndrome (SARS) in southern China in the Spring of 2003.[7]

7. In fact, as early as 1999, the Falun Gong religious movement was already using mobile phones to secretly organize a sit-in that surrounded the party and government leadership compound in Beijing (Shirk, 2011, p. 6). Nevertheless, most people were not aware of this due to heavy censorship.

One of the things that drew my attention during the SARS epidemic, beyond the mundane, daily communication function of mobile phones, was the mobilization of thousands of panicked citizens—driven by text messages—purchasing vinegar, masks, and Chinese herbal medicines. Later, it was again text messages that revealed Chinese authorities initially pinpointed and censored all information put out on the growing number of SARS cases (Kleinman & Watson, 2006; Ma, 2005). Information did, however, leak out and reach the public through Short Message Service (SMS) texts that recipients forwarded to family and friends.[8] For the first time, SARS-afflicted China demonstrated that mobile communication as the main sources of public information had partially threatened Beijing's media blackout and information control (Lim, 2004).

If the 2003 SARS communication shows that the mobile phone has been employed by a population hungry for uncensored information and freer communication during an urgent crisis against a government that regards information censorship and communication control as essential to its power, then, in the subsequent years, reportedly, mobile technologies have enabled people to express their political opinions and engage in political issues on a much wider scale and through more diversified ways than before. The environmental concern over petro-chemical factories, namely the para-xylene plant (PX hereafter),[9] in Xiamen, Southeast China's Fujian Province, was largely ignited by "millions of Xiamen residents frenziedly forward[ing] the same [mobilizing] text message" (Lan & Zhang, 2007), urging each other to join a street protest opposing the local government's PX project in 2007. To figure out possible reasons behind this "unexpected"[10] contention, I carried out three fieldtrips between September and December to Xiamen and interviewed residents about the demonstration.

The experience convinced me of the significance of understanding mobile communication in politics—or politics in mobile communication in contemporary China in particular—through an ethnographic approach to

8. For instance, one text message that read "[China's] Ministry of Health announced that the number of SARS cases has broken through 10,000" was resent over 2.13 million times in several cities, including Chongqing, Guangzhou, Shenzhen, Shenyang, Chengdu, Beijing, Wuhan, Fuzhou, and Shanghai (*Jinling Evening News*, 2003). Another example is the message: "fatal viruses appear in Guangzhou," which was transmitted 40 million times during the day on 8 February, with 41 million on the second day and another 45 million on the third day (Chen & Jiang, 2003).

9. Para-xylene is a petrochemical feedstock used in plastics, polyester, and other synthetic manufacturing.

10. In addition to government's measures to "maintain stability," the residents of Xiamen, particularly those in the middle-class, are well-known for their good temper that would not make them go against the authorities.

investigate "a contemporary phenomenon within its real-life context" (Yin, 2009, p. 18). Ethnography is used for both the nature of contentious collective action and the study of mobile phone uses (see, e.g., similar methods in studies on mobile communication [Ling, 2004, 2008, 2013]). On top of the experience of fieldwork mentioned above, the other main types of research and data collection projects are as follows:

(1) In December 2008, I collected seven telephone interviews about the mass incident on June 22 in Weng'an, a town in Southwest China's Guizhou Province. The incident involved over 20,000 residents smashing and setting fire to police vehicles and local government buildings when an allegation of a cover-up of a 16-year-old girl's "unusual death" circulated via mobile texts and calls (Yu, 2008).

(2) From August to December 2010, as well as in October 2011, I carried out fieldtrips in Xiamen about the anti-PX demonstration. I have collected 18 interviews.

(3) In March 2010, I carried out telephone interviews about the earthquake rumors in Shanxi Province (Lv & Wang, 2010; Wang & Sun, 2010; Yu, 2010). Later, in October 2010, I carried out fieldtrips in Shanxi for further data collection.

(4) In April 2010, I collected six telephone interviews about the taxi drivers' strikes in Fuzhou. In October 2010 and October 2011, I carried out fieldtrips in Fuzhou and Shenzhen about taxi drivers' strikes. In May 2013, I conducted three telephone interviews about the taxi drivers' strikes in Wenling, Zhejiang Province. The strike in Fuzhou occurred on April 23, 2010, in response to a surge in police-issued penalties (*China Daily*, 2010), while the similar one in Shenzhen at the end of October 2010 (eChinacities.com, 2010), with over 3,000 taxi drivers taking part in a three-day strike to protest the failure of the government to address the problems of suburban drivers and the city's inequitable cab fare structure. The strike occurred in Wenling for similar reasons on May 1, 2013 (*South China Morning Post*, 2013). Reportedly, all strikes were organized largely through mobile phones.

(5) From February to June 2011, I carried out field research in Beijing, Shanghai, Guangzhou, Taiyuan, and Fuzhou and interviewed people about the use of mobile phones in their everyday lives with a focus on interpersonal relationships, rumor distribution, and political engagement, if any.

(6) In January and August 2013, I carried out several fieldtrips to Ningbo, Kunming, and Chengdu and interviewed residents about the anti-PX demonstrations in Ningbo on October 24, 2012 (Liu & Yan, 2012) and

at the beginning of May in the other two cities in 2013 (Chang, 2013; Staff Reporter, 2013).

Here it should be pointed out that this study is not an attempt to explain the various factors that caused collective resistance or political protests; instead, the point is to investigate and interpret how and to what extent mobile phones enter these events in the context of political and social constraints in contemporary China. Thus, whether the case succeeded in changing the government's policies through mobile-phone-enabled collective action, for instance, was not a necessary criterion for selection, as there are too many other (contingent) factors influencing government decisions to act or adopt a certain plan. Rather, by focusing on the actual use of mobile phones in specific cases instead of their results, we are able to explore the possible roles and influences of mobile phones in contentious collective action.

For the interview, generally speaking, I follow Flanagin, Stohl, and Bimber's (2006, p. 39) suggestion toward "what people are doing, how they are relating to one another, and what opportunities are afforded them, and from these, examining what organization and structure fit their behavior and help facilitate collective action." When asking questions, I deliberatively avoid the presumption that ICTs in general and mobile communication technologies, in particular, matter in the event. Instead, the interview began by reconstructing the interviewees' personal background and experience using various ICTs, before moving on to their description of experiences during the event, and their self-reflections on the opportunities and threats of these forms of communication.

On top of these first-hand interviews and ethnographic field notes, the book also draws on secondary evidence, including academic works, news reports, and online databases for the comparative study in the last chapter. Nevertheless, I also acknowledge the limit that if the original investigator or reporter did not look for various forms of communication and metacommunication in his or her work, it is unlikely that I would find them for further analysis.

To conclude this chapter, although scholarship has generated a fruitful discussion on ICTs and contentious collective action, the discipline-bound limitation restricts the dialogue between different fields. To overcome this issue, the chapter proposes the centralization of communication in the framework of movements and contention to deliberate (a) the contested role of technologies in movements and (b) the relational dynamics among the interrelated elements in contentious collective action. These two dimensions, including various forms of communication and metacommunication, allow for greater nuance and possible comparison of movement processes across contexts. In the next chapter, I will look at how mobile phones become part of repertoires of contention, before moving to the discussion of the use of mobile phones in political contention.

CHAPTER 3

From Affordances to Repertoires of Contention

The Missing Link in Understanding the Use of (Mobile) Technologies in Contention

Uniformity [in the contentious repertoire] within regimes and differences between regimes result from two interacting influences: (1) actions of central governments that impose limits on collective claim-making within the regime and (2) communication and collaboration among claimants (actual and potential) that pool information, beliefs, and practices concerning what forms of claim making work or don't work. (Tilly, 2008, p. 149)

The use of ICTs in political contention has emerged to become a matter of common occurrence nowadays. While Egyptians and Tunisians largely adopted Facebook and Twitter to disseminate protest information, organize street demonstrations, and raise local and global awareness of up-to-the-minute happenings during the Arab Spring (Howard & Hussain, 2013; Huang, 2011), Hongkongers mainly drew strength from WhatsApp and Facebook to assemble on the street and vent their anger and frustration at Beijing in the Umbrella movement (Lee & Chan, 2018, p. 110). For the Occupy Wall Street protesters in the United States, Twitter, YouTube, and Facebook allowed them to mobilize a surge of movements against social and economic inequality while receiving global attention (Costanza-Chock, 2012; Juris, 2012; Thorson et al., 2013). Why, then, during the political turbulence, did Egyptians and Tunisians depend less on WhatsApp, "the most social tool favoured in the Arab world" (AG Reporter, 2015)? Similarly, why did Hongkongers not use YouTube in their civil disobedience campaigns, even though YouTube has recently enjoyed a spectacular growth of use in Hong Kong (Woodhouse, 2015)?

Much ink has been spilled analyzing the use of ICTs in contentious movements and actions so far, as I recognized at the beginning of this book. While extant scholarship yields a nuanced picture of how people have used ICTs during various contentions, there is more to the story than just looking at the use of specific digital communication technologies. ICTs are not "born" to be used in and for political contention. Rather, people appropriate and maneuver them—*some but not others*, as we see from the cases of the Arab Spring, the Umbrella movement, and Occupy Wall Street—for such purposes, in specific contexts. Consequently, exploring the reasoning behind people's strategic or tactical understandings, choices, and uses of specific (functions of) ICTs helps spell out particular mechanisms that encourage digital communication technologies to become a part of these protestors' repertoires of contention. This process unveils "the microfoundations of political action" by expounding upon the perspective of agency (Jasper, 2004, p. 4) that transforms affordances (Gibson, 1966) of given technologies into aspects of the contentious repertoire. In other words, the answer lies at the heart of the follow-up question: How, and under which circumstances, were decisions made to use ICTs for contention made on the basis of affordances that structure the possibilities of the use of this technology? This chapter offers a less addressed yet vital analysis, i.e., understanding how repertoires of contention in contemporary China are created, with the mobile phone being one example among many possibilities.

In the following sections, I first start with a theoretical grounding that elucidates the relevant, yet rarely addressed, link between affordance and the development of repertoires of contention. Second, I unravel the issue why people employ certain functions of the mobile phone but not others in their protest practices. The process of strategically choosing which functions of their mobile phones that protesters will use in the process of contention is shaped by various forms of communication and their quite distinctive contributions to repertoire selection in the specific context of China. Third, I conclude with thoughts on encouraging a further investigation of the link (or "gap") between affordances to repertoires of contention.

LINKING AFFORDANCES AND REPERTOIRES OF CONTENTION

Affordances and Repertoires of Contention: A Clarification of Some Contested Issues

Before a discussion on the link between affordance and contentious repertoires, it is helpful to begin with a brief review of existing deliberations on ICTs in political contention, focusing on the use of the term "affordance." I then proceed to a discussion of Tilly's seminal term "repertoire of contention." By doing so, I will clarify the conceptions of these two important terms, along with their connections in the discussion of contentious politics.

Among studies that explore the role of ICTs in political contention, the dissection and analysis of affordances emerge as a relevant issue to explore the usage of communication technologies in contention (e.g., Bennett & Segerberg, 2013; Earl & Kimport, 2011; Enjolras, Steen-Johnsen, & Wollebæk, 2013; Papacharissi, 2015). Nevertheless, the inconsistency and, in some cases, inappropriateness of the use of the term "affordance," first coined by Gibson (1966), complicates the understanding of the possible effects ICTs might have on movements. Some take the technology-oriented perspective to address the importance of the material aspects of communication technologies. Largely following Norman's (1988) definition, Earl and Kimport regard affordance to be "the type of action or a characteristic of actions that a technology enables through its design" (2011, p. 10).[1] Along similar lines, researchers employ phrases such as "the affordances of blogging technology" (Graves, 2007), "social media affordances" (Christensen, 2011; Enjolras et al., 2013, p. 891), "affordances of particular social media technologies" (Selander & Jarvenpaa, 2016, p. 333), "Facebook affordances" (Kaun & Stiernstedt, 2014), "the technological affordances of Facebook" (Kaun & Stiernstedt, 2014), "affordance of Twitter" (Jacobson & Mascaro, 2016; Ogan & Varol, 2016), and "affordances of mobile technologies and social networking platforms" (Couldry et al., 2018, p. 180), just to mention a few. Others treat the term rather as the potential outcome of ICT use in movements. For instance, Dahlberg (2011) and Goggin (2013) discuss the "democratic affordances" offered by digital media. Mercea (2013, p. 1309) explains "horizontal collaboration" as an affordance of social media.

---

1. See similar discussions in Gleason, 2013; Penney & Dadas, 2014; Selander & Jarvenpaa, 2016; Thorson et al., 2013; Tufekci, 2014, p. 205; Zuckerman, 2015.

Yet, as Evans et al. (2017) enunciate, affordance is *neither* a feature of the technology *nor* an outcome. While the outcome-oriented perspective ignores affordances as "constant properties" (Gibson, 1977, p. 285) independent of the goals of the actor (Michaels, 2003, pp. 136–137), the technology-oriented perspective, with "language that talks about the affordances *of* or *offered by* specific technologies . . . and positions the affordance as inherent in use based on some material aspects of the technology," fails to acknowledge "the agency present in [the use of] technology" (Evans et al., 2017, p. 39, emphasis in original). In other words, contemporary scholars write as if people are *unambiguously* using Facebook, Twitter, or social media in a straightforward way that is structurally determined by the communication technologies as such. The technologically oriented tendency risks parlous media-centric, techno-centric, or technologically deterministic logic, implying that communication technologies will without doubt lead to, for instance, homogeneity in use (for a critique in the case of the internet, see Hargittai & Hinnant, 2008). Just as Parchoma (2014, p. 361) untangles the issue, "affordances neither belong to the environment nor the individual, but rather to the relationship between individuals and their perceptions of environments." Following this argument, affordance entails *a relational nature* between the actor and the technology in a specific context, which thereby underlines a triadic consideration of "the attributes and abilities of users, the materiality of technologies, and the contexts of technology use" (Evans et al., 2017, p. 36; also see Davis & Chouinard, 2016). In our case, the interrogation of affordances in the study of ICTs and contention postulates not only the discussion regarding particular material features of (mobile) technology but also, more importantly, ideas about the specific perceptions of the selection and use of technology for contentious activities that have been established via communication and metacommunication by various users in different contentious contexts.

If affordances imply the possible uses of technology, then "repertoire of contention" functions as a key term to understand the choice and actualization of some of the possibilities for action in contention.[2] Tilly (1986) reveals the evolution and transformation of repertoires, first in an investigation of the contested process of signaling, negotiation, and struggle in 400 years of modern French history, then in an analysis of the changing features of popular contention in early modern Britain (Tilly, 1995, 2008; for a comprehensive review, see Tarrow, 2008). Tilly writes:

2. For instance, for further discussions on electronic repertoires of contention, see Costanza-Chock, 2003; Rolfe, 2005; Van Laer & Van Aelst, 2010.

The word *repertoire* identifies a limited set of routines that are learned, shared and acted out through a relatively deliberate process of choice. Repertoires are learned cultural creations, but they do not descend from abstract philosophy or take shape as a result of political propaganda; they emerge from struggle. People learn to break windows in protest, attack pilloried prisoners, tear down dishonoured houses, stage public marches, petition, hold formal meetings, organize special-interest associations. At any particular point in history, however, they learn only a rather small number of alternative ways to act collectively. (2005, pp. 41–42)

Therein lies the significance of the contentious repertoire. As a delimited array of contentious claims-making practices and performances, the repertoire in essence is situated in a complex mesh of multifaceted conditions of the moment (Rodríguez, Ferron, & Shamas, 2014). For one thing, structural factors—such as regime type,[3] the history of contention (e.g., prior societal experience and knowledge of contention), and changes in political opportunity—have significant bearing on repertoire selection (Tarrow, 2008, p. 237). For another, people not only closely monitor changes in the political environment, but they also deliberately interpret the actions of others. A repertoire of contention hence "calls attention to the clustered, learned, yet improvisational character of people's interactions as they make and receive each other's claim" (Tilly & Tarrow, 2006, p. 16).

It is significant to keep in mind that, as Tarrow underscores, "repertoire is not only what people *do* . . . it is what they *know how to do* and what others *expect* them to do" (1993, p. 70, emphasis in original). To explore Crossley's definition, a repertoire involves "a tacit recognition of the *know-how* or *acquired competence* involved in specific forms of protest" (2002b, p. 49, emphasis added). This "tactical question," as Van Laer and Van Aelst concur in their discussion on the internet and movement repertoires, "is critical for social movements" (2010, p. 1151). Consequently, in the discussion on the development of the contentious repertoire, the focus should not merely rest on which contentious tactics or strategies people adopt or appropriate, but we must also expand on people's understanding and choice of specific actions, or, more precisely in this study, the perception or know-how of using mobile phones as a means of protest. By doing so, we probe "the social dynamics of the processes by which agents and groups select from that repertoire" (Crossley, 2002b, p. 51).

3. This includes, for instance, whether the regime permits, forbids, or tolerates some aspect of the repertoire (Tarrow, 2008, p. 239).

Furthermore, Crossley draws attention to the notion that "repertoires are not so much forms of action as *of interaction*, . . . [which] connect and belong to sets of actors" (2002b, p. 49, emphasis added). That is, to use Tilly's original statement:

> The action takes its meaning and effectiveness from *shared understandings, memories, and agreements*, however grudging, among the parties. In that sense, then, a repertoire of actions resembles not individual consciousness but a language; although individuals and groups know and deploy the actions in a repertoire, *the actions connect sets of individuals and groups*. (1995, p. 30, emphasis added)

Hence, the contentious repertoire helps articulate into existence the identity of participants in contentious activity or, in other quarters, evolves into the construction of the identity of the agent producing it. Against this backdrop, individuals and groups consolidate further through the deployment of specific contentious repertories with defined meanings and effects.

The investigation above on extant scholarship regarding two key concepts—affordance and repertoires of contention—acknowledges a similarity between them. Both terms entail not essentialism but *relationality*. As illustrated, inherited from the original Gibsonian view, affordance exists in relationships among artifacts, active agents (users and designers), and their context (Davis & Chouinard, 2016, p. 2). Repertoires emerge and evolve, by the same token, in relation with structural variables, exercise (or not) of agency, and the cultural context in which they originate. The same repertoire of possible actions may not be adopted or used in the same way in different contentious environments for reasons other than communication technology per se (Van Laer & Van Aelst, 2010, p. 1151).

Linking Affordances to Repertoires of Contention

Although the notion of affordance and the development of a contentious repertoire, as described above, have been present in various discussions, the connection between them remains obscure. To better understand the linking or transformation from affordance to the development of a contentious repertoire, the following diagram sheds light on the deployment of ICTs in political contention in terms of three issues (Figure 3.1).

First, given its relational nature, the affordances of communication technology may differ or vary significantly among different agents (e.g., social groups) across different contexts. Affordances are, as discussed above,

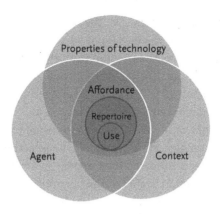

Figure 3.1 The relationship among affordance, contentious repertoire, and use.

possibilities and opportunities for action that emerge from agents engaging with a certain property of technology in a specific context. The same communication technology would therefore denote disparate meanings and result in subsequently dissimilar uses for different people in diverse cultures. For instance, great differences prevail when using social media (Egros, 2011) or the internet (Hargittai & Hinnant, 2008; Hermeking, 2005) among different demographics across divergent cultures or countries.

Second, as illustrated in Figure 3.1, the contentious repertoire essentially develops from—and hence is confined to—the defined affordance(s) of communication technology in a given context. More specifically, for one thing, affordance underpins "the practical constitution of repertories" via "the activities of everyday life" (Crossley, 2002b, p. 49). That is, contentious repertoires grow out of affordance and as "a by-product of everyday experiences" (Della Porta, 2013). For instance, the barricade as an aspect of the protest repertoires developed during the French Revolution emerged from the routine and everyday practice of "neighborhood protection" in sixteenth-century Paris (Traugott, 1993). Protestors then simply chose their protest repertoire from (some affordances of) the available stock. In this sense, affordances of communication technologies in everyday life in a given context offer *preconditions* for possible use of these technologies in contentious activities but do not imply or guarantee that these repertoires will emerge. For another, affordances are only a necessary, but not a sufficient, precondition for the development of repertoires of action. Putting the matter another way, affordance does not equal repertoire, and *not* every affordance will transfer into the contentious repertoire. Rather, contentious practices encompass a deliberative but constrained selection of actions within the repertoire by agents from affordances. In this sense, the transformation from affordances (i.e., the possibilities inherent in the use of a specific technology) to the development of a repertoire of contention (i.e., in the discussion here, the possibilities of technology used as a part of the contentious claims-making practice and performance) embodies strategic choices (Jasper, 2004) that people as agents make in contention. A careful consideration of both structural factors and issues of agency (especially in the case of the development of repertoire of action and tactical innovation) thus untangles the key issue of the selection of repertoires or variations in these repertoires as they appear in contention in different parts of the world as demonstrated at the beginning of this chapter.

Third, contentious repertoires, once established, may constrain further innovative transfer from other affordances to repertoires. In other words, once an affordance becomes a part of a repertoire of contention, people may get used to it and it could become difficult to innovate new uses or strategies. Once labeled, like the case of the so-called Facebook Revolution or Twitter Revolution, protest repertoires tend to overshadow and limit the affordances of the medium. The possibilities and opportunities of digital communication technologies like Facebook and Twitter are transformed and reified by a narrow, specific, and repeated use in certain circumstances. This may stifle further transformation of other possibilities from affordance to repertoire, consequently restraining the diversification of possibilities for contentious use.

To sum up, as Figure 3.1 illustrates, the narrow focus on the actual use of ICTs in contention, valuable though it might be for figuring out people's practices of contention, fails to grasp the dynamic possibilities of human agency and, further, overlooks political and social complexity in favor of a stereotypic rendering of communication technologies. Particular attention should be given to expanding and supplementing empirical research into the investigation of affordances and the establishment of repertoires of contention. Hence, these specific questions:

- What are the affordances of mobile technology for a specific social group in a given contentious context?
- How does the transformation from affordances to repertoires of contention occur?

OBSERVATIONS FROM THE FIELD

This section presents the findings from the fieldwork and the interviews I conducted in China between the years 2010 and 2013. The interviews not only show how various forms of communication flow, but, more importantly, they also probe people's different attitudes and perceptions toward these forms of communication during a moment of political contention. As we will soon see, digitally mediated networked communication has become the dominant channel for the diffusion of contention-related information, especially after coverage of the conflict is suppressed or erased in mass (and often state-sponsored) communication. I found that individuals received and forwarded protest information, including mobilizing calls, and they also learned about mobile phone use for protests largely via networked and face-to-face communications. Official, mass communication usually gets involved either after the proliferation of controversial or mobilizing messages, or after the issue has attracted embarrassing attention from overseas media. Interpersonal, networked, and mass communications coexist, yet they contribute to the diffusion of contention and the perception of mobile technologies as contentious tools in significantly distinctive ways. I will start with an empirical observation regarding mobile and digital communication, as well as interpersonal communication, before moving to the issue of mass communication.

Interpersonal and Digitally Mediated Networked Communications for Contention

Both interpersonal and digitally mediated networked communication lead, for the most part, to the diffusion of information related to political contention as well as the follow-up use of mobile technologies. For 82% (25 out of 30) of the interviewees, digitally mediated communication—including those via mobile calls, text messaging, WeChat, Weibo, BBS, and online forums—functions as the primary means of receiving and circulating contested information. Networked communication is also the most common way to encourage people to adopt certain functions of their mobile phones for protests and demonstrations. Following that statistic, face-to-face communication is also important (18%, or 5 out of 30 interviewees) for exchanging information about protests and for shaping the understanding of mobile phone use as part of a repertoire for action, contributing to the history, knowledge, and experience of contention. Digitally mediated, networked, and face-to-face communications contribute to mobilization and the spread of contention in terms of the following three aspects.

First, digitally mediated, networked, and face-to-face communications increase the visibility of alternative information about politically sensitive topics in society, especially those with contested or controversial contents that have been suppressed or restricted by the authorities.

For instance, in the Xiamen anti-PX case, all interviewees acknowledged that they first heard of the name "PX" and the controversial information surrounding it via text messaging. The message ran rampant within a short time, while, according to a 35-year-old taxi driver, "local media did not mention this issue at all for over three months" (October 5, 2010, personal communication). Texting facilitates face-to-face conversation on the issue and, reportedly, the phrase "did you receive the [PX-related] SMS?" became the opening remark when Xiamen residents met each other between March and May of 2007, the period cultivating the ferment of popular discontent (Zhu, 2007, p. A1). Similarly, in the Weng'an case, the controversy about the death of the local girl proliferated extensively via texts, and therefore directed residents' attention to the issue against the complete silence of official media (Buxi, 2008; Shu, 2009; Zhang, Zhu, & Huang, 2008). Word-of-mouth conversation was the second relevant channel for the dissemination of communication about the "injustice" and the grievances that the family suffered, which the interviewees believed the local authorities ignored. The cases of taxi drivers' strikes show more or less the same situation. Mobile phones, or mobile calls more specifically, functioned as the central means for taxi drivers to exchange information regarding the government's inaction as well as their discontentment toward the authorities. All interviewees emphasized the relevance of mobile calls and conversations for maintaining contact with "fellow drivers" (同伴) and receiving up-to-date messages regarding the progress of the situation. Some also acknowledged face-to-face meetings at service stations for maintaining situational awareness, which they said were equally as important as their mobile channels, if not more so. Again, none of the interviewees mentioned official, mass communication, as they believed, to use one's phrase, "the government did not care so much about us and [did not] want to talk [about the issue]" (a 35-year-old taxi driver in Shenzhen, October 20, 2010, personal communication).

If the above cases encompass relatively the homogeneous functions of mobile phones—either text messaging or phone calls—to receive and spread controversial information, later anti-PX protests saw the adoption of various forms of digitally mediated, networked communication for the same purpose. In the cases of Kunming, Chengdu, and Maoming, local residents mostly resorted to QQ and mobile-based WeChat to disseminate PX-related information, inform their social networks, and initiate discussions, even if, as with the other cases, mass media did not cover the issue at all. Up to 95% of interviewees remembered that the information about the PX project emerged and circulated within their social networks via mobile call, text messaging, QQ, and WeChat. Apart from that, the rest received the information via face-to-face interaction with family or friends, followed by similar messages from their mobile phones. In short, both interpersonal and networked communications in some ways offer people "a broader autonomy" (Della Porta, 2013, p. 2) from the official, mass communication to receive and spread alternative information.

Second, apart from the diffusion of relevant information, people spread mobilizing invitations, either to come for a "stroll (散步)," a euphemism for street demonstrations in anti-PX protests, or to "drink tea (喝茶)," which was the code used for mobilizing strikes in the taxi drivers' protests. These were spread via internet-based platforms like QQ and online forums and, especially, voice calls, text messaging, and WeChat accessed on mobile phones.

In the Xiamen case, the mobilizing message traveled in substance via mobile text messaging, even in the face of local government suppression. In later anti-PX cases, calls for protests expanded via digitally mediated communication such as WeChat, Weibo, and mobile messaging, which became a key part of the mechanism of mobilization (BBC, 2014; Lee & Ho, 2014; Jing, 2013). The easy-to-use features of digital communication technology, and mobile technology in particular, allow people to invite their social networks to collective action without much effort. A 23-year-old graduate from the Kunming case said that she had forwarded the message via WeChat to her whole class and to her relatives, a total of 75 people, by "just twiddling the thumb" (June 2, 2013, personal communication). In the Xiamen case, the apex of the anti-PX movement occurred as "millions of Xiamen residents frenziedly forward[ed] the same [mobilizing] text message around their mobile phones" (Lan & Zhang, 2007), urging each other to join a street protest opposing the government's PX project. The interviewees from other cases also confirmed that they had forwarded mobilizing messages to different social groups they were affiliated with by "copying," "pasting," and "sending" the message or simply pressing the "forward" or "retweet" button on their mobile phones. To sum up, the easy-to-use mobile devices with inexpensive (or, in most cases, "zero-cost") telecommunication fees for information dissemination became the key facilitator—be it through text messaging, mobile-based QQ, or WeChat—to spread mobilizing calls to as many people as possible.

The cases of taxi driver strikes bear a strong resemblance to the anti-PX protests, with mobile phones as the key resource for the diffusion of mobilizing initiatives. Yet, in their strikes, taxi drivers saw a specific mobile technology function– the voice call—as the dominant, or only, means for the dissemination of mobilizing calls. All taxi drivers depended on mobile calls to exchange messages regarding the planning and implementation of the strikes. In practice, mobile calls enable them to share strike initiatives while driving. As one driver said, "Texting creates a lot of visual distraction [while driving], let alone distributing emails or chatting via online instant messaging platforms like QQ. But driving while talking is easy and convenient. For us, the earlier [we mobilize], the better" (a 34-year-old taxi driver in Fuzhou, April 25, 2010, personal communication). Using mobile phones to call for strikes has thus become a convenient, flexible, and practical way for taxi drivers to mobilize collective action "while driving and looking for passengers" (a 34-year-old taxi driver in Fuzhou, April 25, 2010, personal communication).

After receiving these controversial and mobilizing messages, protesters often moved to search engines, microblogging sites, and online forums to look for further information about politically sensitive issues. These digital platforms became major channels for the newly mobilized to explore detailed information about the issues they were concerned with and, more importantly, to retrieve the history and knowledge of previous protests concerning these issues in order to learn from them.

For instance, the interviewees reported that they found out a lot of information about anti-PX protests in other cities as soon as they entered keywords such as "PX" via search engines like Baidu,[4] after which, they read and learned from these experiences. A 33-year-old small clothing-store owner from the Ningbo case described it thus:

> You can find out web pages, online forums, and tweets including photos and videos of the anti-PX protest in Xiamen, [including] the very first one in 2007. This content expands our awareness of the PX project. Most importantly, it shows us ways we can adapt in order to stop the project. (January 15, 2013, personal communication)

While the protest in Xiamen remained "the most renowned anti-PX protest," according to a 27-year-old mobile phone salesperson from the Chengdu case, people can also easily retrieve news, photos, and videos about later ones in Kunming, Dalian, and so on from web pages, microblogging, blogs, and online forums, despite government attempts at censorship. She said,

---

4. It is impossible for censorship to suppress all the information related to protests and demonstrations. Indeed, some of the information arises from official media coverage of the issues at hand. In practice, studies can use search engines to generate a data set of the spread of contention (see Lin & Zhang, 2018).

After checking the internet, we saw several anti-PX protests around the nation. If the project is not toxic or problematic [as the government declared], why would people in other cities oppose it? Why do we need a project that people elsewhere discarded? If they [people in other cities] succeeded in forcing the government to give up the project by protests, we should also do the same! (July 2, 2013, personal communication)

Although such reasoning did not always transform *directly* into offline protest action, it did significantly encourage people to, again, re-distribute the information via digitally mediated communication within their social networks or through face-to-face conversation. In this way, various kinds of information about earlier protests snowballed, allowing many people to know and learn from these experiences.

To sum up, both digitally mediated and interpersonal communications function as a crucial channel for the diffusion of protest information, which includes alternative information about contested issues, mobilizing messages, and past coverage and experiences of protests. These two forms of communication enable people to distribute information that demands immediate attention and action as quickly as possible, as widely as possible. Meanwhile, web pages, online forums, and microblogs provide abundant information, especially about previous protests. Such information substantially shapes people's perceptions about what protest actions are possible and helps people develop their own protest repertoires, thus laying the foundation for further contention.

Mass Communication and the Spread of Political Contention

Generally speaking, news about political contention barely appears on official, mass communication channels, such as newspapers and TV, given its politically sensitive nature and the suppressive policy against it from the regime (King, Pan, & Roberts, 2013; Steinhardt, 2015). Yet, the marketed-oriented mass media with professionalism-endeavored journalists, in some cases, still manage to cover contentious issues before the directive from the authorities that prevents further coverage and discussion, or through the employment of strategic news framing, or after the contention once the censorship is removed (e.g., Kuang & Wei, 2017; Lei, 2017; Zhao, 1998, 2009). Whereas it is definitely not its intention, the coverage by official mass media and its diffusion nevertheless contribute to people's knowledge regarding not just the contention per se but also the specific uses of mobile technologies as means of contention.

The series of anti-PX protests serves as an interesting case to illustrate this issue. In the first case in Xiamen as early as in 2007, the concern over the PX project with its potential petrochemical contamination had been raised during the "Two Congresses" (两会)[5] in March 2007 and was reported by a few national and overseas media outlets, such as the *China Business Journal* (中国经营报) (Qu, 2007) and Hong Kong–based *Phoenix Weekly* (凤凰周刊). However, the coverage failed to be delivered to residents in Xiamen, as local authorities intentionally prevented residents from hearing about the concerns. For three months after the congresses, local media maintained total silence about the issue.[6] Meanwhile, the authorities worked hard from the beginning to censor sensitive words, such as "PX" and "petrochemical," shutting down online forums that contained arguments against the project, and blocking access to overseas coverage of this issue.

Only after the diffusion of warning messages against the PX project intensified via mobile text messages caused residents to worry about environmental protection issues, did local media begin to cover it. Yet, local media, including Xiamen Television and the local party organ the *Xiamen Daily*, rebuked the opposition to the construction of the PX project, calling the messages mere "rumors" that misled the public, which were "deliberately try[ing] to ruin the image of Xiamen," without any elaboration on the project (e.g., Reporter, 2007).

Similar situations occurred in other protests and demonstrations. For the rest of the anti-PX cases, generally speaking, the information from mass communication tried to persuade the public to accept the PX project by citing professional opinions or by claiming that those who spread the messages had ill intent and had falsified or exaggerated the toxicity of the PX project to mislead the public. For taxi drivers' strikes, official media only "denounced" the way in which taxi drivers chose to express their discontentment and requested that they go back to work, after the strikes attracted widespread attention from foreign media (e.g., Branigan, 2008; Watts, 2010; Yang, 2008).

5. The term "Two Congresses" refers to the National People's Congress and Chinese People's Political Consultative Conference, which by principle supervise the enforcement of the Constitution and the operation of all levels of governments; and they handle sensitive political, economic, and social issues, such as corruption, injustice, and unrest that could erode the party-state's legitimacy or question or challenge its power.

6. According to a 35-year-old taxi driver, "local media did not mention this issue at all for over three months" (October 5, 2010, personal communication).

Notably, mass communication failed to change people's attitudes toward the controversies. Instead of the intended suppressive effect, it galvanized further dissemination of contested information; enriched people's knowledge of the protests; provided successful, learnable examples to follow; and acted as a *deterministic* element to encourage citizens, in an indirect way, to adopt digital technologies like mobile phones as protest tools.

More specifically, mass media's coverage of the controversies and objections to the PX project acted as a catalyst to ignite widespread contention against the project, as people perceived the emergence of the coverage as both the removal of censorship and an admission of the danger of the PX project by the authorities. In practice, mass media's coverage of PX-related information failed to turn up until the information had already proliferated within interpersonal and networked communications. This significant change in coverage over the controversial issue was interpreted by residents as a release of censorship regarding the debate over PX. The interviews showed that people believed that, following mass media coverage, they were allowed to argue against the PX project *publicly*. A 38-year-old IT professional said, "even the government had to admit the dangers of the PX project in [mass] media. Why can't we oppose it?" (December 13, 2010, personal communication).

Second, mass media coverage of protests elsewhere emboldened people to learn from earlier strategies for collective action and encouraged their adoption. For instance, according to the interviews, various official mass media outlets, such as the *People's Daily* (人民日报), the official newspaper of the Communist Party of China, *China Newsweek* (中国新闻周刊), published by China News Service, the second-largest state news agency, and national and regional level newspapers such as the *Southern Metropolis Daily* (南方都市报), covered the anti-PX protests. To them, the coverage implied that "the government had accepted 'the stroll,' or street protest, as a *legitimate* way of opposing the PX project" (36-year-old taxi driver in Chengdu, July 8, 2013, personal communication, emphasis added). Especially, the reports of the protest in Xiamen (Lan & Zhang, 2007; Xie & Zhao, 2007) became not only a benchmark of anti-PX protest but also *a successful, politically accepted* example for people elsewhere to learn, follow, and duplicate in later cases. A 42-year-old university lecturer from the Kunming case offered the following explanation,

the media will not be allowed to cover the protest in Xiamen if it is an illegal act. Now it [the protest] appears in the news, which means the government recognized this activity as a *legitimate* form of public participation in the PX issue. Thus, we can take to the streets as people in Xiamen did [to march against the PX project]. (June 5, 2013, personal communication, emphasis added)

It is clear from the above that mass media coverage about the protests, as a form of knowledge about collective action (Koopmans, 2004), helps to motivate concerned citizens to act collectively as others have done elsewhere in earlier protests.

Third, and more importantly, mass communication plays a key role in influencing the perception that mobile technologies, among other digital communication technologies, can be used as a tool for contention, hence conferring a decisive influence on the adoption of these technologies for later protests. The way official media covered the anti-PX protest underlined the relevant role of various digital technologies in initiating and organizing protests. These reports served as examples for people to learn from the past by adopting and appropriating various digital devices, in particular mobile technologies, in their repertoires of contention. For instance, the interviewees from several cases mentioned a report they read in *China Newsweek*. Titled "The Power of Mobile Messaging" (Xie & Zhao, 2007, pp. 16–17), the report detailed how residents used mobile messaging to organize protests. People treated this report as a signal from the authorities giving *tacit consent* to use mobile phones for successful protest organization. A 36-year-old accountant from the Chengdu case recalled,

> even the authorities acknowledged *the power of mobile phones* for successful protest. We just copy the [call for the] "stroll" in Xiamen by using our mobile phones to distribute protest information and organize similar protests [against the PX project]. This successful example [of using digital media such as the mobile phone] shows a way that is *recognized* by the government to oppose the project. (July 5, 2013, personal communication, emphasis added)

Similarly, in later coverage of the anti-PX protests, mass media reported the use of various digital media in citizens' protest repertoires, which consequently becomes the main driving force that inspires and encourages people to "replicate" the successful example of the past by employing their available digital media for protest.

To summarize, and similar to other observations (e.g., Ganesh & Stohl, 2013), the diffusion of protest-related information through mass communication coincides with those sent via networked and interpersonal communication during protest events. Although its role is different from interpersonal and mobile-mediated communication, mass media still plays a critical role in shaping people's knowledge of protests from the past and in facilitating similar protests thereafter. Even though the media coverage did *not* announce that the protests were legal, the stories were considered to be a removal of censorship over contested issues and as giving the go-ahead for the implementation of protest activity. Similarly, the way these reports covered the contention played a fundamental role in shaping people's attitudes and actions. The coverage on the use of mobile technologies had been perceived as encouraging people to adopt "the successful models" of the past by using their mobile devices for collective action, which has consequently incited and sustained the use of mobile technology within various repertoires of contention.

MOBILE PHONE AS CONTENTIOUS REPERTOIRE: WHY CERTAIN FUNCTIONS BUT NOT OTHERS?

The question raised at the beginning of this chapter was, why did Egyptian protesters rely less on WhatsApp and instead choose Facebook and Twitter, while Hongkongers drew their strength not from Facebook or Twitter but WhatsApp? A similar phenomenon from empirical materials catches my attention: Why did people in the anti-PX cases take advantage of multiple functions of their mobile phones—starting with text messaging, taking photos (during demonstrations), using WeChat and QQ—to document and facilitate protests, while taxi drivers in different cities basically relied on voice calls during their strikes? Put differently and perhaps more succinctly, why do some people adopt certain functions of the mobile phone but not others as part of their contentious repertoire? The answer consists of two parts: (a) the affordance, observed through habitus (Crossley, 2002b, p. 57), shapes repertoire choice, and (b) various communications and metacommunications popularize, modularize, and legitimize repertoire selection.

Habitus, Affordance, and Formation of the Contentious Repertoire

To unmask the affordances in mobile-mediated contentious behaviors to better understand people's perceptions of the uses of mobile phones, it is helpful to introduce the term "habitus." In further developing our discussion on repertoire selection, I would like to invoke Crossley (2002b, p. 52; 2003, p. 49), who suggests an integration of Bourdieu's notion of *habitus* as a way of contextualizing and looking beyond intense and short-lived contentious moments, or what Zolberg (1972) describes as "moments of madness." Bourdieu's original idea is as follows:

> The habitus is a set of dispositions, reflexes and forms of behaviour people acquire through acting in society. It reflects the *different* positions people have in society, for example, whether they are brought up in a middle-class environment or in a working-class suburb. (Bourdieu, 2000, p. 19, emphasis added)

In the sociology of movements, Crossley contends that "[t]he concept of habitus allows us to reflect upon and explore the way in which agents' life experiences and trajectories shape the dispositions and schemas which, in turn, shape the ways in which they choose from the repertoires of contention that prevail within their society" (2002b, p. 52). More specifically, people develop "perceptual and linguistic schemas, preferences and desires, know-how, forms of competence and other such dispositions" (2002a, pp. 171–172) over the course of their lives. Meanwhile, "activists' statuses, skills and social connections all shape their possibilities for protest and this is reflected in their different ways of doing so" (2002a, p. 132). Consequently, the involvement of habitus "opens up the question of the manner in which activist choices (of repertoire amongst other things) are shaped by activist histories . . . [and], analytically, the procedures and methods of practical reasoning that structure those choices" (2002b, p. 52).

Crossley's suggestion largely falls in with scholarship that underlines not only visibility but also latency in social movements (e.g., Almanzar, Sullivan-Catlin, & Deane, 1998; Buechler, 2000; Melucci, 1985, 1989; Reed, 2005). Visibility, or the political or social action that is visible to the outside world, refers to that which is already manifested and easily recognized (e.g., demonstrations or riots), while latency, or the social or political activity that remains invisible, is embedded and submerged in everyday life but underpins, structures, and informs the manifest activity (Melucci, 1985, pp. 800–801). In actuality, these two parts are inseparable, reciprocally correlated, and are integral to the understandings of social movements. The emphasis here points out that the locus of social movements is not only situated in spaces of open defiance such as political conflicts, but, more importantly, it also resides in structures of everyday life—in this case, in the very Bourdieuian habitus as "not only a structuring structure, which organizes practices and the perception of practices, but also a structured structure" (Bourdieu, 1984, p. 170). As the key—but *hidden*—nature of social movements, the elements of habitus, or these structures of everyday life, become visible when engaged in overt political conflict.

If protesters' contentious repertoires grow out of their habitus, then an interrogation of habitus, especially as it relates to ICT use, is essential for the depiction of its affordances, i.e., the relational understanding of specific communication technologies to certain agents in a particular context. In other words, in the cases outlined above, a careful probe of people's routine attitudes and practices with the mobile phone spells out affordances as the underlying and necessary, but not sufficient, foundation of repertoire selection.

The roots of mobile phone use as protest repertoire are to be found, first of all, in the widespread availability of mobile phones as a simple yet substantial necessity for everyday life. The affordance of *availability* (also see Schrock, 2015, pp. 1236–1237) indicates that both the artifact, i.e., the mobile phone, and its user are an always-on resource. Notably, all interviewees shared more or less the same understanding of the mobile phone: "whatever happens, the very first thing is to check the mobile phone . . . to ask [relatives, friends, etc.] and to inform others [in our social networks]" (36-year-old accountant in Chengdu, July 5, 2013, personal communication). Availability establishes a taken-for-granted perception of the individual's connections via mobile communication in everyday life (Ling, 2013). Said differently, people have all become habituated to connecting and being connected, communicating and being communicated with, activating and being activated through their mobile phones, anytime, anywhere. Moreover, due to the *un*availability, or lack of institutional support and resources for political contention under China's unique institutional context and authoritarian control, people are getting used to the limited available resources—in this case, their mobile phones, a means of habitual communication—for receiving and circulating alternative or contested information against the authorities. Consequently, as the cases illustrate, people exploit their mobile phones as the most readily—in some cases, the only—available resource for protest distribution, organization, and mobilization, even for those who have little technological know-how. As one taxi driver conceded, "apart from mobile phones, we do not have any other thing [for protesting]" (35-year-old taxi driver in Shenzhen, October 20, 2010, personal communication). Availability therefore institutes the adoption of mobile phones, a quotidian, habituated tool, for "improvisation" (Tilly, 1986, p. 390) of political activism.

Second, it is nevertheless not the mobile phone in a general and abstract sense, but rather its specific functions that help build the contentious repertoires of divergent populations in different contexts. A close observation of variations in repertoires in different cases reveals that, even though mobile technology per se is the same, given its distinctive affordances to disparate social groups that can be detected through the habitus of agents, protest repertoires differ significantly case by case.

For taxi drivers, the mobile phone affords the voice call as the most convenient way of talking to each other as well as keeping in contact with their social networks in daily life. This is especially true considering the danger or impracticality of the driving-while-reading—let alone texting—practice. These interviewees rarely mention functions other than voice calls in their work routine. Instead, to use one interviewee's vivid description, "[to us], 'the mobile phone' indeed means 'phone call.' . . . [A]ll the time, we [use mobile phones to] call each other; and others [taxi drivers] are expecting to be contacted via calls" (54-year-old taxi driver in Shenzhen, October 22, 2010, personal communication). Calling and chatting on mobile phones consequently came to be the habitus of taxi drivers.

In practice, voice calls involve affordances of *immediacy* and *emotional embeddedness* that taxi drivers take advantage of during strikes. Immediacy refers to synchronous or real-time interaction and feedback, which brings instant confirmation of participation and hence improves the *self-perceived* effectiveness of mobilization. As Chadwick (2013, p. 193) observes, "Real-time response is itself a mechanism that generates the substantive resources of authenticity and legitimacy." Taxi drivers clearly recognized the difference between voice calls and other functions, like text messages, and regarded the former as a more "effective means of mobilization." As one noted:

> When talking via mobile call, you are able to get an immediate response to your mobilization request. The confirmation of participation offers a sort of guarantee of the effectiveness [of mobilization for strikes]. . . .To make a call is thus essentially distinguished from sending out text messages . . . [which means] you are always unsure whether and when you will receive feedback [to your text]. Without [an instant] reply, it is impossible to estimate the results [of mobilization]. (37-year-old taxi driver in Fuzhou, April 25, 2010, personal communication)

As we will see in more detail in the next chapter, although a text message arrives at its destination almost instantaneously, this form of transferring information does not guarantee an immediate response, which compromises the self-perceived effectiveness of the intended mobilization. That is to say, possibly delayed replies due to the asynchronous interactions inherent in text messaging dramatically hinders participant motivation due to the uncertainty engendered by the effectiveness of the mobilization effort. Another interviewee agreed, "without response from [the text message recipient], you have no idea about whether the mobilization message has been received, read, or accepted . . . you have no idea who, or how many people, will join the strike. How could you decide [to join the strike if you weren't sure who else would be joining]?" (43-year-old taxi driver in Fuzhou, April 25, 2010, personal communication.)

The synchronous voice call, on the contrary, invites immediate interaction as soon as the connection is established, consequently creating "a feeling of greater propinquity" (Walther, 1992, p. 75) with others. The instant connection and conversation with the feeling of propinquity guarantees the effectiveness of the transmission of the mobilizing message, fundamentally lowering the uncertainty inherent in organizing high-risk collective resistance (McAdam, 1986) under authoritarian regimes like China. Immediate confirmation via phone call therefore encourages more recruitment practices. As one striker recalls, "when I got my friend's confirmation, it made me confident [about the organization of the strike]. . . . Right away, I made another call to invite one more friend" (36-year-old taxi driver in Wenling, May 13, 2013, personal communication). By establishing a connection quickly and efficiently, transferring mobilizing messages via voice call results in a higher rate of success for collective action.

No less importantly, voice calls elicit the affordance of emotional embeddedness—that is, the articulation and expression of people's emotions through vocal elements such as tone, pitch, and volume. These elements easily generate a sense of cohesion and solidarity, and they invite political engagement. When drivers were calling and speaking with each other regarding the strikes, one said:

> [Y]ou can feel the strong emotion and attitude from the other side [via phone call], including the grievance of unfair treatment by the police and the anger over government's inaction. Such feelings resonate with your own experience. . . . [You know that] you are not alone. . . . From the tone [of the conversation], you can also recognize people's willingness to engage in the strike. It really makes you feel empowered for emotional togetherness [about the strike]." (43-year-old taxi driver in Fuzhou, April 25, 2010, personal communication)

As the interviewee elaborates here, vocal communication expresses, transfers, and articulates—in short, metacommunicates—communicators' feelings and emotions (Scherer, Johnstone, & Klasmeyer, 2002). While most forms of mobile communication—such as text messages and email—have reduced social interactions to the barebones transfer of textual elements, speaking through the mobile phone establishes "live interactions with human beings" (47-year-old taxi driver in Wenling, May

12, 2013, personal communication). Emotion has long been recognized as a key driving force to motivate passionate movement action (Aminzade & McAdam, 2002; Goodwin, Jasper, & Polletta, 2009; Jasper, 2011) and, for this reason, promotes engagement in strikes.

While vocal interaction unfolds and evokes a large degree of emotion, the articulation of emotions and feelings functions as an essential component of collective mobilization, as it involves shared experiences of empowerment and collective effervescence, which greatly affects the transformation "from framed emotion to action and from individual to collective" (Flam & King, 2005, pp. 4–5; also see Yang, 2000). Beyond passing on a call to strike, the conversation via voice calls during the taxi strikes became a method of emotional expression, accumulation, and mobilization through which the taxi drivers articulated their suppressed experiences and were able to empathize with each other's suffering, which together helped form group cohesion. On top of that, through vocal conversations taxi drivers recognized that, instead of being separate individuals, they were "networked individuals" enjoying the support of their colleagues, friends, and social networks. This feeling of solidarity and empowerment pushes an increasing number of people toward mobilization via mobile phones and makes them much more likely to engage in protests.[7]

Distinguished from the cases of the taxi strikes, the anti-PX protests exemplify a totally different picture of affordances, with protesters, most of whom reportedly came from the middle class (see Zhu, 2007), clearly maneuvering much more diversified functions of mobile technologies, such as texting, photo-taking (e.g., during contention), WeChat, and so forth as part of their repertoires of contention. In other words, diversified uses of the mobile phone as a part of the protest repertoire in the anti-PX protests resulted from different affordances of mobile phones, embodied in these participants' habitus, including *visibility* and *networking*.

The affordance of visibility, or "whether a piece of information can be located, as well as the relative ease with which it can be located" (Evans et al., 2017, p. 42), contributes to the proliferation of both contested information about the PX project and later mobilizing messages against the project. Leonardi (2014, p. 797) remarks that digital communication technologies increase visibility "by loosening the requirement to select a target audience through email carbon copy features or the instant messaging forward feature. Instead, the sender can create a public communication platform that

---

7. For a detailed discussion on the mobilization mechanism via mobile communication, see Chapter 4.

can be accessed by team members." Protesters in the anti-PX cases clearly utilized this affordance as part of their protest repertoire to either make calls for mobilization or share stories of past protests with greater visibility by snowballing these politically sensitive messages via, for instance, group messaging functions, as well as sharing their discontentment toward the silence, false accusations, or censorship from official media.

The "affordance of networking" refers to the capacity of building and maintaining social networks and activating (selected) contacts from these networks. The interviewees concur that the mobile phone is a central means for relationship maintenance and seeking help in their everyday lives. Consequently, the habituated practice of circulating messages within one's social networks to inform each other of relevant matters and gather available network resources to help each other easily adapts itself to political mobilization in contention.

Given the observation here about distinctive affordances—and subsequent protest repertoires—to different social groups in diverse contexts, a key issue stands that affordance, as I underscore, has a decisive effect—in terms of both facilitation and constraint—on later repertoire choices. On the one hand, taxi drivers hardly ever consider using their phones to mobilize support for protests by using text messaging. As voice calls occupy an inseparable role in their work life, it is not surprising that they would pick up their mobile phones and call for mobilization. On the other hand, residents in a series of cities who were protesting against the PX project prioritized SMS or WeChat group messaging, as these functions allowed for a mass distribution of relevant information within their networks to quickly muster support, as these people generally do in their daily lives.

The third point regarding habitus, affordance, and repertoire is the following: it is the process of repertoire selection that constructs and consolidates the identity of a contentious population in its collective struggles against a suppressive regime. In other words, to employ text messaging or voice calls within one's contentious repertoire goes beyond an improvised act, rather, as Tilly (1995, p. 30) correctly notes, it is a clustered action that connects sets of individuals. To choose certain aspects of a protest repertoire but not others tends to metacommunicate a sense of togetherness in contention. To use one interviewee's words, "we are [doing exactly] the same as other people [do for protest]" (34-year-old taxi driver in Fuzhou, April 25, 2010, personal communication). Repertoire choice in this sense reduces heterogeneity within the protest population, such as age, career, gender, job, and so forth. By the very adoption of the same repertoire—such as "the distribution of information [against the PX project via SMS] as quickly as possible to as many people as possible" (residents in Xiamen, December 2010, personal communication)—people with different backgrounds come together as a collective, consistently with certain functions of their mobile phones as part of their protest repertoire against the authorities.

To summarize, a relevant, yet less commonly addressed, issue comes to light in the discussion of the use of mobile phones as part of a contentious repertoire: the affordances of the very same technology, i.e., mobile phones, varies significantly among different social groups in different contexts, which entails the habitus of mobile phone uses that fundamentally determines repertoire choice. As we can see from the cases here, the political use of mobile phones among the same group label, like "Chinese people," is indeed not homogeneous, but rather is a *heterogeneous* collection that embodies distinctive affordances of mobile phones among different groups. When people do not have sufficient experience or knowledge about contention, they simply "improvise" (Tilly, 1986, p. 390) out of their habitus in using mobile technology. Habitus embodies specific affordances, and these affordances further facilitate and constrain repertoire choice and actual use of mobile phones. A nuanced view that integrates the consideration of affordance—and further repertoires of contention—hence avoids an oversimplified and homogenized understanding of communication technologies.

Communication, Metacommunication, Modularity, and Legitimation of Protest Repertoires

The establishment and development of contentious repertoires may take different forms, among which communication performs a crucial role to facilitate the process. Scholars in this field have especially delineated how diffusion of contention operates as a key mechanism to disseminate, modularize, and institute certain contentious forms as aspects of protest repertoires in society (McAdam, 1995; Traugott, 1995b; Wada, 2012).

The diffusion of contention suggests sharing "word of successful—and learnable—collective actions" to be spread to more groups and localities for mimetic struggles and, as Tarrow suggests, "be sustained far longer than the episodic and cathartic collective actions of the past" (Tarrow, 1993, p. 83). The diffusion further provides "modular repertoires" (Tarrow, 1993, p. 82; Tilly, 1986, p. 6) that manifest in the capacity of forms of collective action to be used in a variety of conflicts by a number of different social actors and by coalitions of people against a variety of opponents (Tarrow, 1993, p. 77). As such, the spread and modularity of contentious activity allows for the transferability of repertoires into different contexts (Wada, 2012), as "the demonstration effect of collective action on the part of a group of 'earlier risers' triggers a variety of processes of *diffusion, extension, imitation,* and *reaction* among groups that are normally more quiescent and have fewer resources to engage in collective action" (Tarrow, 2011, p. 205, emphasis added). These processes hence engender an indirect effect on the structure and constraints of political opportunity, i.e., earlier challenging the authorities increases the leverage of other groups to join the challenge and elevates their own power or privilege later (McAdam, 1995, pp. 221–222). The subsequent borrowing or imitation leads to cycles of certain types of protest in a society. In this cyclical process, a stock of these inherited tactics or forms of contentious actions that become *habitual* and that transfer across different contentious contexts consequently become "the permanent tools of a society's repertoires of contention" (Tarrow, 1993, p. 284).

Communication in this cyclical process involves different actors, via different channels. Some recognize the relevance of organizations (e.g., social movement organizations) or associational networks in the process of distributing information on contention in established networks of communication as a precondition for diffusion (McAdam, 1995, p. 232; Minkoff, 1997). Others advocate the significance of mass media in the process of disseminating the news about protests beyond immediate social settings (Myers, 2000; Oliver & Myers, 1999, p. 39). Studies recount that mass communication plays a critical role in the progression of protest diffusions by broadcasting action strategies of the transmitter to potential adopters, connecting otherwise unconnected individuals via a shared response to events covered, shaping the public opinion and framing of contention issues, and routinizing protests as institutional politics.[8] The increasing ubiquity of digitally mediated networked communication facilitates the transfer of "protest ideas and tactics quickly and efficiently across national borders" (Norris, 2002, p. 208). Boyle and Schmierbach (2009), for instance, dissect the emerging role of alternative media (i.e., the Web) in prompting both traditional and protest participation.

8. For detailed discussions, see Gamson & Wolfsfeld, 1993; Oliver & Maney, 2000; Oliver & Myers, 1999; Tarrow, 2011, p. 201.

Similar to other scholars who observe different flows of interaction and communication coexisting in contention (e.g., Lim, 2012; Tufekci & Wilson, 2012), the cases I examine here epitomize a complex picture of various communications and associated metacommunications that spread information related to political contention, including those involving mobile phones, which develops into "learned conventions of contention" (Tarrow, 2011, p. 29) in later struggles. In this process, interpersonal, mass, and networked communications provide disparate contributions to the use of the mobile phone as part of a repertoire of contention and to further changes in political opportunities. The following discussion starts with digitally mediated networks and interpersonal communications and is then followed by mass communication.

Both interpersonal and networked communication centrally lead to the diffusion of information related to political contention as well as the follow-up use of mobile phones as a means of protest. Many-to-many networked communication, including via mobile calls, text messaging, WeChat, Weibo, BBS, and online forums, functions as the primary source to receive and circulate contested information as well as to encourage people to adopt certain functions of their mobile phones for protests and demonstrations. Following that, face-to-face communication matters when exchanging information about protests and shaping the understanding of mobile phone use as part of a repertoire of action, i.e., the history, knowledge, and experience of contention. As observed from the field, these two kinds of communication increase the visibility of alternative information about politically sensitive topics in society—especially those with contested or controversial contents that have been suppressed or restricted by the authorities. Further, they help proliferate mobilizing initiatives and popularize knowledge of protests from earlier struggles.

In the repressive political environment in China, participants in political contention face great political risk and can encounter harsh political suppression by the authorities (e.g., King et al., 2013; O'Brien, 2009). Against this backdrop, the mere diffusion of contentious information—or, for most people, simply knowing about alternative information or mobilizing calls via interpersonal or networked communication—is not sufficient to inspire political action. Instead, protesters exploit official ideologies through, for instance, "the innovative use of laws, policies, and other officially promoted values" (O'Brien, 1996, p. 32) to legitimate their resistance and protests (also see O'Brien & Li, 2006). A fact that emerges and should not be ignored among the cases is that, contrary to expectation, it is indeed the official, mass communication that legitimizes the contention, establishes mobile phones as important parts of the contentious repertoire, and encourages the emergence of assimilation in the long run.

To understand the issue here, a brief discussion about the role of official, mass communication in China is essential.[9] As studies of the issue illustrate, mass communication in China is not at all like its Western counterpart in bringing news to the general public and influencing the perception and understanding of reality. A key role of mass communication in China, through its service as part of the stock of socially constructed and distributed knowledge created for the general public to make sense of the changing environment (Chang, Wang, & Chen, 1994), is to legitimize and maintain the Communist Party's rule and their continued policies (Brady, 2009). A longitudinal analysis of AIDS coverage in the *People's Daily*, for instance, illuminates an emergence of news stories with positive words in the discourse about AIDS, "suggesting approval of governmental efforts to tackle the problem" (Dong, Chang, & Chen, 2008, p. 370). In other words, official media functions as the party's mouthpiece that metacommunicates policy while following the government's stance. This special understanding of mass communication in China, deeply ingrained among the general public, makes an *unexpected* contribution to mobile phones as part of the protest repertoire.

O'Brien noted in the study of rural contention that increased media penetration cultivated villagers to be "more knowledgeable about resistance routines devised elsewhere" (1996, p. 41). A similar situation occurs in the cases we have presented here. Apart from the knowledge of protests elsewhere, the news coverage about contentions implies that previously politically sensitive issues were no longer a political taboo. To the general public, the coverage thus metacommunicates a signal that these issues are all but "tolerated" (Tarrow, 2001, p. 7) by the ruling regime. In other words, as the interviews show, the protests have been recognized as "a form of officially legitimate public action" (Thireau & Linshan, 2003, p. 87) among the general public, as soon as they have been publicly covered by official media (see Oliver & Myers, 1999, pp. 44–45). This is especially so when the coverage comes from a national-scale news agency (e.g., *China Newsweek*), beyond the control of local authorities but considered as "an extension of state power" (Shi & Cai, 2006, p. 329), it significantly persuaded locals that their protests against local authorities had been tolerated and accepted with the connivance of the central authority, thereby establishing opportunities for later contention. This "schemata of interpretations" (Zhao, 2010, p. 42) perceived and shared by the public as a significant institutional policy change regarding the protest consequently expanded

9. For more detailed discussions, see Lee, 1990, 2000, 1994, 2003; Zhao, 1998, 2009.

political opportunities for contention and encouraged the adoption of such a form of collective action against similar issues for successors elsewhere. In short, the metacommunication of traditional media's coverage increases the influence of contention by legitimizing the protests as a kind of "partially sanctioned resistance" (O'Brien, 1996, p. 33) and by consequently encouraging widespread duplication.

Reports on protests in mass communication do not merely legitimate earlier acts of contention. Details about the use of mobile phones for protests in news coverage have led to the use of mobile phones as an essential facet of the contentious repertoire and further encourages imitation by late-comers. For instance, the interviewees recalled clearly that mass communication addressed the adoption of digital communication technologies as a unique and successful aspect of the protest (Center for Public Opinion Monitor, 2014; Zeng, 2015, pp. 112–113). News title like "The Power of Mobile Messaging" (Xie & Zhao, 2007) not only depict the political influence of mobile texts but also leaves an impression of binding protests and the adoption of mobile phones together. This kind of spread of information generates a demonstrative effect by offering key tactics as "mobilizing information" (Lemert, 1984, p. 244) and serves as a slogan to encourage people to adopt their mobile media for protests. In this way, mass communication plays a key role in giving impetus to the knowledge of mobile phone use as part of a repertoire of contention by establishing, modularizing, and facilitating patterns of mobile-mediated contentious behaviors that "can be learned, adapted, routinized, and diffused from one group, one locale, or one moment to another." (Traugott, 1995a, p. 7). As we can see in later contentious activities held elsewhere, the anti-PX protest has consequently become a typical, successful model that crystallizes and acclaims mobile-mediated political activism in the process of struggling against authority and finally forcing it to change its policies. In a long-run perspective, the coverage and diffusion by mass communication allows people to adopt modes of contention easily by learning from the past and duplicating it, facilitating its transferability into other cases, and furthering the popular perception of mobile technology, or its specific function, as a repertoire of contention in society.

CONCLUSION: THE SOCIAL CONSTRUCTION OF MOBILE TECH AS REPERTOIRE OF CONTENTION

This chapter started with the proposal that advocates for the relevance of the link between affordances and the development of repertoires of contention fills a gap to understand the role of ICTs in political contention. Since the development of repertoires of contention involves specifically what people *know* how to do during protests (Tarrow, 2011, p. 39), a narrow focus on the use of ICTs alone limits a relational understanding of agency, technology, and context. As the cases in contemporary China illustrate, repertoire choice derives both from habitus of media use that manifests particular affordances and from the learned experience of the contested means of the past in official mass communication. Variations in repertoires occur largely due to distinctive affordances. Metacommunication in mass communication further brings the possibility of institutional change by engendering an indirect effect on the political opportunity structure and constraints, as people, with specific functions of mobile phones, challenging authority increase the leverage of other groups to also challenge authorities and elevate their own power or privilege (McAdam, 1995, pp. 221–222). A nuanced investigation of affordance and its connection to contentious repertoires hence shed significant light on similarities and differences regarding the perception of mobile phones as part of a contentious repertoire among different social groups in different contexts. It advances the field and calls for further consideration in terms of the following three aspects.

First, given distinct affordances, the meaning of communication technology (Jackson, 1996) is hardly univocal and universal but rather varies significantly depending upon various agents in different contexts. As a result, instead of assuming that there is a single logic by which protesters are using ICTs in movements, focusing on discrete instances of political activism and ICT use forces us to face the possibility that there may be as many different understandings of affordances as there are distinct ways of using digital communication technologies in the protest repertoires for contentious collective action. This further bears significant relevance for understanding and explaining the uses of mobile apps like the hugely popular, do-everything-in-one WeChat, through which people would have distinct understandings and subsequent uses of even the same app. In this way, both affordance and repertoires of contention consequently have an advantage in straightening out fine-grained yet essential nuances in respect of their relational nature. A comparative agenda beyond the specific case of China, for instance, will further forward such understanding against different national contexts.

Second, an understanding of the development of the contentious repertoire, along with other things in "moments of madness" (Zolberg, 1972), requests an extension in order to capture, reflect, and assess the political ferment in and around the routine—or habitual use of digital communication technologies in this study—in everyday lives. Stated differently, "the contentious moment cannot be examined in isolation from the context of everyday life that has come to generate and influence it" (Liu, 2017, p. 421). Habitus, in this case, offers an analytical approach to inquire into the political relevance of the mundane and the everyday in structuring and underpinning specific contentious moments.

Third, an interrogation on what people both *do* and *do not do* with communication technology is relevant to disclose specific dynamics behind repertoire selection and constraint. That is to say, the reasoning behind protesters' decision to not take up certain activities within the protest repertoire is as equally important as protester's decisions regarding the adoption of specific activities.

Over and above all this, whereas digital communication technologies, as Van Laer and Van Aelst (2010, p. 1146) criticize in the case of the internet as contentious repertoire, are "unable to create the necessary trust and strong ties that are necessary to build a sustainable network of activists," the uniqueness of mobile communication technology, with the embedding of strong social ties and reciprocal networking, may transform this weakness—which is the focus of next chapter.

CHAPTER 4

More Than Words

The Integrative Power of the Mobile Phone as a
"Reciprocal Technology" for Micromobilization

[M]obilization does not occur through recruitment of large numbers of isolated and solitary individuals. It occurs as a result of recruiting bloc of people who are already highly organized and participants. (Oberschall, 1973, p. 125)

Among the topics that have drawn longstanding interest and are still central to the study of contentious collective action is that of mobilization, i.e., the process by which individuals come to organize and initiate action of their own volition, to involve themselves in political action collectively, and to influence and recruit potential participants and resources (Beinin & Vairel, 2013; McAdam, Tarrow, & Tilly, 2001; McCarthy & Zald, 1977; Melucci, 1988; Munson, 2010; Oberschall, 1973; Olson, 1975; Rogers, Goldstein, & Fox, 2018; Tilly, 1978). Since mobilization is of great significance to contention, as contentious movements "come into being through a process of mobilization" (Marx & Wood, 1975, p. 384), what are the most effective mechanisms for individual and collective mobilization concerning various forms of political action? Which factors account for individual participation and recruitment?

Numerous studies intending to explicate mobilization as well as its underlying determinants and implications have demonstrated both the complexity and diversity of mobilization processes, ranging from the macro-, meso-, to micro-levels and the linkages among them. On the macro-level, studies tend to explore historical, economic, and social dynamics as contexts for potential mobilization (Corcoran, Pettinicchio, & Young, 2011; Dalton, Van Sickle, & Weldon, 2010, pp. 53–56; McAdam et al., 2001). Mesomobilization deals with mobilizing structures through which organizers seek to cooperate and negotiate toward mobilization and recruitment of participants (e.g., Boekkooi & Klandermans, 2013; Gerhards & Rucht, 1992; Staggenborg, 2002). Mobilizing structures correspondingly involve all those "meso-level groups, organizations, and informal networks that comprise the collective building blocks of social movements and revolutions" (McAdam, McCarthy, & Zald, 1996, p. 3). Structure alone, nevertheless, is insufficient to mobilize individuals to act and join movements (Klandermans & Tarrow, 1988). An analysis of micromobilization hence scrutinizes the ways in which individuals come to participate in movements by revealing the relevance of interpersonal ties and networks (Marwell, Oliver, & Prahl, 1988; McAdam, 1986, 1988; Snow, Zurcher, & Ekland-Olson, 1980), frame alignment processes (McCaffrey & Keys, 2000; Snow, Worden, & Benford, 1986), or emotion (Flam, 2015; Jasper & Poulsen, 1995).

While studies have advocated the confluence of macro-, meso-, and micromobilization in order to expound mobilization and recruitment (e.g., McAdam et al., 2001), recently, widespread adoption of ICTs in contention has facilitated a special focus on micromobilization (e.g., Bekkers, Beunders, Edwards, & Moody, 2011, p. 210; Bekkers, Moody, & Edwards, 2011; Maher & Earl, 2017; Nekmat, Gower, Gonzenbach, & Flanagin, 2015; Valenzuela, 2013. p. 922). The increasing prevalence of personalized communication technologies (e.g., email, mobile phones, and social media), along with their speed and linking potential, enable horizontal, mass self-communication (Castells, 2007) based in well-connected collective or connective action networks (Bennett, 2012; Bennett & Segerberg, 2012, 2013). These networks enable large-scale political mobilization and recruitment, activities that were traditionally dominated by top-down organizations. This process entails a more essential contribution by individuals—their interactions and communications as a new organizational dynamic (Bennett & Segerberg, 2012, 2013)—to the course of mobilization and recruitment.

THEORETICAL AND EMPIRICAL BLIND SPOTS AND SHORTCOMINGS

Extant literature, however, remains vulnerable on three fronts with respect to the mobilization issue.

First, the most striking shortcoming is the tendency to over-generalize the role of digital communication technologies under umbrella terms such as "ICTs," "new communication technology," or "digital media," just to mention a few, at the expense of the different properties inherent in various forms of communication technology and their (potentially) respective influences on mobilization, if any.[1] To be clear, these terms stand as shorthand for a wide range of different digital materialities and technological modalities (Gershon, 2010; Mortensen, Neumayer, & Poell, 2019; Siles & Boczkowski, 2012), making it a complex plurality of networked communicative capacities. Among these networked communications, as Bennett and Segerberg (2012, p. 752) concede in their seminal work on digitally enabled mobilization, not all online (read "digital") communication works in the same way. Different digital materialities and modalities, each with their own communicative characteristics, in turn, are subject to various conditions of use and may embody separate mobilization potentials. Generally speaking, internet-based communication is better able to distribute beyond existing personal networks, and thus characterizes the development of the flexible "weak tie" (Granovetter, 1973) that increases the diversity of information (e.g., Enjolras, Steen-Johnsen, & Wollebæk, 2013; Kim, Chen, & Gil de Zúñiga, 2013; Van Laer, 2010; Weber, Loumakis, & Bergman, 2003), expands the probability of recruitment (e.g., Gil de Zúñiga & Valenzuela, 2011; González-Bailón, Borge-Holthoefer, Rivero, & Moreno, 2011; Tang & Lee, 2013), and promotes collective identities and solidarity across geographically dispersed individuals, communities, and nations for collective causes (e.g., Bennett, 2012; Bennett & Segerberg, 2012; Della Porta & Mosca, 2005; Juris, 2005; Walgrave, Bennett, Van Laer, & Breunig, 2011). By contrast, *mobile-mediated* communication is shared predominantly within networks with strong, close, and personal ties—and this communication further strengthens these ties (e.g., Katz, 2003a; Wellman & Hampton, 1999; Wellman & Tindall, 1993). Furthermore, these networks are "central [to] social influence and normative pressures (Burt, 1984, p. 127)" (cited from McPherson, Smith-Lovin, & Brashears, 2006, p. 355; also

---

1. For instance, see Anduiza, Jensen, & Jorba, 2012; Fung, Russon Gilman, & Shkabatur, 2013; Howard & Hussain, 2013; Walgrave, Bennett, Van Laer, & Breunig, 2011. For a similar critique on "computer-mediated communication," or CMC, see Yzer & Southwell (2008, p. 10), who castigate that "it [the term] often does not speak directly to the impact of differences in technological interaction modalities."

see Kobayashi, Ikeda, & Miyata, 2006, pp. 585–586).[2] Treating the internet and the mobile phone as a single mode of digital communication fails to recognize specific affordances[3] and their distinctive influences on mobilization. In line with Campbell and Kwak's view (2011, 2012), I believe the observation that mobile communication for mobilization is unique from other communication channels and deserves more attention both theoretically and empirically; hence this chapter speaks directly to the question at a finer-grained level.

Second, organizations remain a pivotal focus in mobilization processes in most scholarship on the issue, even though ICTs may promote self-organized mobilization "without central or 'lead' organizational actors . . . [or] . . . with conventional organizations deliberately kept at the periphery" (Bennett & Segerberg, 2012, p. 755; see, for instance, Abul-Fottouh & Fetner, 2018; Bennett, Breunig, & Givens, 2008; Van Laer, 2010). Against this backdrop, many studies have illustrated that, as "an additive role" (Vitak et al., 2011, p. 113), ICTs *complement* rather than replace traditional social movement organizations in mobilization processes (e.g., Bekkers, Beunders, et al., 2011; Bekkers, Moody, et al., 2011; Van Laer, 2010). The remaining essential role of organizations here reminds us of the relevance of liberal and democratic contexts from which these cases emerge. In such settings, organizations enjoy relative autonomy from the state and contribute fundamentally to mobilization (e.g., Bennett, 2012; Bennett et al., 2008; Bennett & Segerberg, 2012; Juris, 2005, 2008). However, we need to ask what may happen in a opposite context, where organizations fall under the stern control of and restriction by governmental and ideological authorities, and are therefore unable to play the roles they do in liberal democracies. The case of China, where nongovernmental organizations, "especially the ones that criticize government policies . . . have encountered a policy of containment, even destruction" (Jacobs & Buckley, 2015, p. A4)—let alone the ones that initiate or engage in mobilizations—yields a much-needed understanding of mobilization initiated and sustained

2. For discussions on mobile technology and strong ties, see Campbell & Russo, 2003; Katz, 2003b; Katz & Aakhus, 2002; Ling, 2004, 2008, 2013. For discussions on mobile-related participation, see Campbell & Kwak, 2011, 2012. For a similar discussion on the difference regarding synchronous and asynchronous communication in email, instant messaging (IM), and mobile phones, see Tseng & Hsieh, 2015, p. 1159.

3. For discussion on "affordance" see Chapter 3.

solely by individuals *in the absence of* movement-encouraging networks from SMOs.[4]

The third and final aspect, while fruitful discussions have been developed in the established democracies with cases from North America and Europe, scholarship with examples from authoritarian regimes has recently emerged, mostly from the Arab countries (e.g., Allagui & Kuebler, 2011; Hermida, Lewis, & Zamith, 2014; Howard & Hussain, 2013; Khondker, 2011; Wolfsfeld, Segev, & Sheafer, 2013). An interrogation of the case of China, the largest authoritarian regime with the largest internet and mobile population in the world, contributes to a better understanding of the mobilization mechanism of digital communication technologies in contention and further offers opportunities for both comparative studies and theoretical generalization.

In short, this chapter delves into the role of mobile communication, which is the most available personal communication channel today (Castells, Fernandez-Ardevol, Qiu, & Sey, 2007; Ling, 2008), in the process of mobilization and recruitment in authoritarian China, where social organizations hardly contribute to movements under intensified suppression. In the following, I first synthesize and expand upon the research on distinctive aspects of mobile communication and, in particular, the mobile phone as a *"reciprocal* technology" (Ling, 2013, p. 160, emphasis added). Second, I elaborate the role of social ties and networks in collective action mobilization, with a focus on the relevance of reciprocity and on *guanxi*, understood as "personal connections" or "social networks" in Chinese. Third, I explore the mechanism of mobile-mediated mobilization with empirical cases from China. Fourth, by summarizing the findings, I theorize the role of mobile communication in political mobilization with the embedding of reciprocity and suggest potential directions for further study beyond the case of China. All in all, this chapter by no means advocates for a simplistic technocentric account of mobilization, but rather argues against a monopolistic view that ignores or discards specificities in investigating ICTs and mobilization.

WHAT MAKES THE MOBILE PHONE UNIQUE? DISTINCTIVE ASPECTS OF MOBILE COMMUNICATION

While studies are increasingly recognizing the considerable use of mobile phones as a resource for political mobilization and recruitment (e.g.,

---

4. See examples of political contention without organization-based mobilization involved in Lin & Zhang, 2018, pp. 35–36.

Rafael, 2003; Rheingold, 2002, 2008; Shapiro & Weidmann, 2015; Suárez, 2006), few works systematically and theoretically interrogate the uniqueness of mobile communication in the mediating structures for mobilizing people to act collectively (Pierskalla & Hollenbach, 2013, p. 221). As mentioned earlier, scholarship on this topic tends to blend mobile communication into an overarching framework of digital communication technologies, and thus treats mobile phones and other ICTs as undifferentiated and homogeneous with regard to mobilization (e.g., Allagui & Kuebler, 2011; Bennett et al., 2008; Castells, 2012; Eltantawy & Wiest, 2011; Hands, 2011; Hofheinz, 2011; Howard & Hussain, 2013). Yet, increasingly, studies are acknowledging that the mobile phone entails a mobilization potential that is significantly distinct from other communication technologies. Indeed, as "an explosive tool for insurgents" (*The Washington Times*, 2005), mobile phones share attributes in common with other digital communication technologies used for mobilization, such as fast and easy communication, reduction of transaction costs, facilitation of alternative information, and coordination of contentious activities across geography (Ball & Brown, 2011). Meanwhile, we should not ignore the fact that it is exactly this unique set of mobile communication technologies that encourages "new forms of mobile action" (Monterde & Postill, 2014, p. 431). Campbell and Kwak (2010, 2011, 2012) in their studies of mobile communication and political participation convincingly identify distinctive aspects of mobile communication, including its intimate networks of strong ties, mobility and flexibility ("anytime-anywhere social affordances" [Campbell & Kwak, 2012, p. 262]), and the "heightened degree of selectivity and control" (Campbell & Kwak, 2011, p. 1007) over communication processes that can support active political deliberation and engagement. What makes mobile communication especially distinct from other communication technologies, as Campbell and Kwak contend, is its foundation of "a large number of close and trusted discussion partners [that] helps boost the salience and personal relevance of supporting views, creating a discussion environment that is not only safe, but also robust and therefore more meaningful" (Campbell & Kwak, 2011, p. 1018; see similar discussion in Katz, 2006; Wei & Lo, 2006).

Among studies that examine the embedding of mobile communication into society, Ling's path-breaking work (2004, 2008, 2013) offers relevant theoretical insights to understand the distinctive functioning of mobile communications. Being a direct interpersonal means of communication on the basis of strong social ties, as I see it, three relevant aspects uniquely entrench mobile communication by delineating the mobile phone as, to use

Ling's phrase, "essentially a *reciprocal* technology" (2013, p. 160, emphasis added).

First, mobile communication features flexible, individual *addressability* that makes each user "personally addressable" (Ling, 2008, p. 3) anytime, anywhere, as *mutually expected*. Addressability involves the reciprocal expectation (Ling, 2016) of an *immediate response* in view of the idea that we are perpetually connected by mobile communication (Katz & Aakhus, 2002). For instance, Ling notes "a common expectation that we can always quickly respond to calls and texts. If we're not available, the situation becomes awkward" (2013, p. 171).

Second, mobile communication embodies *social reflexivity* (Ling, 2013, p. 13), the appropriate understanding of socially constructed expectations of both ourselves and our communication partners as well as the subsequent actions of both sides. As Ling (2013, p. 175) explains, "we have to imagine how our interlocutor will receive and interpret the communication. In addition, we need to calibrate how much effort we want to invest in the communication." "[A]bove and beyond . . . special content" (Simmel & Hughes, 1949, p. 254), sociability inheres in mobile communication and hence complicates the meanings of interactive practices via the mobiles, as the consideration should go beyond the current situation that is under way to, more broadly, involve reciprocally determined ethical issues like "the nature of . . . friendship [between the communicating partners] and how the person receiving the communication will react" (Ling, 2013, p. 177). Functioning as social glue, mobile communication hence engages self-reflective, mutually defining individuals and "ties us securely into the expectations of our social networks" (Ling, 2013, p. 185).

Third, mobile communication encompasses both instrumental, task-oriented and expressive uses of mobile technologies (Ling, 2004, 2008; also see similar discussions by Katz, 2003b, 2006, 2008; Katz & Aakhus, 2002). While the former, referred to as "micro-coordination" (e.g., arranging everyday logistics and coordinating plans with other), the latter as "hyper-coordination," or "social and emotional interaction" (Ling & Yttri, 2002, p. 140), establishes solidarity and maintains allegiance between individuals for social cohesion (Ling, 2008). In this sense, we may say that under certain circumstances (e.g., everyday life or movement mobilization), the social functions of the mobiles go over and above instrumental functions, as social functions are essential to conserve the social fabric in society. The observation here hardly stands alone but resonates well with current scholarship. In the same vein, Johnsen points out that "the communication [via the mobile phone] has . . . a very important function apart from the instrumental exchange of information. It becomes an information-carrier without necessarily having content or function *except* to sustain the idea of a social fellowship" (2003, p. 163, emphasis added). Acknowledging that the transmission of both information and affect are highly important via mobile communication, Katz (2006, p. 107) also concurs that greater attention should be devoted to the symbolic and affective sides of mobile uses (also see Katz & Aakhus, 2002). A specific examination of the hypercoordination via mobile phones that is laden with "expressive-symbolical content" (Johnsen, 2003, p. 164) would act as a fruitful approach to dissect the cohesive properties of mobile communication (Campbell & Park, 2008).

Despite being addressed individually here, these three aspects are closely correlated to each other and, together, they play a critical role in making mobile communication unique. The issue of individual addressability involves social reflexivity concerning the imagination of expectation from others, while the latter internalizes social expectations and norms of interaction and accessibility in the social place, further necessitating individual addressability (Ling, 2016). Social reflexivity, or sociability, significantly underpins the affective dimension of mobile communication and, as a consequence, contributes notably to shaping interactive practices via mobile communication. That is to say, mobile communication enables "a feeling for, by a satisfaction in, the very fact that one is associated with others and that the solitariness of the individual is resolved into togetherness, a union with others" (Simmel & Hughes, 1949, p. 255). In some extreme cases, as Ling observes, "peer pressure [from mobile communication] seems to be more important than the essential meaning" (2008, p. 8). On the whole, this peer pressure carries a non-negligible potential for collective expression, which so far has received scarce attention[5] and thus is the focus of this chapter. Current discussions largely view mobile communication from a personal, or individual, perspective, and feature the perception that mobiles function as "personal miniature representative[s]" (Katz, 2006, p. 57), or they describe the mobiles' influence on "personal communication society" (Campbell & Park, 2008; Castells et al., 2007), or they celebrate the "more fine grained and individualized way" (Ling, 2016) that the mobile phone enables us with regard to our personal utility. How may the mobile phone, as a reciprocal technology with strong expectations for sociability,

5. For instance, in his analysis of mobile uses for political changes in Arab societies, Ibahrine reveals not just the way that mobile communication mobilizes existing networks as "more personal, more direct, and easier to use than the Internet" (2008, p. 267), but also the very affective dimension in the use of mobile phones—hypercoordination—for greater freedom for collective action (p. 264).

affect *collective* mobilization? Following Ella Baker's definition, mobilization in this study is "more sporadic, involving large numbers of people for relatively short periods of time and probably for relatively dramatic activities" (Payne, 1989, p. 897). To answer the question, we should especially draw from literatures on social ties and reciprocity in mobilization and on reciprocity in the special context of China, which sets the focus of the next section.

SOCIAL TIES, RECIPROCITY, AND *GUANXI* IN MOBILE COMMUNICATION FOR MICROMOBILIZATION

Micromobilization: From Face-to-Face to Mediated Communication

Earlier work on collective action mobilization assumes that atomized individuals make isolated, independent decisions about their actions (e.g., Olson, 1975). More recent network-based or structural perspectives discard this proposition and instead underscore the principle of interdependence in mobilization (e.g., Diani & McAdam, 2003; Marwell et al., 1988; Snow et al., 1980). While the influence of personal networks over individual orientations, beliefs, and behaviors has long been recognized (e.g., Lazarsfeld, Berelson, & Gaudet, 1948; Rogers, 1962), social ties and networks establish a significant "microsocial model" (Marwell et al., 1988, p. 503) of mobilization and recruitment (also see the similar discussion on "microstructural" analyses in Snow et al., 1980).

The microsocial model of the mobilization process, or micromobilization as we discussed at the beginning of this chapter, especially delves into the salience of social ties and networks as an effective mobilization avenue (Gould, 1991; Kitts, 2000; McAdam, 1986; Stark & Bainbridge, 1980; Tindall, 2004). Since it is one of the most well-established findings in the studies of micromobilization, strong and dense ties play a much more prominent role than weak ties in interpersonal mobilization and recruitment. In brief, "recruitment among acquaintances, friends, and kin is generally more successful than recruitment among strangers" (Snow et al., 1980, p. 797).[6] Still, as Gould correctly points out, "[s]imply observing that social ties affect mobilization is not much of a contribution" (2003, p. 237). Similarly, as Kitts (2000, p. 242) reminds us, "no one has identified any intrinsic property of social ties that unequivocally promotes protests,

---

6. For further discussions on mobilization through friends, see, for instance, Kitts, 2000; McAdam, 1988; Passy, 2003 and through family, see Sherkat & Blocker, 1994.

collective, or organizational participation." To pinpoint the contribution of social ties, or the specific dimension of social ties (Passy, 2003, p. 22), studies have attested to exactly how and why strong or dense social ties are important to mobilization and recruitment through the examination of, for instance, tie strength and number (Schussman & Soule, 2005); network density and centralization (Fernandez & McAdam, 1989; Marwell et al., 1988; Oliver, Marwell, & Teixeira, 1985; Oliver & Marwell, 1988); the exposure to mobilization information (Snow et al., 1980, p. 797); the articulation of grievances, identities, and strategies of contention (Friedman & McAdam, 1992; Kitts, 2000; McAdam, 1988; Passy, 2003); or the exchange of the norm of fairness (Gould, 1993; Snow et al., 1980). Strong ties stand prominently, especially in "high-risk/high-cost activism" (McAdam, 1986) that puts individual's safety in danger or entails a time, financial, or other type of cost to the individual.

Meanwhile, a large portion of scholarship on social ties and micromobilization has developed on account of face-to-face, rather than mediated, communication (e.g., Lim, 2010; McAdam, 1986, 1988; McAdam & Paulsen, 1993; Walgrave & Wouters, 2014). Studies on mediated communication, social ties, and micromobilization remain inchoate.[7] From a broad picture, the pervasive adoption of ICTs on political contention further complicates the picture. While a widespread critique argues that digital communication technologies might be plausibly regarded as facilitative of mobilization, as studies underscore, strong ties, with organizational entities in most cases, are still an essential determinant of mobilization (e.g., Bond et al., 2012; Diani, 2000; Gladwell, 2010; Schradie, 2018). Scholars examining this issue have thereby been especially careful *not* to exaggerate the general theoretical implications of the role of ICTs in their findings. As Walgrave and Wouters accurately suggest, the mediated communication channel—including "digital channels and social online networks" (2014, p. 1700)—becomes a potentially fruitful subject to study in order to tease out the exact determinant by which collective action mobilization and recruitment emerges on the *mediated, interpersonal* level.

Given this consideration, I focus on the embedding of reciprocity in mobile communication for mobilization and recruitment. This embedding of reciprocity is one specific kind of interdependence on the microlevel, that is, the emotional function of social ties. To be clear, individuals may take account of reciprocity when using their mobile phones as they make their own decisions about contributing to a collective action. The thoughts

---

7. But, see Snow et al., 1980.

underlying this proposition are twofold. For one thing, mobile communication favors particularly strong and dense ties from "the intimate sphere of friends and family" (Ling, 2008, p. 159). Furthermore, as discussed in the last section, mobile phones are growing into a reciprocal technology that especially accentuates the social and tacit dimension of reciprocity. For another, with the embedding of strong ties, mobile communication entails reciprocity, or introduces reciprocity as a causal mechanism to micromobilization. A theorization of reciprocity in mobilization and in the discussion of *guanxi*, the Chinese expression describing interpersonal ties and connections, will be presented separately.

Theorizing Reciprocity in Mobilization

The term reciprocity captures some key properties of the social tie in the maintenance of social support in a wide variety of human societies (e.g., Antonucci, Fuhrer, & Jackson, 1990; Gouldner, 1960; Putnam, 2000; Putnam, Leonardi, & Nanetti, 1993; Uehara, 1995). Among various studies on reciprocity, Gouldner's work on "the norm of reciprocity" (1960) provides a classic yet underdeveloped framework to investigate the effectiveness of reciprocity in social ties as a facilitator of collective action. As a universal and relevant "causal force" (Uehara, 1995) in social life, reciprocity refers to the dynamic through which interdependence among individuals is realized, reassured, and reproduced. Besides reciprocity as a pattern of exchange, Gouldner emphasizes "a generalized moral norm of reciprocity which defines certain actions and *obligations* as repayments for benefits received" (1960, p. 170, emphasis in original). More specifically, being a general moral norm rather than a specific one, reciprocity "evokes obligation toward others on the basis of their past behavior" (Gouldner, 1960, p. 170) *without* the inducement of material incentives or special normative mechanisms. Here, as a self-perpetuating phenomenon (Uehara, 1995, p. 484) regarding social support, reciprocity permeates socially supportive interaction with the connotation that "each party has rights *and* duties" (Gouldner, 1960, p. 169, emphasis in original) to support those with whom they share social ties, even without returning these benefits immediately. With this connotation, to use Gouldner's words, reciprocity "mobilize[s] egoistic motivations and channel[s] them into the maintenance of the social system" (1960, p. 173). People who fail to return benefits as reciprocal repayments will instead suffer certain social penalties. Generically, the reciprocity norm of social support systems, as a sort of moral belief, acknowledges, motivates, and guarantees "a mutually gratifying pattern of exchanging goods and services . . . in the long run" (Gouldner, 1960, p. 170). The internalization of moral obligation and debt to respond to the request from those who offer benefits therefore maintains the reciprocal dependency of social ties and further contributes to social cohesion.

Reciprocity, as the dynamic of moral support that binds together social ties, acts as a reservoir or resource for recruitment and mobilization. For Tilly (1978), the governing power of reciprocity that arises from "netness," or relational connectedness, is crucial in engendering mutual obligations and stimulating collective action. For Putnam, Leonardi and Nanetti, "the norm of generalized reciprocity serves to reconcile self-interest and solidarity" (Putnam et al., 1993, p. 172), hence overcoming problems of collective action. From the French commune (Gould, 1995) and the Russian Revolution (Bonnell, 1983) to the 1964 Mississippi Summer Project in the United States (McAdam & Paulsen, 1993) and the Maoist movement in India (Cody, 2016; Shah, 2013), examples of insurgencies and movements around the world uncover mobilization and recruitment through reciprocity among relations of intimacy, such as bonds of family and kinship, as the core mechanism of various political movements. Consequently, this study asks:

> Given that mobile phones are a deeply reciprocal technology, how will mobile communication, integrating the reciprocal nature of social ties, affect the mobilization process?

To answer the question, we turn to the Chinese context where reciprocity enjoys a particularly central role in networking.

A Characterization of Reciprocity in *Guanxi*

Reciprocity seizes a pivotal position in *guanxi*, the pervasive and dominant system of social ties constituting "the entire [Chinese] society throughout much of its historical, political, and economic contexts" (Lin, 2001, p. 159; also see Bian, 2017, 2018; Smart, 1993; Wu et al., 2006; Yan, 1996). Before we elucidate the characterization of reciprocity in *guanxi*, we first briefly discuss *guanxi*.

Guan signifies "to connect" or "to close up," while *xi* denotes a chain, "to tie up," or "to link." The combination, *guanxi*, connotes the relation-oriented social ties that exist among parties that make up intricate social networks in the Chinese society (Gold, Guthrie, & Wank, 2002; Kipnis, 1997; Yan, 1996). In a Chinese Confucian view, the nature of a person is that of "a relational being, socially situated and defined within an interactive context" (Bond & Hwang, 1986, p. 215). Following this argument, the individual in Chinese society is always considered as an entity *within* the interlocking social networks of *guanxi* (Fei, 1992, pp. 65–67), the social ecology of relational interdependence and reciprocity, which necessitates proper and moral ways of relating to others (i.e., relational others) in social practices.

Guanxi involves complex, unwritten, and implicit rules that differ from other relationship systems. Beyond its literal translations as "relation" or "personal connections," *guanxi* implies intangible emotional bonds and ethical obligations that are established by reciprocity between two or more individuals (Christensen & Levinson, 2003, p. 573; Gold, Guthrie, & Wank, 2002, p. 4). Among many studies on *guanxi*, Barbalet (2015, p. 1040) summarizes its definition as "a practice of social exchanges, expressed through reciprocal favour-seeking and provision of benefit. The reciprocal nature of *guanxi* relations encourages continuity of engagement, entailing emotional attachment and a morally charged sense of obligation."

As can be seen from above, the moral force of reciprocity is of central importance to the conduct and maintenance of *guanxi* (Yang, 1994, p. 70), as it underlines proper exchange behaviors as not only instrumental but also expressive or sentimental (Barbalet, 2015; Bian, 2017)—therefore entailing *ethical* and *essential* performance of indebtedness and obligation.[8] Similarly, as Bian underscores, "the norms of reciprocity, besides anything else, are deterministic about the continuation or termination of a *guanxi* tie" (Bian, 2018, p. 616). Given this consideration, some studies have advocated the inappropriateness of using, for instance, tie strength for an understanding of *guanxi* (Barbalet, 2015, p. 1043), even though *guanxi* typically operates through strong-tie links (e.g., Bian, 1997). Rather, reciprocity and its consequential effects would serve as a better and more reliable predictor to indicate the functioning of *guanxi* (Barbalet, 2015, p. 1043).

A characterization of reciprocity in *guanxi* is delineated in its four key properties as follows.

First, reciprocity forges reliability (*xinlai*, 信赖)[9] in personal networks in China. The stronger the reciprocity, the closer and more reliable the *guanxi* and vice versa (Chan, 2009, p. 718, also see Bian, 1997, p. 369). In other words, reciprocity implies the expectation of long-term, mutual reliability

8. For instance, the discussions of *"renqing"* (human sentiment, 人情) and *"mianzi"* (face, 面子) (Hwang, 1987; Park and Luo, 2001).
9. Some studies may use the term "trust" instead. Nevertheless, I follow Barbalet's suggestion here, as the term "reliability" implies "a sense of unconditional acceptance of dependence on another" (2014, p. 56).

by both parties in *guanxi* (Barbalet, 2014). In particular, Chinese society is characterized by weak legal institutions that have failed to provide "a trusted third party adjudication and enforcement of private agreements" (So & Walker, 2006, p. 114) with concomitant "unpredictable risks of arbitrary bureaucratic intervention" (Smart, 1993, p. 404). Against this backdrop, acts of reciprocity bring credibility into personal networks and social supports, including trustworthiness and dependability. The maintenance of *guanxi* is also dependent on an ongoing demonstration and constant cultivation of reliability and trustworthiness (Barbalet, 2015), or, as Barbalet elucidates, "trust as both a mechanism and an outcome of *guanxi*" (2014, p. 55).

Today *guanxi* still dominates people's lives in China (e.g., Xie, 2017) and is even more significant (for a comprehensive review, see Bian, 2018) despite the fact that Chinese people have become less socially and more individually oriented (Yan, 2009). As studies discern, the decline of social trust in recent years reinforces the role of *guanxi* in everyday life, leading "one to trust only those individuals in one's personal networks and to behave in accordance with a particularistic morality" (Yan, 2009, p. 286). Consequently, "[t]o seek a new safety net, or to re-embed, the Chinese individual is forced to *fall back to* the family and personal network or *guanxi*" (Yan, 2009, p. 288, emphasis added).

Second, reciprocity induces obligation, which, as studies note, is "the most important characteristic of *guanxi*" (Barbalet, 2015; Bian, 1997, p. 369). The moral code in reciprocity denotes a mutual, iterated obligation for both sides to act in accordance with behavioral codes that define the relationships between them. Hence, moral performance is culturally evaluated in light of the relationship and its consequent expectation in China, rather than the absolute principles of right and wrong as in the West (Bedford & Hwang, 2003, p. 133). More specifically, Bedford and Hwang anatomize that, as harmony is an important component of relational identity in Confucian China, "*wrong* and *right* are socially (and relationally) defined" (2003, p. 133, emphasis in original). To be clear, relationally defined guidance cultivates subjective (relational) morality that imposes obligations and duties on the (relational) other (Bedford & Hwang, 2003). Those who fail to uphold their relational obligations would be isolated in society, would suffer from losing face, and could even risk the ultimate price of being deprived of their *guanxi* resources and social ties (Cheng & Rosett, 1991; Hwang, 1987; Park & Luo, 2001; Smart, 1993; for a detailed discussion on guilt and shame see Bedford & Hwang, 2003). In practice, the extent or degree of felt relational obligation also functions as a mechanism of social control to monitor people's agency (Bedford & Hwang, 2003, p. 139).

Third, reciprocity transforms participants in *guanxi* into "resource mobilizers" (Bian, 2017, p. 265). "[G]*uanxi* not only promotes trust and sentiment in the relationship, it also expects resource exchanges" (Lin, 2017, p. 273). In actuality, reciprocity entails the requirement to mobilize *guanxi*-embedded resources for carrying out a series of actions and exchange of favors among members to access the resources from the *guanxi* network. Whether it is to influence job-control agents to allocate occupations for someone (e.g., Bian, 1994, 1997; Bian & Ang, 1997) or to acquire institutional or non-institutional support for business (e.g., Davies, Leung, Luk, & Wong, 1995; Tsang, 1998; Wank, 1996; Xin & Pearce, 1996), reciprocity promotes favor-exchange practices—in both instrumental and expressive senses—by allowing members of a shared community to serially tap into their *guanxi*-embedded resources in networks beyond specific individuals. The utility of reciprocity also implies that these *guanxi*-embedded resources are mutually expected to be reciprocally accessed and activated among members through networks of ongoing social relationships (Bian, 2018).

Fourth, the necessity and significance of reciprocity propel people into the cultivation of *guanxi* as an *end* itself through its expressive aspect. Indeed, given its reciprocal nature, as we can see in most cases, *guanxi* serves to instigate purposive acts of favoritism for one another. This is what can be described as *guanxi*'s instrumental (Barbalet, 2015, p. 1039) or utilitarian aspect (Farh, Tsui, Xin, & Cheng, 1998, p. 473). Meanwhile, of greater significance is that reciprocity also entails the expressive and sentimental aspect, or what Bian refers to as "influence" (1997, 2018), that cultivates and preserves relationships *in the long run* (Barbalet, 2015, p. 1039). As Bian (2018, p. 11, emphasis added) comments:

> In a granter–receiver dyad, the granter does a favour for the receiver, and the receiver repays the granter with a different form of favour either immediately or later . . . What is the main form of favours involved in this first part of the exchange? It is *the influence of power*, not merely information, that is possessed and exercised by the granter . . . the influence of power is felt and effective when it is used to help the receiver of the favour.

As Farh, Tsui, Xin, and Cheng propose, given the relation-centered world in China where "social relations are accorded great significance, . . . relationships are often seen as ends in themselves rather than means for realizing individual goals" (Farh et al., 1998, p. 473). For instance, "interpersonal favors and generosity are rendered with the anticipation that they will be reciprocated" (Farh et al., 1998, p. 473). In short, Chinese people not only rely heavily on *guanxi* to obtain social resources to meet needs and adapt themselves to changing environments but also actively engage in *guanxi* through performing reciprocation and fulfilling obligations to anchor their roles in social networks.

Thus, the case of China, where reciprocity seizes an imperative position in social ties, offers an appropriate example to dissect how reciprocity may affect collective action mobilization and recruitment. As a potent asset for survival in Chinese society, *guanxi* is naturally imbricated in mobile communication (e.g., Chu, Fortunati, Law, & Yang, 2012; Chu & Yang, 2006; Wallis, 2013). In an earlier paper, I coined the concept of the "*guanxi*-embedded mobile social network" (Liu, 2013, pp. 175–177) to exemplify that *guanxi* dynamics have been incorporated into mobile communication in the wake of the increasing popularity of mobile devices and the huge rise of the use of mobile devices in maintaining social relations in Chinese society. Similarly, Wallis (2013, p. 105) reveals female migrants' heavy reliance on existing *guanxi* and, particularly, the participants' norms of reciprocity during their mobile communication practices. Three focal questions further structure the inquiry into the ways in which the mobile phone as a reciprocal technology affects the mobilization process with the integrative power of reciprocity in China.

First, what are the microstructural avenues of mobilization enabled by mobile phones with the embedding of reciprocity?

Second, what are the processes by which mobile communication is deployed for mounting mobilization?

Third, what implications does mobile-mediated mobilization have for the spread and growth of political contention?

It should be noted that these explorative questions are not intended to apply to *all* processes of mobilization or all kinds of activism initiated by mobile phones. However, I believe that these questions promise to yield new understandings in an important, yet understudied, category of political mobilization facilitated by mobile communication.

MOBILE PHONE USES AND MOBILIZATION: HOW DO PEOPLE GET MOBILIZED?

This section presents the empirical material regarding mobile phone uses and mobilization in cases. First, it briefly discusses the selected cases (for detailed information about the methodology, see Chapter 2 and Appendix). Second, the section segments the empirical data in terms of two specific focuses: (1) How and why people used their mobile phones for mobilization, and (2) the ways in which people perceived and responded to the mobilizing messages received on their mobile phones and why.

The Cases

The sampled cases were drawn from contentious events involving the use of mobile phones as a resource for mobilization. The cases include the text-messaging fueled, anti-PX demonstration in Xiamen in 2007 (Xie & Zhao, 2007), the mobile-communication-facilitated mass protest in Weng'an in 2008 (Yu, 2008), and the taxi driver strikes in Fuzhou and Shenzhen in 2010 (*China Daily*, 2010). A brief description of the cases is presented as follows.

The anti-PX demonstration in Xiamen in 2007 was one of the largest middle-class protests in recent years, in which local residents challenged the installation of a petrochemical factory they perceived as a health threat. Reportedly, it is the first time that a demonstration was organized primarily by mobile communication. Credited as "the power of text messaging" (Xie & Zhao, 2007), the role of mobile phones and, not least, mobile text messaging has been highlighted in collective mobilization and political action. Similarly, on June 28, 2008, thousands of mobile-phone-mobilized local residents torched a police station and smashed county government office buildings in southwest China's Guizhou Province (Yu, 2008). The unrest was triggered by allegations of a cover-up of a 16-year-old girl's "unusual death" and the injustice her relatives suffered at the hands of the government and policemen (Ding, 2008; Ma, 2008).

The taxi drivers' strikes further exemplify the mobile-mediated mobilization. Discontent with rigid regulation enforcement and increasing fuel prices and rental fees, taxi drivers staged consecutive strikes in more than 10 cities between 2008 and 2011, primarily by calling and texting with mobile phones. This section investigates the strikes in Fuzhou (*China Daily*, 2010) and Shenzhen (eChinacities.com, 2010) to examine how taxi drivers employed their mobile devices, among other means, to mobilize strike actions collectively.

A snowball sampling strategy was applied to locate participants in contention, with the initial "seeds" for sampling provided by local journalists or editors from my contacts. Normally, it is easier for journalists and editors to find out about sensitive information like political contention, although they are not always allowed to cover these protests. After sampling, face-to-face interviews were conducted for data collection. The interview specifically delves into how interviewees feel about the influence of mobile communication on mobilization and recruitment, if any, in their own words (for details of the interview questions, see the Appendix: Methodological Reflections). As mentioned in the methodological note (in Chapter 2), I deliberately started the interview with a general picture regarding various forms of communication (face-to-face, mass, and networked communication) before moving toward specific case- and media-based questions to avoid the risk of inducing the focus on a specific communication practice or technology explicitly. A total of 37 face-to-face interviews were conducted in Chinese for data collection, with each around one-and-a-half hours in duration.

From Texts to Calls: Mobile Phone Use for Collective Action Mobilization

The interviews show that mobile phones played an essential role in mobilization and recruitment for all cases. *All* interviewees underscored that calls and texts through their mobile phones acted as "the primary channel" (participants in the Xiamen case and taxi drivers in Fuzhou and Shenzhen, October 2011, personal communications) to learn information about the events and, further, allowed them to circulate (mobilizing) messages and to coordinate contention against government censorship and suppression. To be clear, interviewees heard about the action and disseminated the mobilizing calls via mobile communication in their personal networks, which involved family members, relatives, friends, and people from school or work. Face-to-face communication stands as the second relevant channel through which people shared and discussed information related to mobilization (30 out of 37, or 81.8%). Yet, these kinds of conversations and discussions were always alongside mobile communication, i.e., they tended to occur *after* people received messages through their mobile channels. A little under half of the interviewees (15 out of 37, or 40.5%) noted that mass communication channels, i.e., newspapers and television, also mentioned the contention, but these messages discouraged mobilization, in unison with the authorities.

Why did the citizenry rely so much on mobile communication? In effect, the stringent control over public communication from the authorities pushed people into employing their *guanxi*-based personal communication channels, i.e., mobile communication devices like mobile phones. In the Xiamen case, more specifically, local government officials tried to prevent residents from knowing about or denouncing the controversial PX project by banning reports covering this project, blocking related words on the internet, and shutting down online forums that engaged in discussion about the project. Furthermore, asserting that the negative messages about the project were "rumors,"[10] the local government launched a crackdown on so-called rumormongers. This move had a chilling effect on public communication platforms, especially online forums. One interviewee noted, "The [online] discussion on the PX issue reduced significantly, as people turned silent on public platforms in the face of such intimidation from the government" (Resident in Xiamen, September 13, 2010, personal communication).

Subsequently, mobile phones played a key role in both circulating a "warning" message about the PX plant[11] and proliferating a "mobilizing text"[8] for later demonstrations. The mobilizing text read, "For the sake of our future generations, take action! Participate with 10,000 people, June 1 at 8 a.m., opposite the municipal government building! Tie hands with yellow ribbons! Pass this message on to all your Xiamen friends!"

Residents spread the messages via their mobile phones as interpersonal communication channels to break the censorship by calling upon relatives, friends, and social connections to "distribute this information as soon as possible to as many people as possible" (residents in Xiamen, December 2010, personal communication). With the help of the flexibility of mobile text messaging, one interviewee noted, "you just need to twiddle the keyboard with your thumbs" (resident in Xiamen, December 15, 2010, personal communication) to forward calls. These types of messages were transmitted so widely through mobile communication that, as *Southern Weekend* (南方周末) records (Zhu, 2007, p. A1), the phrase "did you receive the [PX-related] SMS?" became the opening remark when Xiamen citizens met each other face-to-face in the following three months. Reportedly, the mobilizing text had been relayed "more than 1 million times" via mobile phones until it had reached practically every citizen in Xiamen (Lan & Zhang, 2007).

A similar situation can be observed in the Weng'an case. Besides the control over mass media and communication, local authorities ordered a few "tech-savvy teachers" to post comments favorable toward the government on the internet in an attempt to "guide online public opinion." The authorities' monopoly over public communication channels left rural residents with their mobile phones as the *only* available tool to communicate

10. For a detailed discussion on rumor, see Chapter 5.
11. The message read: "When this massive toxic chemical product goes into production, that will mean an atomic bomb has been released over all Xiamen Island. The people of Xiamen will live with leukemia and deformed babies . . . "

"with their own voices" (a journalist in Weng'an, December 22, 2010, personal communication) beyond mouth-to-ear interactions about the grievance of the girl's family. To make such grievances heard, local residents circulated messages through their mobile devices, claiming that instead of getting justice, the local government and policemen had physically assaulted the victim's relatives. Such messages eventually mobilized almost 10,000 people who went to the public security bureau building where they smashed and burned all the police vehicles parked there.

The situations in the two strikes show similarities to the above descriptions of the control over communications, including mass communication and communication, though in different contexts. Taxi drivers have long shown widespread discontent about the increased operating costs and traffic fines from taxi companies and the government. Nevertheless, their discontent had been largely ignored, and local media were not allowed to discuss drivers' grievances and anger. Meanwhile, some taxi drivers attempted to post their discontentment on the internet (Lee, 2011), but most of this information was censored. Dissent was brewing and, again, mobile communication provided heat for the pot. In both strikes, mobile interaction functioned as the sole means to spread strike messages and to call for strikes. Specifically, voice calls as contentious repertoire played a fundamental role in circulating strike information and in recruiting colleagues (Liu, 2014). One interviewee elaborated:

> The reason [we use mobile phones to organize strikes] is very simple: it [calling] is very easy. . . . It is impossible to text while we are driving, let alone surf the internet [to post something online]. But driving while talking is possible . . . and convenient [for spreading the word]. For us, the earlier [we mobilize], the better. (34-year-old taxi driver in Fuzhou, April 25, 2010, personal communication)

In this way, mobile communication encourages the dissemination of strike messages within a short time and enables "flash" strikes "on the move," i.e., mobilizing and driving simultaneously. Meanwhile, face-to-face meetings for discussion and sharing mobilizing messages took place at service stations where taxi drivers gathered to take their breaks. Nevertheless, to avoid being impeded by the authorities, taxi drivers deliberately chose *not* to talk about the strike explicitly and openly when they met. Rather, they "simply nodded to each other when getting together" for a short time and "got to know that the other side has already known [about the strike], then [when they got] back [into their taxis, they] continued to diffuse [mobilizing] messages further [via their mobile phones]" (34-year-old taxi driver in Fuzhou, April 25, 2010, personal communication). In other words, face-to-face communication, albeit with no words, also encourages mobile communication.

In summary, participants in the four cases relied on both the text and call functions of mobile phones to initiate contention and to recruit participants. In addition to the obvious advantages of mobile phones, such as ease of use and instantaneity, the crucial reason people employ their mobile phones as a mobilizing tool is that the mobile phone as a personal communication device is more or less the *only* available means for them to express their discontentment, to air their grievances, and act collectively when the authorities have snatched up all the public communication channels.

Mobilizing *Guanxi* via Mobile Phones

While mobile phones allow people to disseminate mobilizing messages, the question of how this communication process via mobile phones encourages people to follow such messages and to engage in contention remains a key issue regarding understanding the process of mobilization and recruitment. The interviews indicate that in the process of mobile interactions, people activated and deployed their *guanxi* for mobilization. As I present below, the involvement of *guanxi* and, precisely, a strong sense of moral duty and ethical obligation from reciprocity act as the driving forces for recruitment and participation in contentious cases.

Interviewees reported how they perceived the influence from their *guanxi* networks when they exchanged messages through mobile communication. One interviewee noted:

> [T]he [mobilizing] texts show care and kindness from my friends' network, as they wanted to inform me of the potential pollution from the [PX] project. It also shows that they are asking me to expand [the text's] dissemination. . . . It is my *duty* to forward this information straightaway to my friends, as I also care about them and hope they are aware of this issue and spread it within their [mobile] social network to get more support. (23-year-old university student in Xiamen, December 8, 2010, personal communication, emphasis added)

The above statement epitomizes that when people received messages via their mobile devices, what they apprehended was more than just being informed about the concrete content of the messages. Instead, the message metacommunicated and hence reminded the receiver of the *guanxi* between the senders and themselves, on the one hand, and their duties in their *guanxi* network regarding such relevant information on the other hand. This feeling, largely *self-perceived* given the basic reciprocal nature of *guanxi*, urges people to diffuse mobilizing messages throughout their *guanxi* network as both a form of social support and a fulfillment of their obligations in *guanxi*. As one explained, mobilizing your network resources by disseminating messages via mobile device "is a crucial way to demonstrate that you are a reliable friend, even if it concerns joining a demonstration [about a politically sensitive issue]" (37-year-old taxi driver in Fuzhou, October 4, 2011, personal communication).

In this way, the proliferation of mobilizing messages expands the contention's influence not only by informing and inviting more individuals but also by engaging and recruiting more *guanxi* networks into the diffusion practice. In the Xiamen case, for instance, government agents "never anticipated that mobile users involved in spreading . . . calls [would] surge past [a] million people within only three days" (26-year-old civil serviceman, September 15, 2010, personal communication), as a civil serviceman from the local government acknowledged, not least when the authorities had already taken measures to prevent collective action from occurring. In short, circulating messages through one's mobile phone has become a crucial way to activate one's *guanxi* resources as social support, which consequently becomes a crucial force to promote the proliferation of mobilizing calls through mobile networks.

Beyond delivering mobilizing messages, the activation of *guanxi* via mobile communication pushes and encourages people to join protests to fulfill their obligations. According to the interviews, when people receive mobilizing messages via their mobile devices, the messages imply an invitation to include receivers into an activity, in this case a politically sensitive one in China (i.e., political action). Nevertheless, the embedment of *guanxi* largely addresses people's attention to the relevance of social ties and relationships instead of the politically sensitive nature of such activity. A typical answer goes,

> Apart from the mobilizing initiative, the [mobilizing] message is, more relevantly, an appeal from your *guanxi* network . . . the people you knew or have a close relationship with are seeking your response, help, and support. How could you thrust aside this kind of appeal? (33-year-old taxi driver in Fuzhou, October 2011, personal communication)

Similarly, when people distributed mobilizing calls within their *guanxi* network via mobile phones, they also believed that receivers would respond to their requests in terms of the consideration of *guanxi* between them. For instance, participants in the anti-PX event asserted that when they sent messages to their best friends, they trusted that "given our *guanxi*," friends would "definitely respond to their requests and provide help [to them], regardless of the [politically sensitive] reason" (residents in Xiamen, October 2010, personal communications).

On the contrary, those who declined to respond to mobilizing messages or recruitment for collective action are considered to have failed to fulfill their duties to others within their *guanxi* network. The refusal to participate in mobilization is no longer the focus of the issue here. Instead, it implies "a refusal to fulfill your duty and moral obligation in the *guanxi* relation" (43-year-old taxi driver in Fuzhou, April 25, 2010, personal communication), consequently raising the social costs of non-participation and eroding one's social networks in a long run. Therefore, interviewees distributed mobilizing messages via their mobile phones while both engaging themselves and recruiting other people in their *guanxi* networks into collective actions.

Furthermore, the more times people received mobilizing messages from their social networks, the more willing they became to distribute these messages and join collective actions. One interviewee elaborated,

> The multiple [mobilizing] messages illustrate that the people you know all agree with this issue [to participate in strikes or protests]. And they are urging you to be one of them. . . . So we [both senders and receivers] are "comrades-in-arms in the same trench" and need to consolidate against the authorities. (35-year-old taxi driver in Shenzhen, October 20, 2010, personal communication)

As such, the idea of collective cohesion also plays to mobilization dynamics. The more people receive and distribute the messages via mobile communication, the stronger their sense of solidarity becomes.

Clearly, as has been consistent with extant literatures on movement mobilization, the activation of social ties and relationships, *guanxi* in this case, exerts a direct impact on recruitment and mobilization. More important for our central questions is that such activation occurs through mobile communication, which entails and motivates reciprocity that, in turn, generates an influence over people's attitudes, opinions, and behavior toward political engagement.

BEYOND WORDS: MOBILE COMMUNICATION, RECIPROCITY, AND MICROMOBILIZATION

This section expounds the role of reciprocity in mobile-mediated mobilization for self-selecting recipients for recruitment, engendering obligations for participation, legitimating mobilizing appeals, generating solidarity for collective action, and accumulating social ties and resources. The uniqueness of mobile communication underpins and forges this process of micromobilization. Close observation of mobile phone uses for protest mobilization in these cases reveals that the uniqueness of mobile communication and the embedding of reciprocity in *guanxi* mold collective action mobilization and recruitment in two significant ways.

Micromobilization with Immediate Effect

Mobile communication establishes micromobilization with immediate effect. The flexible, individual addressability of mobile communication releases people from fixed locations to maintain, activate, and mobilize their connectivity in order to exchange information, interact with others, or access resources embedded in their social networks. Such addressability hence offers "the presence of interpersonal networks which facilitate recruitment to activism" as "structural availability" (Schussman & Soule, 2005, p. 1086) anytime, anywhere for movements mobilization and recruitment. The direct, immediate access to individuals via their mobile phones prompts *instantaneous* mobilization and recruitment at the individual level, even when people are busy with their daily work routine (e.g., driving). Remarkably, the initiative of mobilization and recruitment enters into force with effect at once, as the reciprocal expectation toward the recipient in mobile communication requires an instant response to the (mobilizing) inquiry.

In practice, the interviewees acknowledged that they "replied to the [mobilizing] messages *right off* when receiving them" (emphasis added) because "the other side is waiting for . . . . You should not make others wait" (Resident in Xiamen, December 12, 2010, personal communication). The recipients thus had to make their decision about participating as soon as they received the message from their mobile phones. A similar expectation exists on the sender's side. As one taxi driver narrates, "of course . . . you just wait for the response [from the recipient via the mobile phone] as soon as you send it out . . . they [the recipients] should respond to it very soon" (35-year-old taxi driver in Shenzhen, October 20, 2010, personal communication). Otherwise, the relationship may suffer if the recipients fail to respond to the message upon receiving it. Or, according to the interviews, in rare cases, the senders might send the message again to "make sure [the recipient] received [it] and responds."

Clearly, mobile-mediated mobilization characterizes a synchronous process of micromobilization, which becomes very similar to traditional mobilization and recruitment in the face-to-face situation, where people are expected to receive an immediate result to their mobilization initiative. This synchronicity in the process of micromobilization differentiates mobile communication from other asynchronous communications without the expectation of immediate reaction, where people may decide later (e.g., respond to an inquiry on Facebook or Twitter).

Reciprocal Reflexivity as the Mobilization Agent

Mobile communication incorporates reciprocal reflexivity as the mobilization agent for collective action beyond concrete contents. The reciprocity in mobile-mediated mobilization guarantees reliability, reinforces obligations, legitimates mobilization appeals, strengthens empathy, and consolidates solidarity for recruitment and participation.

With the reciprocity of *guanxi*, mobile communication induces mutual reliability during collective mobilization. The sense of reliability—the idea that individuals appeal to and draw strength from their social ties—has been a part of what makes mobilization via mobile communication a highly self-directed (Castells, 2007, p. 248) and continuously expanding process.

In earlier studies on social movements, Marwell, Oliver and Prahl (1988, p. 512) denounced mass media as leading to "the 'waste' of communicating with people who are not potential contributors." Without doubt, the prevalence and low cost of digital communication resources today may further lower communication costs significantly. Nevertheless, the capacity to disseminate mobilizing message to anyone does *not* infer the efficiency of mobilization, as the sender cannot control to whom the message might next be sent. In other words, even though in many-to-many networked communication eases the spread of information and especially broadens its scope, it remains ambiguous in most cases with regard to the identity of the "many" in many-to-many communication. Nor does the sender control or influence the interpretive orientations of the (mobilizing) message that performs as a necessary condition for participation (Snow et al., 1986).

Mobile communication takes on a different look in terms of its basis of interpersonal interaction. More specifically, participants started the interaction process by selecting recipient(s) of mobilizing calls (in their mobile phones' directory) on their own. The choice is hardly random but, rather, is highly selective. People chose to send the calls to those social ties with whom they have reliable relationships to reduce the possibility of being identified and exposed as they distributed politically sensitive information. In other words, the decision about who should be the recipient fundamentally relies on the sender's perception of reliability toward the other side on the basis of established social ties and relationships. Hence, what I observed in these cases comprises two issues. For one thing, considering political costs and risks in high-stakes activism in a repressive context like China, organizers may not want or be able to communicate with all the people they know. Furthermore, it might not be possible to communicate with members of the general public as freely as they might want. In this context, the mobile-mediated, self-selective mobilization process ensures that recruitment and participation is low risk but highly efficient in consideration of reciprocity. In other words, the reliability of reciprocity entailed in mobile communication overcomes anxiety and fear in the authoritarian context and guarantees low potential risk when making mobilization public. The self-directed communication and mobilization via mobile phones therefore exemplify a strength of mobile phone use for mobilization and recruitment in an authoritarian context: Selectivity, or people's ability to concentrate their mobilizing efforts on "some faction of the people s/he knows and could potentially organize" (Marwell, Oliver, & Prahl, 1988, p. 502), stems from a consideration of reliability.

Next, the expressive dimension of mobile communication, or emotional interaction, dramatically shapes the interpretive orientations (Snow et al., 1986, p. 464) and follow-up response to the mobilizing message as soon as it is received. The recipients view the message as an appeal from their *guanxi* networks rather than as a simple piece of mobilizing information. In other words, mobile interactions between people who know each other already—such as family, intimate friends, close colleagues and the like—have established a rather different connection compared to a "cold call" (Gergen, 2002). In turn, it is the social dimension, or social influence in mobile communication that encourages recipients, as morally good and reliable people, to respond positively to (mobilizing) requests from their mobile social networks. As we can see from the interviews, the emphasis on "the people you knew or have a close relationship with are seeking your response, help, and support" (33-year-old taxi driver in Fuzhou, October 13, 2011, personal communication) undoubtedly prioritizes sociability and weights the social dimension of relationship much more heavily than the content of the message. This, again, is in line with observations from the classic sociology of movements. McAdam and Paulsen, for instance, direct attention toward social influence instead of information for mobilization, arguing that "at the microlevel, ties are less important as conduits of information than as *sources of social influence*. And the stronger the tie, the stronger the influence exerted on the potential recruit" (McAdam & Paulsen, 1993, p. 655, emphasis added).

So, what would "the influence exerted on the potential recruit" (McAdam & Paulsen, 1993, p. 655) be in mobile communication for mobilization? The communication process, first and foremost, epitomizes the way in which reciprocity legitimates the practice of distributing political mobilizing messages and participating in protests in a repressive context like China. Technology alone is not sufficient to legitimate mobilization practice; instead, the external force beyond technology plays a key role in the process of legitimating mobilization (Diani, 2000; Rafael, 2003).[12] In the *absence* of movement-encouraging networks from organizations, reciprocity from social ties legitimates mobilization appeals by underlying the *norm* of responding to support requests from one's social networks. This emphasis shifts the attention from "should I respond to—and participate in—the call for collective action" to "should I respond to the request for help/support from my social network?" Then, as the recipients perceive it, how they deal with the request definitely affects how the senders handle appeals from them in the future beyond the (mobilizing) issue at hand. Such a sentiment, generated by *self-perceived* duties and responsibilities, given the basis of the reciprocal nature of *guanxi*, encourages recipients to respond positively to the request immediately as a sort of moral support and ethical fulfillment of their duties in a social relationship. In other words, given the duty and obligation from reciprocity, in particular the fear of losing social support in the long run, the answer to the (mobilizing) request is usually "yes." The reciprocal duty and obligation inherited from *guanxi* accordingly legitimates mobile-mediated mobilization by generating *pressure* to respond in positive ways to the request to participate in collective action. As such, the moral dimension in the norm of reciprocity decisively exerts influence on people's decisions concerning recruitment and participation in contention.

Second, the expressive dimension of reciprocity nurtures a "shared awareness" (Shirky, 2011, pp. 35–36) through mobile communication, which embodies empathy and consolidates solidarity for micromobilization. As Shirky (2011, p. 36) states, shared awareness allows people to be aware of the thoughts and feelings of those within their social networks, further engendering a sense of togetherness during the process of micromobilization. In the cases of mobile-mediated mobilization,

12. Rafael, for instance, identifies the Catholic Church as "an authority outside the [mobilizing] text messages themselves" (2003, p. 409) in "People's Power II."

through engaging themselves in the process of participation and recruitment, people are conveying their attitudes toward mobilization as well as sharing their feelings toward mobilization: The implicit position of the metacommunication is "I agree with and support this action." Such micromobilization consequently articulates a sense of shared awareness that enables mobile users to recognize that others in their *close* social network have a common understanding of certain situations that every individual in the same social network may have to face. Individuals in the same (mobile) network would thus expect that they were not alone when disseminating mobilizing messages; they were also *identified* networked individuals who enjoyed reciprocal support from recognizing one another due to their shared awareness. In other words, the support is derived from having recognized members of one's reciprocal relationships, such as friends, classmates, relatives, rather than anonymous sources. The empathy accordingly engenders a strong sense of solidarity and cohesion between participants during mobilization, as people know that those in their *guanxi* networks are "in the same camp" (54-year-old, taxi driver in Xiamen, October 13, 2011, personal communication).

In summary, the embedment of *guanxi* in mobile communication and, in particular the reciprocity obligated by it, is a pivotal facilitator of engagement in and recruitment for contention. The process of mobile-mediated mobilization entails a practice of articulating social ties and fulfilling reciprocal obligations between communicators. During the process of mobile interaction, the reciprocal nature of social ties generates mutual reliability, legitimates mobilization appeals, addresses obligations for both sides, and engenders solidarity, a combination which facilitates mobilization and recruitment. In this way, the cultural importance of reciprocity acts as a key force for the expansion of the uniqueness of mobile communication in the process of collective action mobilization and recruitment.

BEYOND HOMOGENEITY: MOBILE-MEDIATED "RHIZOMATIC NETWORKS" AND POLITICAL IMPLICATIONS

Indeed, mobile communication or mobile-mediated mobilization, given its basis in strong ties, suffers from certain disadvantages. One of the key concerns regarding what Gergen (2008) calls "monadic clusters" consists of mobile-based, tightly knit networks. As Koskinen notices, " . . . [i]n these clusters [of small and like-minded network ties], people focus on immediate life and microrelationships at the cost of civic concerns" (2008, p. 241). Consequently, these mobile-based or facilitated clusters constrain or hinder political dialogue and participation at broader levels of civil society (Campbell & Kwak, 2011, p. 1019; also see Campbell & Kwak, 2012). While these observations primarily come from the Western cases, what about the cases of mobile-mediated mobilization in China? Are they the same as or different from the Western cases?

The answer to the that question is both "yes" and "no." It is "yes" because, as the interviews demonstrate, the embedding of reciprocity from *guanxi* makes recruitment and participation via mobile communication largely *guanxi*-driven practices. While "social ties may constrain as well as encourage activism" (McAdam & Paulsen, 1993, p. 645), so does mobile-mediated mobilization with the embedding of social ties and relationships. Participants tend to be more concerned more about the maintenance of their social ties and relationship via mobile communication instead of contention per se. Even though they disagreed with the government's plan for the PX project (the Xiamen case), were angry about the injustice the girl and her family have suffered (the Weng'an case), and shared discontent toward the controversially rigid manner of enforcing traffic regulations by local authorities (the Fuzhou and Shenzhen cases), few interviewees acknowledge that these reasons are the key driving forces behind their participation in various acts of contention. What is even more noteworthy is that, after an experience of contention, regardless of whether it succeeds or fails, people rarely consider that what might be potential institutional change would better protect their rights. This undoubtedly—and unfortunately—restricts the long-running impact of contentious activities on Chinese society.

Yet, the answer is also "no," given the specificity of *guanxi*. As "resource mobilizers" (Bian, 2017, p. 265), *guanxi*—its relational ethics and structural features, such as quasi-group formation—also provides for the ability of an individual to reach a much wider segment of society through the *guanxi* of *guanxi*, or "rhizomatic networks" as Yang coins the term. In her study on *guanxi* practices, Yang (1994, p. 294) advocates for the significance of an investigation of "rhizomatic networks" comprised of "informal group and individual units for the seeds of an autonomous social realm in China," particularly due to the environment in the Chinese political context that discourages the formation of independent organizations. By the lights of Deleuze and Guattari's work (1987), Yang describes "rhizomatic guanxi" with "a 'conjunctive' process of addition . . . creating an outwardly expanding network of lateral relationships" (Yang, 1994, pp. 308–309). Within this rhizomatic *guanxi*, the ethics of reciprocity from kinship, friendship, and so on bind people together to meet their needs and desires of everyday life. "Thus guanxi are rhizomatic or vinelike growths extending across state arborescent organizations and offices to form their own linkages" (Yang, 1994, p. 308). In this way, *guanxi* can assume the role that formal groups and associations play in Western civil societies, with its unique political significance in China.

This *guanxi* polity poses as an alternative system of relational ethics and social integration subverting and displacing state structures. Thus, the power of official channels, state rules, and state regulations are neutralized. They are made to bend and change with the circumstances and with each particular constellation of persons involved. In the art of *guanxi*, personal and private ends are attained ironically through a process and an ethics that breaks up any unitary construction of the individual by stressing obligation, indebtedness, and interpersonal loyalty. Therefore, through the art of *guanxi*, it is possible to recuperate from the state's monopoly on the category of "public" and return it to the realm of the social (Yang, 1994, pp. 308–309).

Rich evidence that *guanxi* functions in such a capacity with compelling political implications but remains relatively unarticulated and underexplored. Yan's (1996) investigations of rural communities exhibit that *guanxi* as a defense mechanism supports local residents to win battles with local cadres. Against the decline of political control systems in universities, relational, peer-influence networks among students of the same or nearby dormitories nurtured the connections necessary for movement mobilization and participation during the 1989 Chinese Student movement (Zhao, 1998). *Guanxi*-based kinship and acquaintance mobilization or demobilization has become a new mode of organization (Shan, 2010; Shan & Jiang, 2009) and even of repression (Deng & O'Brien, 2013) in contemporary rural contentions.

Exactly this kind of *guanxi* polity, but now mediated by mobile communication, exemplifies as observed above. Mobile-mediated mobilization is not simply a matter of involving more individuals, but each new member, in turn, recruits their whole personal network. In the Xiamen case, this is demonstrated as the mobilizing message was sent to almost every and each resident. For this reason, the growth of the movement is not mere arithmetic, rather, it is a *geometrical* expansion, consequently reaching many different levels and segments of society. Given the difficulties of establishing civic organizations in China's repressive context, the flexible and temporary quasi-groups that form around a common purpose and are sustained and activated via mobile communication, but are not formally registered as social organizations, become important components of the struggle against the authorities and their possible demobilization efforts (e.g., sending out warning messages against mobilizing messages). In other words, despite the absence of social organizations, these kinds of quasi-groups based on personal networks are especially helpful in building a mobilizing structure that is "submerged" (Melucci, 1985, p. 801) in everyday life but can reemerge and become active when a specific issue arises. This recognition also allows us to avoid the risk of reducing "networks to individual-level counts of social ties" (Gould, 1991, p. 716), A further interrogation of *guanxi*-embedded mobile communication should produce fruitful research to detect "an independent social realm in China . . . in expanding circles of private relations and networks" (Yang, 1994, p. 311), mediated and facilitated by mobile communication, as an alternative and even subversive realm of operations, weaving webs of personal relationships which crisscross and overlie one another (Yang, 1994, p. 308). Regardless of its temporariness, mobile-mobilized, *guanxi*-based quasi-groups nevertheless help move toward a Chinese version of "civil society,"[13] better termed *"minjian,"* or "a realm of people-to-people relationships" (Yang, 1994, p. 288) as an oppositional power reacting against the repressive state.

MOBILE COMMUNICATION FOR MICROMOBILIZATION

To highlight the relevance of mobile *communication* in the process of micromobilization resonates with the argument in social movement scholarship that treats ongoing interactional processes and hence the "influence process" (Gould, 1993, p. 185) by which people come to participate in a social movement as the "underlying causes of the act" (Snow, Zurcher, & Ekland-Olson, 1980, p. 795). As Snow et al. remind us, "the 'motives' for joining or continued participation are generally emergent and interactional rather than pre-structured. That is, they arise out of a process of ongoing interaction with . . . its recruitment agents" (1980, p. 795). That is to say, networks function to structure movement recruitment and growth, but they do not tell us what transpires when people get together. Consequently, connections or social relationships alone function insufficiently as causal determinants for understanding mobilization but work better as "conduits of processes affecting the likelihood individuals will support a movement, be motivated or participate, and/or actually participate" (Ward, 2016, p. 859). Rather, emphasis should be placed on "the kinds of communication that individuals use to activate personal networks" (Bennett, Breunig,

13. For more discussions on the application of the concept "civil society" in the case of China, see, for instance, Huang, 1993; Yang, 1994, Chapter 8. This topic, nevertheless, goes beyond the scope of this chapter.

& Givens, 2008, p. 286). Indeed, as we can see from these cases, it is in the process of interaction and communication—and through mobile communication technologies—that the embedding of social ties activates the social expectation of reciprocity and its further influence on mobilization and recruitment.

Moving forward, the widespread accessibility of social media like the mobile messaging service WeChat accentuated by mobile phones further enhances new potentials of reciprocity-based mobilization. Being increasingly a structural part of daily life in China, WeChat fundamentally rests upon personal, closely knit social circles (*Economist*, 2016). The inherent power of a high degree of reliability and reciprocity from WeChat's friend and relative circles (e.g., Wei, Huang, & Zheng, 2018), in turn, encourages politically sensitive discussions or *guanxi*-embedding mobilization (see, for instance, army veterans' protests in 2018 [Buckley, 2018, p. A11]) based on these personal contacts and networks (*Economist*, 2014). Far more than a messaging platform, WeChat-based communication, with its integration of personal, reliable network resources, offers further opportunities to assess and advance the reciprocity-based mobilization and recruitment discussed in this chapter.

MEDIATED COMMUNICATION, RECIPROCITY, AND MOBILIZATION: BEYOND THE CASE OF CHINA

Little headway has been made in pinpointing the uniqueness of mobile communication in political mobilization and recruitment (but, see Campbell & Kwak, 2010, 2011, 2012). The first shortcomings of much of the work involves the tendency to make claims in terms that are too general (e.g., ICTs or digital media), as if there were one or two overarching mechanisms that could account for mobilization via digital communication technologies, regardless of the variations in their modalities. The second shortcoming concerns the lack of examination of cases of mobilization *without* organizations or organizational supports that still dominate contemporary mobilization. A third shortcoming deals with the deficits of non-democracies, or authoritarian cases that hinder either comparative studies or theoretical generalizations to understand communication technologies in movement mobilization.

Accordingly, this chapter contributes to current scholarship from the following three perspectives. First, it canvasses and further theorizes the characteristics of the mobile phone as a reciprocal technology that differs from other communication technologies, with the embedding of strong and dense social ties as vital resource for mobilization. Second, this chapter analyzes reciprocal expectations and influence with regards to the use of mobile technologies that strengthen reliability, reinforce obligations, legitimate mobilization appeals, engender empathy, and nurture a sense of solidarity, which energize and consolidate collective action recruitment and participation. This mobile-mediated micromobilization matters especially in authoritarian regimes like China where social organizations have been under stern suppression and where people avoid involving themselves in formal, organized movements. Third, to put reciprocity at the center affords a further advantage to facilitate comparative studies beyond the current authoritarian context.[14] As Gouldner (1960, p. 171) points out, "a norm of reciprocity is universal." Studies would argue that *guanxi*, as what Geertz (1983) calls "local knowledge," may carry tremendous differences compared to social networks in the West. Nevertheless, an investigation of reciprocity would instead serve as a common ground for integrating results from China and beyond. Further careful measures of reciprocity in both Chinese and Western contexts would accordingly encourage follow-up studies from the comparative perspective around the world and guide future research on the role of (mobile-) mediated communication and social ties in mobilization. The fact that mobile communication technologies have deeply penetrated people's everyday lives hereby creates a mobilizing structure with "structural potential for action" (McAdam, McCarthy, & Zald, 1996, p. 5). This chapter further calls for more comparable studies concerning (mobile-) mediated communication and reciprocity in social ties for collective actions in different contexts beyond China to specify the extent to which various (mobile-mediated) mobilization processes may vary across contexts. In this way, the discussion regarding reciprocity and contention mobilization here will encourage theoretical enrichment, augmentation, and refinement.

In addition to the activation of reciprocity for collective mobilization, mobile communication also facilitates the mobilization of subversive emotions, and the mobilizing force of emotions via mobile communication becomes the focus in the next chapter.

---

14. For a further discussion on contributions from Asian values like *guanxi*, face, dharma, and karma to indigenous digital communication, see Lim & Soriano, 2016.

CHAPTER 5

"To Retweet Each and Every Rumor"

Mobile Rumoring as Contention

A rumor is a spontaneous vie for the right to speak. (Kapferer, 2013, p. 7)

Rumor is one means by which a collectivity, albeit a temporary and unstable collectivity, emerges from an aggregate. (Peterson & Gist, 1951, p. 160)

As "the oldest form of mass media" (Kapferer, 2013, p. 1), spreading rumors remains a noteworthy social phenomenon that has attracted considerable and ongoing attention from various disciplines, including psychology (Allport & Postman, 1947; Knapp, 1944; Rosnow, 1980), economics (Banerjee, 1993; Bommel, 2003), social psychology (Bordia & DiFonzo, 2004; Rosnow & Fine, 1976), sociology (Morin, 1971; Peterson & Gist, 1951; Shibutani, 1966), political science (Huang, 2015; Layman & Green, 2005), and communication (Harsin, 2006; Pendleton, 1998; Rosnow, 1988). Studies of rumor and rumoring traverse different historical periods, societies, and cultures (e.g., Kapferer, 2013; Li, 2011b; Neubauer, 1999; Prasad, 1935; Shibutani, 1966). Rumors especially abound and prevail nowadays as the widespread adoption of ICTs gives rumor—originally spread by word of mouth—digital wings, thereby easing, accelerating, and widening rumor circulation with an unprecedented impact on societies (e.g., Chen, Lu, & Suen, 2016; Fisher, 1998; Kwon et al., 2016; Rojecki & Meraz, 2016; Sunstein, 2009). In actuality, researchers are increasingly concerned that rumor—that is, inaccurate, misleading, or false claims—may cripple political campaigns (Garrett, 2011; Kolbert, 2009), sabotage business reputations (Solove, 2007; Weinberg & Pehlivan, 2011), escalate mass panics (Kleinman & Watson, 2006; Kwon et al., 2016), or even compromise the outcomes of democratic elections (Weeks & Southwell, 2010; Weeks & Garrett, 2014).

Rumor and rumoring—i.e., the communicative practice of sharing rumors—on digital media platforms, such as online forums, the instant-messaging service QQ, Weibo, and the mobile messaging app WeChat, have emerged as a prominent issue in contemporary China (*China Youth Daily*, 2012; Li & Liu, 2017; Ng, 2015). The survey by the official newspaper of the Communist Youth League of China, *China Youth Daily* (中国青年报), reports that over 80% of interviewees agree that rumors flourish in society today, with the top three rumor mills being the internet (85.8%), face-to-face communication (58.6%), and mobile messages (53.6%) (Xiang, 2011b). The official English-language newspaper *China Daily* portrays Weibo as "filled with rumors" (*China Daily*, 2014). The report from the state-run Chinese Academy of Social Sciences acknowledges that 6 in 10 WeChat users have encountered rumors, and over 2.1 million suspected rumors are deleted daily on WeChat (Chen, 2015; Liu, 2015). Frequent occurrences of internet and mobile phone-disseminated rumors have hit the country, turning it into the "People's Republic of Rumors" (Larson, 2011, 2012), aggravating social tensions, and evoking collective actions in recent years (*China Daily*, 2014; China Youth International, 2011; Li, 2014; Li & Zhao, 2010; Lv & Wang, 2010; J. Yu, 2008; S. Yu, 2010). Cracking down on the rumor mill and snuffing out rumor diffusion on the internet and mobile phones have consequently become an essential part of the government's work (Dong, 2017). Under the direction of the authorities, governmental agencies, telecommunications services, and internet companies have established stringent mechanisms of rumor monitoring. They have launched recurrent campaigns against rumor spreading, and have quashed so-called rumor-mongers with "ulterior motives"—i.e., in terms of the official narrative, their intent is to disturb social order, disrupt public security, produce unhealthy social effects, or incite the overthrow of state power (e.g., *China Youth Daily*, 2012; China Youth International, 2011; Li & Liu, 2017; Wu, 2011; Xiong, 2011; Zhang, 2010).

Even though Chinese authorities have made great efforts to stem the spreading of rumors, they still spring up one after another and swirl on digital platforms, frequently putting the whole society in a state of anxiety and nervousness. Remarkably, more than 90% of people have been exposed to rumors on their mobile phones, and 45.9% of the rumors originated on WeChat and Weibo in 2015 (Liu, 2016). More intriguingly, rumor rebuttal from the authorities fails to prevent rumor diffusion; on the contrary, the attempts push its dissemination even further (e.g., Wong & Geng, 2014), with the public "believing in the rumor [rather] than government's word" (Yiyin, 2011). Why do rumors and rumoring persist and intensify in the face of authoritarian surveillance and harsh suppression, even flaring up after official rumor rebuttal (e.g., Xinhua, 2014)? What gives digital media special potency for the persistence of rumors in contemporary China?

This chapter specifically discerns mobile rumoring, i.e., the practice of diffusing rumors via mobile phone. By exploring rumors and rumoring via mobile communication, this chapter presents one of the first studies of what I call the *politics of rumoring* and advances our understanding of the political challenges that mobile technologies pose to authoritarian regimes like China. The politics of rumoring is about more than the political effects of rumor diffusion. It is about the underlying politics that drive and influence the communication of rumors, or more precisely, the communicative act of forwarding and circulating rumors, including the political implication of rumor experience and rumoring practice. It is about how seemingly non-political acts in everyday life, with the embedding of mobile technologies, become an issue in politics and embody "changes to the category of the political itself" (Zayani, 2015, p. 13).

To unravel the politics of rumoring, this chapter dissects not only people's belief in rumors but also (the meaning behind) their reaction to rumors, namely, how people deal with rumors and why they deal with rumors in specific ways (via their mobile phones). Throughout in-depth interviews with people during three rounds of fieldwork and second-hand data collected from existing literature and newspapers, I reveal the understudied contentious nature of rumor communication, not least in a highly repressive context. This is evident in mobile rumoring as "covert resistance" (Scott, 1985, 1990) against omnipresent censorship and social control in everyday life in contemporary China.

Taking rumoring as a form of contention contributes to current literature in three ways. Above all, central to the explanation of the persistence of rumor in digital media in current Chinese society is the contentious aspect of rumor communication that has not been given enough consideration in previous studies. Second, this chapter shows how various forms of communication—specifically in terms of rumoring as a phenomenon—interact and articulate contentious elements. As such, allegations or accusations of rumoring in official discourse can instead open a window of political opportunity that triggers public engagement in rumoring as contentious collective action par excellence. The call for rumoring via mobile phones—like the phrase in the chapter title articulates, "to retweet each and every rumor"[1]—emerges as both a frame for collective action and an action that entails and metacommunicates civil disobedience against the abuse of exploiting the term "rumor" as an excuse for political suppression. Beyond rumor content as such, rumoring as a *counter-power* embodies dissenting emotion and contested identity. Third, this chapter demonstrates that Chinese people have not only incorporated mobile technologies into their repertoire of contention in rumor communication but have also redefined what counts as the political itself. Understanding rumoring is hence a way of appreciating the significance of digitally mediated, contentious "micropolitics" (Deleuze & Guattari, 1987, pp. 208–231) in everyday communicative practice.

The next section gives a theoretical discussion on rumor by integrating its transmission and communication or, better, ritual aspects (Carey, 2008) beyond two dominant, dichotomous traditions in rumor studies, rooted in psychology and sociology respectively. The theoretical part further highlights the understudied dimension of contention as an essential part of rumor communication. After that, I examine the repressive context in which the control of and crackdown against rumoring has developed into a key part of social control in everyday life in contemporary China. This analysis is followed by an interrogation of people's beliefs and practices toward spreading rumors on their mobile phones in several cases, in both urban and rural areas. A nuanced account then elaborates the call of rumoring as a frame for collective action and rumoring as a resentment-venting behavior in contemporary China. The communicative act of rumoring releases citizens from internalized prejudices about both the rumor and the rumormonger, develops an identity of resistance against the stigmatization of the rumor phenomenon, and emblematizes "bounded solidarity" (Portes & Sensenbrenner, 1993, pp. 1324–1327) among the rumor public (Peterson & Gist, 1951, p. 160). This process demonstrates the mobile phone as one essential ingredient that empowers rumoring as a "weapon of the weak" (Scott, 1985). The conclusion extends the findings to general issues in studying the communication of rumor and other similar concepts such as misinformation and fake news in the digital age.[2]

---

1. This phrase, in Chinese as "有谣必转," or "to forward each and every rumor [you receive]," came from one of my WeChat group chats on March 8, 2017, 14:23.

2. The two terms "rumor" and "fake news" become interchangeable with negative implications in some studies (e.g., Shao, Ciampaglia, Flammini, & Menczer, 2016; Vosoughi, Roy, & Aral, 2018) and news coverages (e.g., Meyer, 2018).

RUMOR: AN AMBIGUOUS AND CONTESTED CONCEPT

A Tale of Two Rumors

Although the phenomenon of rumoring in society has long been discussed, different concepts of "rumor" vary significantly,[3] which may lead to distinct approaches and attitudes toward rumoring in reality. Generally speaking, two dominant but contrasting definitions have been given in previous studies, which can be tracked back to a pair of distinguished traditions of thinking in psychology and sociology.

One of the dominant traditions in the study of rumor is defined mostly by a psychological analysis, which treats rumor as a piece of information (Caplow, 1947; DiFonzo & Bordia, 2007a; Rosnow, 1974), a message (Berenson, 1952; Buckner, 1965; Chen, Lu, & Suen, 2016, p. 90; Morin, 1971), or a proposition (Allport & Postman, 1947; Knapp, 1944; Rosnow, 1980; Rosnow & Fine, 1976; Rosnow & Kimmel, 2000). The classic Allport and Postman's (1947) psychological study of rumor, for instance, defines rumor as "a specific (or topical) proposition for belief, passed along from person to person, usually by word of mouth, without secure standards of evidence being present" (p. ix). With a focus on the content per se, this tradition underlines variations of authority and quality of a given piece of information in the process of transmission among individuals. Rumor, in this view, has been considered as a false, unverified (DiFonzo & Bordia, 2007a, p. 273; Peterson & Gist, 1951, p. 159), unconfirmed (Buckner, 1965, p. 55; Caplow, 1947, p. 299), unauthenticated (Knapp, 1944, p. 22; Rosnow & Kimmel, 2000, p. 122), or distorted piece of information with deleterious effects on society due to distortion in transmission (Sunstein, 2009). It arises in contexts of ambiguity, uncertainty, danger, or risk (Allport & Postman, 1947). Under this premise, the motive underlying rumoring, or information-distorting and information-circulating behavior, be it psychological or political, deserves attention. This understanding determines both techniques and methods for studying rumor phenomena and actions and attitudes both toward the rumor and the rumormonger. Methodologically, rumor phenomena have been approached essentially as a chain of transmission among individuals (Banerjee, 1993; Buckner, 1965), mostly in laboratory experiments or quasi-experimental designs, to identify the reason behind the variations of the content in serial reproduction and dissemination. Practically, potential detrimental effects of rumor as disinformation or misinformation necessitate its control and crackdown.

---

3. For the difference between "concept" and "conception," see Jensen, 2013, p. 204.

Rumor studies of digital media so far largely follow the psychological tradition to explore how unsubstantiated, distorted, or exaggerated information travels via digital communication and affects people's beliefs and behavior (e.g., Bordia & DiFonzo, 2004; Dalziel, 2013; Garrett, 2011; Rojecki & Meraz, 2016; for the case of China, see Huang, 2015; Zeng, Chan, & Fu, 2017, but also see Hu, 2009). Most current studies in this vein juxtapose rumor with falsehoods, lies, and misinformation (e.g., Garrett, 2011; Rojecki & Meraz, 2016; Rubin, Chen, & Conroy, 2015; Shin, Jian, Driscoll, & Bar, 2017), which affect politics and society "in destructive ways" (Berinsky, 2015, p. 1).

By contrast, and unlike the content-based definition of rumor in the psychological tradition, the sociological tradition moves rumor outside of the accusation of falsehood, distortion, and exaggeration (e.g., Kapferer, 2013; Shibutani, 1966).[4] Instead, it views rumor not as a deviant phenomenon but as an essential part of social processes. More precisely, rumor is a routine, collective problem-solving process in an "inadequately defined situation" through dozens of communicative acts, which goes beyond "any particular set of words" (Kapferer, 1990, p. 50; Miller, 2005; Prasad, 1935; Shibutani, 1966, p. 16). One of the most influential sociological studies of rumor can best be traced back to Shibutani's (1966) work that coined rumors as "improvised news" during the Second World War. According to Shibutani, rumor is "a recurrent form of *communication through which men caught together in an ambiguous situation attempt to construct a meaningful interpretation of it by pooling their intellectual resources*" (1966, p. 17, emphasis in original). Human beings generate rumor as "improvised news" through "a collective transaction" to cope with the uncertainties or ambivalences of life when the formal communication channel breaks down, does not exist, or cannot be trusted to provide them with badly needed or trustworthy information. Of importance, as Shibutani argues, is that "the transformation of rumor content—usually called 'distortion'—is actually part of the developmental process through which men strive for understanding and consensus" (1966, p. 17). Consequently, "falsehood is not a necessary feature of rumor" (Shibutani, 1966, p. 17; also see Neubauer, 1999, p. 3), and "[r]umor is not so much distortion of some word combination but what is held in common." Following the argument, "[t]o focus attention upon words, then, is to misplace emphasis" (Shibutani, 1966, p. 16; for similar discussions, see Donovan, 2007; Pendleton, 1998, p. 70).

4. Also see, for instance, the discussion on "honest rumors" (Bommel, 2003).

The sociological tradition of rumor studies offers a critique of some of the stereotypes in the psychological tradition and, furthermore, of its methodological deficiencies in the following two specific aspects: On one hand, rumor is a collective rather than individual action. Different from the psychologically rooted definition that sees rumor as a product of an individually based, chain-wise transmission, the sociological tradition believes rumor grows out of collective interactions to interpret a problematic event or issue (Knapp, 1944, p. 31). As a result, rumor not only embodies personal relevance but rather entails a *collective* sense-making and enacting through the "social interaction of people caught in inadequately defined situation" (Shibutani, 1966, p. 17). An emphasis on the inherently collective, interactive nature of rumor thereby underlines the relevance of communication—and metacommunication, if any—in rumor situation. As Bordia and DiFonzo stress, "[i]t is communication that provides rumor with substance" (2002, pp. 56–57). Moreover, the collective-oriented perspective sheds light on the role of rumor as "a homogeneous medium" in building cohesion of a previously loosely bound collectivity "by stimulating a common feeling and perception of the situation" (Rosnow, 1980, p. 585). This process in turn encourages rumor transmission, which further strengthens the effects of homogeneity in the rumoring situation (Knopf, 1975). In this sense, the collective nature of rumor lends itself to being an alternative, bottom-up form of public opinion (Peterson & Gist, 1951) or even to the disclosure of "the deeper structure of public opinion" (Knapp, 1944, p. 28).

On the other hand, social structure and social context—rather than content—matter in the attempt to understand rumor phenomena. Studies have castigated the oversimplification of the laboratory paradigm in the psychological tradition of rumor studies. This tradition fails to replicate real-life situations within which rumors emerge, develop, travel, and generate meaning (Caplow, 1947, pp. 300–302; De Fleub, 1962, p. 55; Schachter & Burdick, 1955). Allport and Postman acknowledge that "[b]y forcing serial reproduction into an artificial setting, we sacrifice the spontaneity and naturalness of the rumor situation" (1947, p. 64; also see Rosnow, 1980, p. 582). To overcome this methodological deficiency, researchers suggest taking a naturalistic approach, such as a field study, to capture the nuance of rumor situations (Caplow, 1947; Festinger et al., 1948; Peterson & Gist, 1951). By doing so, such studies are able to expound both social context (Rosnow, 1988), i.e., the circumstance surrounding rumors, and social structure, i.e., "the structure of the social relationships and interaction patterns that constitute rumor situations" (Miller, 2005, p. 507). Aligning with the collective dimension of rumor, the social structure of rumoring involves "group (or social) influences, such as group norms, feelings of ca-maraderie or affiliation, and a shared representation of reality" (Bordia & DiFonzo, 2002, p. 50; also see Prasad, 1935).

Bringing Two Approaches Together

Without being well-recognized, the above two contrasting approaches of rumor studies clearly (read coincidentally) resonate with two conceptions of communication: the transmission view and the ritual view (Carey, 2008). The center of the transmission view explores "the transmission of signals or messages over distance for *the purpose of control*" (Carey, 2008, p. 15, emphasis added). Here, in line with the psychological tradition of rumor studies, the overarching transmission view underscores the motives behind the transportation of messages in space—be they religious, polit-ical, or mercantilistic (Carey, 2008, p. 16)—by delving into the effect of messages (e.g., propaganda [Smith & Lasswell, 2015]). Equally important yet less recognized is the ritual view of communication that is "directed not toward the extension of messages in space but toward the maintenance of society in time; not the act of imparting information but the representation of shared beliefs" (Carey, 2008, p. 18). Here, in a similar vein as the socio-logical tradition of rumor studies, the ritual view, which exhibits features of metacommunication (Goffman, 2008; Ruesch & Bateson, 1951), speaks to the effects of communication in daily lives on the creation, maintenance, and alteration of community (e.g., "a rumor public" [Peterson & Gist, 1951, p. 160] in the case of rumor) and, further, of society. Beyond the dissem-ination of messages, communication establishes social life as the sharing of experience, and it undergirds society as "a process by which reality is created, shared, modified, and preserved" (Carey, 2008, p. 33).

While the sociologically oriented approach of rumor studies disregards the psychological one as being "less social" (Bordia & DiFonzo, 2002), Carey's discussion offers a suggestion that would allow for the existence of both definitions of communication—and hence rumor—as complemen-tary. As he writes in the relationship between the transmission and the ritual views:

> Neither of these counterposed views of communication necessarily denies what the other affirms. A ritual view does not exclude the processes of information transmission or attitude change. It merely contends that one cannot under-stand these processes aright except insofar as they are cast within an essen-tially ritualistic view of communication and social order. Similarly, even writers

indissolubly wedded to the transmission view of communication must include some notion . . . of ritual action in the social life. (Carey, 2008, pp. 21–22)

Given Carey's suggestion, more leeway is granted to an integrated framework for understanding rumor communication, not just in terms of its content but also its ritual enactments. This chapter thus examines the "dual aspect" (Carey, 2008, p. 31) of rumor communication—both the rumor content and the symbolic meaning behind rumoring as communication—to provide "the elaboration of rumor" (Scott, 1990, p. 144). Just like Fitzpatrick (1996, p. 286) emphasizes, "rumor is as much a medium for the expression of popular as for the dissemination of information." Particularly, this chapter centers on the ritual facets of rumor communication that attract people to voluntarily share and socially engage.

Contention: A Relevant, Less-acknowledged Dimension of Rumor

Of the many characteristics of rumor and rumoring, one of the most relevant yet least understood and theorized in current literature is the contentious one. As discussed above, moving beyond the quality and authority of its content, the sociological tradition disregards stereotypical conceptualizations of rumor as being an unauthenticated, distorted, or exaggerated piece of information and subsequent accusations of those involved in rumoring as irrational, malicious, or suggestible (Miller, 2005). As Peterson and Gist (1951, p. 160) argue, "the common-sense assumption that rumor is abnormal or pathological reflects the fact that the persons involved are normally expected or accustomed to rely upon authority or upon a different kind of authority." In other words, the stigmatization of rumor implies a compulsion over people to comply, follow, obey, and submit to authority or else be treated as anomalous for their belief in the rumor or their engagement in rumoring. Kapferer further elucidates,

the phenomenon of rumor is as political as it is sociological. The notion of an "official" source is a political notion: it is governed by a consensus about who has the juridical authority to speak. . . . A rumor constitutes *a relation to authority*: . . . it constrains authorities to talk while contesting their status as the sole source authorized to speak. A rumor is a spontaneous vie for the right to speak. . . . It often involves *oppositional* speech: it remains unconvinced by official disclaimers, as if "official" and "credible" did not go hand in hand. It attests thus to a questioning of authorities, of "who has the right to speak about what." As information that runs alongside and at times counter to official information, rumors constitute a *counter-power*, i.e., a sort of check on power. (Kapferer, 2013, p. 14, emphasis added)

Hence, it is important to consider rumor as essentially unofficial (Shibutani, 1966; 1968, p. 579) and, in some situations, contentious and anti-authoritarian. Rather than a pathological phenomenon, it emerges as "the routine social act of defining ambiguous but important situations" (Miller, 2005, p. 505) to question or contest officially sanctioned definitional authority. Taking rumor as a routine, communicative act with unofficial, counter-power initiative that develops on a collective basis not only reformulates the concept of rumor beyond a falsehood with deleterious effect but also offers a broader framework for thinking of rumor— and therefore rumoring—as a type of contentious collective action. It aims at challenging definitional authority and airing disputes with the official line in ambiguous or chaotic phenomena and events through collective, communicative practices (Shibutani, 1966, pp. 31–62). This process generates "a rumor public" (Peterson & Gist, 1951, p. 160), a homogenous collective that has been consolidated by rumoring—collective sharing of a common object of attention and emotion—in the same situation and that may further engage into rumor diffusion given its homogeneity. In short, consideration should be given to both the contentious dynamics of rumor communication and the formation of a rumor public with common interests and a sense of solidarity with regard to an issue or event through rumor dissemination.

RUMOR COMMUNICATION IN CHINA: CASES

This section offers a brief presentation of the cases. The overall strategy is exploratory in nature and seeks to identify a set "diverse cases" of rumor and rumoring that are intended to represent "a full range of variation" (Seawright & Gerring, 2008, p. 301).

Chronologically, the six selected cases include the anti-PX demonstration in southeast China's Xiamen, Fujian Province from May to June 2007; the mass incident in western China's Weng'an, Guizhou Province in June 2008; the earthquake panic in central China's Shanxi Province in January 2010 (*China Daily*, 2010; Li & Zhao, 2010; Lv & Wang, 2010; Wang & Sun, 2010); a chemical factory's pollution scare in eastern China's Xiangshui in Jiangsu Province in February 2011; the mass incident in southern China's Zhengcheng city in Guangdong Province in June 2011; and the anti-PX demonstration in northeast China's Dalian in Shandong Province in

August 2011. According to news reports, the internet and, in particular, mobile phones have become key means of rumoring in these cases (*China Daily*, 2010; Han & Lu, 2007; Lai, 2010; Li & Zhao, 2010; Lv & Wang, 2010; Yu, 2010). Selected cases cover diverse categories of rumor situations, i.e., natural disasters (earthquake) and man-made crises (pollution and mass incidents) in rural (Weng'an, Xiangshui, and Zhengcheng) and urban (Xiamen and Dalian) areas. In other words, I seek to detail the workings of similar processes in widely varying forms of rumor phenomena.

A key issue related to case selection should be clarified here in advance. So-called rumors and rumoring in the cases selected here are called thus in accordance with government statements and news reports. However, that does not mean that this study shares the government's or news media's position of viewing these messages as "fabrications deliberately spread with a malicious intent." To be clear, I aim to explicate the reasons behind the homogeneity of the cases, i.e., how and why these officially alleged "rumors" emerge, spread, and flourish through mobile communication, even in the face of rumor crackdown or rumor rebuttal. It is beyond the scope of this study to explore the origin of rumors, to verify their accuracy, or identify the so-called ill-intentioned mastermind(s) behind a thriving rumor.

Furthermore, I adopt the "situational approach" to examine rumor and rumoring in cases, when possible. As Shibutani explains:

> If rumors are viewed as the cooperative improvisation of interpretations, it becomes apparent that they cannot be studied fruitfully apart from the social contexts in which they arise. They are not isolated reports but phases of a more inclusive adjustive process, and the analysis of symbolic content alone is not likely to yield adequate understanding. An appreciation of any rumor requires some knowledge of the sensitivities shared by the people and the manner in which they are mobilizing to act. (Shibutani, 1966, p. 23)

In my view, this approach allows the study to complement most existing scholarship, which is usually based on either archives (Huang, 2005; Li, 2005, 2011a; Smith, 2006, 2008) or news reports (Hu, 2009; Zhou, 2010). Moreover, unlike these studies that have mostly revolved around content, I also look at how people treat and use various communication channels (e.g., mass communication and mobile communication) when they encounter and trade rumors. Specific attention has been given to mobile communication, or more accurately, the dynamics that drive how people use their mobile phones in rumor situations. Taken together, a careful examination of the social, cultural, and technological factors provides a richer and more comprehensive illustration and understanding of not just the rumor and rumoring but also the role of mobile phones in rumor phenomena.

RUMOR CRACKDOWN AS SOCIAL CONTROL
IN CONTEMPORARY CHINA

To get a precise picture of rumor and rumoring in contemporary China, it is necessary to first delve into the territory where rumormongers and rumoring would face severe repression. The naming of some piece of information a rumor, and the subsequent rumor allegation and crackdown function as key strategies for control in contemporary Chinese society. For one thing, the authorities denounce the false, fabricated, defamatory, and irrational nature of rumor to legitimize their anti-rumor actions. For another, exploiting "rumor" as a catch-all term to embrace query, speculation, criticism, and misinformation online, government officials aim not just to quell unauthorized or counter-authority messages but, most importantly, to also establish an impressively pervasive uncertainty about the boundaries of acceptable communicative norms and practices in everyday life.

The allegation that a piece of information is a mere rumor and is therefore factitious, and further that those involved in rumoring are irrational, suggestible, or even anti-government dominates the official discourse. News coverage frequently condemns rumor as "a 'new-style' political weapon" by certain foreign forces as a way to attack the leadership of the ruling party (Chen, 2011; Liu & Zhang, 2016; Smith, 2006), draw colorful parallels between rumors and "pornography, gambling and drugs" as online crimes (Chen, 2011; Ren, 2011; Xinhua, 2014), or endow rumormongering with a counter-revolutionary initiative (Smith, 2006). Apart from alleged "rumormongers," official narrative further blames those who believe in or are involved in rumoring as "the masses completely in the dark." Without or even disregarding fact-checks, they are highly sequacious and easily misled by rumor. The report from the Chinese Academy of Social Sciences, for instance, attributes digital media being a rumor mill feeding off the "three lows" of its users, which refers to low age, low level of education, and low income (Lam, 2013). It clearly puts the blame on impressionable character and poor education as the root causes of rumor proliferation on digital platforms.

Much more perturbing is the fact that, as portrayed in official accounts and media reports, *every* mass protest is attributed to having been the tragic outcome of "a few rumormongers with ulterior motives, taking advantage of the many being unknowing accomplices," with authorities stating that "rumors have played a damaging role in every incident" *(China Daily*, 2009). Consequently, it would be no surprise that rumoring has been labeled as a "necromantic delusion" *(yaoyan,* 妖言) (China Youth International, 2011; Lv, 2003), a public nuisance (Xin & Wen, 2012), or "a malignant tumor" (Chen, 2011; Forsythe, 2011) in society, resulting in "discredit to the innocent and caus[ing] panic or even social unrest if not clarified in time" (Chen, 2011). Taken together, rumoring has turned into an ethically and politically unacceptable practice in the official discourse, or, quoting *The People's Daily*'s rhetoric, "[an act] stepping over the fundamental bottom line of both morality and law" (China Radio International, 2010).

Against this background, the accusations of "spreading rumors to mislead people" and "fabricating rumors to erupt disturbances" have legitimized the persecution of rumormongers and the suppression of rumors. People have been detained in recurrent anti-rumor campaigns for allegedly spreading rumors to pursue commercial gain, deteriorate morality and values, and cause public disorder (Cao, 2014; Xinhua, 2014). "To ensure the good image of government, local stability, and economic development," for instance, a national-scale crackdown on online rumors detained many hundreds of internet users within 12 days, from high-profile Weibo users to ordinary citizens, who were accused of rumor fabrication and dissemination in August 2013 (Liu & Ju, 2013). Ongoing efforts to monitor, dispel, and combat rumors also lead to the widespread establishment of rumor-busting platforms on the internet and mobile applications, such as "The National Platform to Refute Rumors," jointly launched by the Ministry of Public Security and Sina Weibo, as a key component in China's extensive campaign against rumors (Liu, 2016).

What needs attention especially is the fact that rumor control coincides with a too-broad use of this term by the Chinese authorities for the sake of social control. Without a clear definition, as Smith (2006, p. 408) discloses, "the authorities considered 'rumor' to be any information or opinion at variance with the official construction of reality." Put differently, as an elastic term, "rumor" develops into a phrase that would encompass all manner of messages and opinions about contemporary events and policies that, in the eyes of the authorities, are simply different from—let alone contesting—official narratives (also see Human Rights Watch, 2015; Ng, 2015). By all accounts, in the allegation of rumor, people have been persecuted or detained for political speech, unsanctioned opinions, criticism of the government, mocking government officials, or questioning official stories (e.g., Hille, 2013; Kan, 2011; Liu & Huang, 2014; Rajagopalan & Rose, 2013). Legal and regulatory provisions further strengthen the punishment for spreading rumors, still without a clear definition of the term, to ensure rumor crackdown in accordance with law. A controversial law jointly issued by the Supreme People's Court and the Supreme People's Procuratorate of the People's Republic of China (PRC) in the anti-rumor campaign in 2013, for instance, stated that people will be considered has having committed "severe" breaches of the law and would face up to three years in jail if any posts or messages they create online turn out to be "rumors" and are visited or clicked on more than 5,000 times or reposted more than 500 times (Kaiman, 2013; the Supreme People's Court of PRC and the Supreme People's Procuratorate of PRC, 2013,; also see the revision in China's Criminal Law, in which spreading "rumor," again, lacking a clear definition, will lead to up to seven years in prison [Human Rights Watch, 2015]).

Consequently, rumor control has turned into an effective strategy by the authorities to chill political discourse and encourage self-censorship in everyday communication. In their discussion on punishment and control over public professionals including journalists and lawyers, Stern and Hassid uncover the rule of uncertainty by the regime: i.e., "ambiguity about which actions political authorities consider off limits. Confusion over the boundaries of tolerance, in turn, leaves citizens unsure whether any given action will be encouraged, forbidden, or ignored" (2012, p. 1242). Rumor control and crackdown, in a similar vein, clearly target a broader, general public beyond specific groups of public professionals. The stiff punishment for rumor mills and, especially, *the uncertainty of the boundary of permissible communicative activities* prevents people from speaking freely, let alone criticizing officials, and forces them to observe an extra degree of self-awareness and self-censorship in routine life. Even though they do not see themselves as dissidents or even political, citizens still face the danger of being persecuted as officially alleged "rumormongers," so long as officials treat the messages they have posted or circulated as "rumors." Several human rights lawyers, such as Mo Shaoping and Ma Gangquan, contend that rumor crackdown aims not to suppress so-called rumor, but rather is "an excuse" to cover the infringement on freedom of expression (Rajagopalan & Rose, 2013; Xin & Yang, 2013). The fear of detention due to pervasive, intensive, but also ambiguous rumor crackdown leads people "to think twice about sharing information which might or might not be 'sensitive'" (Kan, 2011), or, as civil rights lawyer Zhou Ze describes, "[everyone must] talk less, and more carefully" (Rajagopalan & Rose, 2013, also see Human Rights Watch, 2015). As an important component of the emerging "rule of fear" (Pei, 2016) in recent years, such a "scare tactic," along with recurrent anti-rumor campaigns, aims at internalizing social control from the regime, cultivating "the knowledge that such enforcement *could* happen at any time" (Roberts, 2018, p. 119, emphasis in original), harnessing public communication, and therefore reducing the political agency of individuals in Chinese society.

By halting public discussion and communication, rumor control further attempts to magnify the authority of the official voice in society. In reality, "the crackdown on rumors has made the passing-along of news (even news that has nothing to do with politics) seem dangerous unless it comes from an official source" (Custer, 2014). Again, the ambiguity of the term "rumor"—and, consequently, of the limits of political tolerance—coerces people into reining in unsanctioned, unofficial, or even non-official messages for fear of charges of rumormonger and, in turn, accepting official stories as the only permissible "truth." In broad strokes, the dissipation of the possibility of regular people receiving (political) alternatives and pursuing social change exemplifies the regime's initiative to consolidate the monopolization of official stories and maintain a widespread acceptance of the status quo.

To sum up, rumor control and crackdown are some of the most notable political phenomena in contemporary China. Far beyond uncorroborated claims, rumor has been officially "demonized" and negatively portrayed as morally problematic and politically dangerous in order to assert its stigmatized dimension. The ambiguity of the term "rumor" and its associated uncertainty with the boundaries among forbidden, tolerated, and prescribed communicative practices involve an initiative from the authorities to discipline the people's communicative behaviors at the routine level. At the same time, social control takes place in the guise of rumor crackdown and rumor control, with rumor allegation widely seen as a fear technique to silence public discussion and mold a docile populace.

TO SPREAD OR NOT TO SPREAD: DISTRUST AND DISOBEDIENCE IN RUMOR COMMUNICATION

Control and repression, however, backfire, with rumor communication increasingly being a prominent phenomenon against rumor control and crackdown. The interviews show two reasons that motivate rumor communication even in the face of rumor rebuttal and rumor crackdown: the expression of public distrust toward the authorities, and the struggle against social control in the disguise of rumor.

"I Would Rather Believe in the Rumor Than the Government's Words"[5]: Rumor Communication and Public Distrust

Feelings of suspicion and distrust toward the authorities undergird the necessary basis of rumor proliferation. As several studies have pointed out, rumor seems to thrive where there is a dearth of trust toward formal sources of information (DiFonzo & Bordia, 2007b, p. 201; Shibutani, 1966). In other words, people compensate with informal speculation, or rumor, when they distrust formal news sources.

Rumor dissemination in China aptly exemplifies such a phenomenon with its effects in revealing the public's widespread, deeply ingrained discontentment with censorship practices. Official censorship generates highly non-transparent circumstances, erodes government authority and media credibility, and undermines public confidence. The lack of transparency is therefore increasingly becoming a major trigger of the unrestrained rumor mill in Chinese society. According to a survey from *China Youth Daily*, the official newspaper of the Communist Youth League committee, 73.1% of Chinese people attribute the proliferation of rumor to a lack of transparency from the authorities (Xiang, 2011a). Such a circumstance leaves people highly suspicious and distrustful of information coming from the authorities. An ingrained belief prevails among people that the "government would never have censored information had they not had anything to hide or refuse in the first place" (Bai, 2010, p. 93). Furthermore, some believe that censorship sometimes even comes with the aim of "stability maintenance" (维稳) while sacrificing people's lives. For instance, some people believed that to prevent earthquake panic, the government suppressed earthquake predictions before the 2008 Wenchuan earthquake, presumably resulting in 70,000 people losing their lives and over 374,000 people being injured (Zhang, 2008). This kind of pervasive distrust becomes the soil that easily nurtures unsanctioned *content* and encourages its spread.

The distrust and further discontent resulting from the authorities' lack of transparency has become even more obvious when people are situated in uncertain or ambiguous situations. In the case of the earthquake rumor in Shanxi, when local residents suffered from emotional distress due to fear of an impending earthquake, one interviewee complained, "there is no announcement or explanation at all on why these [fire and earthquake] drills had been carried out" (35-year-old civil servant in Shanxi, March 3, 2010, personal communication). "We cannot help discussing why the government and local media remain silent," explained another interviewee.

---

5. Cited from Yiyin, 2011.

"There was consequently a widespread belief that the government intentionally hid information [about earthquakes] because it feared triggering public panic [from earthquake prediction]" (54-year-old laid-off worker in Shanxi, October 7, 2010, personal communication). Rumor, in this situation, "services as a vehicle for anxieties and aspirations that may not be openly acknowledged" (Scott, 1990, p. 145) by the authorities. A similar situation existed, for instance, in the Xiamen case, where there was a widespread belief that local government deliberately held back pollution-related information to prevent public objection to the petrochemical project.

With such an interpretation in mind, forwarding this kind of government-hidden or government-censored content—what people believe that the authorities are preventing them from knowing—becomes a crucial way to break through the censorship imposed by the authorities. To be clear, people engage in rumor communication because they are convinced that "too much information is currently covered up by government" (54-year-old laid-off worker in Shanxi, October 7, 2010, personal communication) and that rumor content is the very *truth* that the authorities prevent the populace from knowing. In reality, with no access to the whole truth, either from the government or from the (government-controlled) media, the public struggles to uncover and spread the truth—or, at the very least, what they perceive as "the truth"—for themselves. As one interviewee described it:

> [T]o go against the monolithic system of newscasting permitted only by government, the most important thing is to reveal those stories hidden or banned by the authorities. The officially alleged "rumor content" is always the truth censored by them. (35-year-old civil servant in Shanxi, March 3, 2010, personal communication)

Social discontent never eases even after governmental rumor rebuttal. In actuality, people treat rumor rebuttal as a means of mitigating their anxiety or anger in an attempt to avoid panic or collective action instead of "true" rumor rebuttal. Put differently, because the public does not believe the authorities to be a credible source of information, official rumor rebuttal has been perceived as just another way for the authorities to cheat the public with the intention of calming the panic-stricken populace without letting them know the truth. As one interviewee complained about rumor rebuttal in the Shanxi earthquake case:

> There would be no "rumors" if the government would explain the reason first [for the drills]. However, the government remained silent [for around 40 days], ever since the emergence of the first [earthquake] rumor at the beginning of

January. Only after realizing that it was unable to control [the panic] did it deny the rumors, but still without any explanation at all. (Resident in Taiyuan, Shanxi Province, March 13, 2011, personal communication)

Similarly:

[T]he only thing the government is good at is to define "rumor" and to scotch what it asserts [to be] "rumors." Labeling a message as a rumor becomes the simplest tactic for them [the government] to clean up their responsibilities [for this event]. They never consider a case's specific situation. Because no matter what the situation is, it is presented as though it is the rumor's fault. Nor do they take people's feelings and voices into account. (35-year-old lawyer in Taiyuan, March 6, 2011, personal communication)

The above statements clearly demonstrate people's rancor and distrust toward a government that repeatedly conceals facts from its populace or tries to shirk responsibility and shift the blame onto the elements of the so-called rumor. Against this backdrop, even *The People's Daily* admitted that people would "believe in the rumor [content], rather than the government's words" (Yiyin, 2011). The situation is exacerbated when the authorities resort to the blame game whenever anxiety or conflict arises. Rumor accusations and rebuttals rather reinforce perceptions of censorship and non-transparency among the public, with subsequent discontent against and anger toward the authorities intensifying. In reality, it becomes obvious that rumor crackdown actually draws attention to the rumors the authorities are hoping to quash (Hu, 2009, p. 82). Consequently, official rumor rebuttal deteriorates the government's relationship with the public, leaving people to circulate officially designated "rumor messages"—even after the rumor rebuttal comes out—in order to inform each other of "the truth" and to vent their discontentment and anger toward the government's lack of transparency and censorship. To conclude, the deep-seated distrust toward the authorities not only constitutes a fertile constituency for rumor communication, it has also been expressed through the act of sharing rumor messages that have been perceived as "truth" by the public.

"To Retweet Each and Every Rumor": Rumor Communication Against Social Control

Notably, not all people join in rumor communication because they perceive the content as being censored truth. The interviews uncover that, while some believe the rumor content, others have forwarded so-called rumors regardless of their contents. In other words, people take part in rumor dissemination *even if* they do not care about or, in some cases, disregard the content. In this situation, the struggle against social control under the veil of "rumor crackdown" motivates rumor proliferation. Rumor communication hence affords a relevant outlet for rising public discontentment with the authorities' adoption of repressive approaches to suppress and intimidate everyday communicative activities in the guise of "rumor crackdown."

In the Xiamen case, for instance, some residents continued circulating officially asserted "rumors" regardless of whether the content about the PX project was true or they themselves were being cautioned by public security forces. One interviewee explained:

> It is difficult for we ordinary people to make a judgment on whether they [potential environmental hazards of the PX project] are true without professional background. . . . Regardless of the truth, however, you [the government] must not stop people from speaking about this issue by prosecuting them as "rumormongers" arbitrarily. (45-year-old taxi driver, Xiamen, October 7, 2010, personal communication)

Similarly:

> So-called rumor is just another excuse for the government to . . . ban discussions [on the issue]. They think people dare not to argue or even talk about this controversial issue once the authorities label it as rumor. . . . Because then they [the authorities] can easily hamper different points of view by making political charges, such as fabrication or distortion of facts to interfere with the social and political order . . . the charge of so-called rumormonger against Professor Zhao Yufen . . . is a living example. (28-year-old university student, Xiamen, October 11, 2010, personal communication)

The above statements exemplify that interviewees have treated rumor allegation mostly as a "political persecution" by the authorities. The persecution aims not just at eliminating specific pieces of information as dissenting voices. Rather, it reveals the attempt of a broader tightening of social control from the authorities by using ambiguous rumor rhetoric to suppress communicative practices and discipline public order. One interviewee commented: "The government has overemphasized stability and harmony. . . . Now they try to repress daily communication in the name of 'rumor rebuttal'"! (35-year-old migrant worker, Guangzhou, May 11, 2011, personal communication).

To fight against such an attempt, rumor communication has been developed into an act of civil disobedience. In practice, people are not afraid of being accused of violating the law as "individual lawbreakers" who are committed to the rumor mill as a "highly inflammatory cause." The anger toward official attempts to control routine communicative practices stimulates people to resend and spread so-called rumors, disregarding the content. Several interviewees have come up with Evelyn Hall's saying "I disapprove of what you say, but I will defend to the death your right to say it" to underscore their right to free speech. One stressed further:

> Failing to provide prompt information . . . is one thing. Dampening the vigor of public discussion and, worse yet, muzzling ordinary communication in the name of "dispelling rumors" are quite another. . . . You [the authorities] must not stop us from talking to each other. We have the right to openly express our opinion. (27-year-old white-collar worker, Beijing, October 27, 2010, personal communication)

The phrase in the title of this chapter, "to retweet each and every rumor," exactly epitomizes this contentious initiative. To literally translate the original Chinese phrase, it can also be read as "making sure to forward each and every rumor you receive." This phrase clearly shows a strong motivation that invites people to participate in rumor dissemination *not* in terms of the content but rather because a certain message has been labeled a rumor by the authorities.

In this situation, the official labeling of certain messages as mere rumor and those sharing the messages as rumormongers, as well as later rumor rebuttals, dramatically provoke growing discontent among the public. To be clear, the rumor accusation shifts the focus from the specific content itself to the authorities' repressive policy, which consequently unearths larger scale discontent, prompts outrage among the populace, and results in increasing numbers of people involving themselves in forwarding officially alleged rumors. To struggle against social control in the name of rumors, inspired citizens further "ask recipients to forward the messages [via mobile phone] to as many people as possible." "They [the authorities] try to ban any discussion on these topics. What we want, exactly the opposite, is to be a lot more involved in communication" (38-year-old university teacher, Xiamen, September 23, 2010, personal communication). Consequently, something notably common happens after an official rumor accusation and rumor rebuttal. For one thing, officials tend to deny the rumors under a barrage of public criticism. For another, officially labeled rumors tend to be more aggressively disseminated after government declarations. The more vehemently refutation comes out, the more likely it is that people will tend to forward so-called rumors and the more fiercely those rumors reignite.

To summarize, scrutiny of the reason behind the dissemination of rumor demonstrates two different, sometime overlapping, motivations that lead to hardly controlled rumor phenomena in contemporary China. For one thing, rumor *content* matters, as people take it as the censored truth, or, specifically, what the authorities do not want the populace to know. Rumor communication allows people to battle the government over the censorship of certain specific content—such as an earthquake or a deleterious project—by diffusing these pieces of information in society. For another, beyond specific pieces of information per se, rumor communication incorporates a strong contention against the overuse and misuse of the accusations of something being a rumor or certain people being rumormongers to stifle communicative practices and consolidate authoritarian control. Considered together, in both situations, official rumor allegation and rebuttal only add fuel to the counterattack fire and stir up even further dissemination of rumor instead.

RUMORING AS CONTENTION: COLLECTIVE ACTION FRAME, EMOTION, AND SOLIDARITY

With rumor communication encompassing contentious initiatives against information censorship and social control, the call to spread certain rumors turns out to be a collective action frame that predisposes citizens to problematize the official stigmatization of rumor phenomenon, articulate long-suppressed discontentment in a rumoring-as-pathological context, and turn emotional affronts toward authorities into collective behaviors. From a ritual perspective, rumoring—the communicative act of forwarding so-called rumors via mobile phones in this case—galvanizes "bounded solidarity" (Portes & Sensenbrenner, 1993, pp. 1324–1327) among members of the public and articulates the rumor public as a resistance identity. The tactical use of the rumor frame, along with communicative competences amplified by mobile technologies, offers political leverage for the public to quickly mobilize its network and communicative resources on a massive scale for further collaboration and movement.

The Call for Rumoring as a Collective Action Frame

Meaning construction, negotiation, and contestation are widely recognized as crucial factors in the mobilization, unfolding, and outcomes of collective action (e.g., Benford, 1993a, 1993b; Ellingson, 1995; Oliver & Johnston, 2000). Scholars who take this perspective underscore that it is both the individual and collective interpretation and appropriation of the meaning of action that are at stake in these forms of collective involvement and mobilization. In particular, the framing perspective on collective action mobilization acknowledges the relevance of "interactively based interpretive processes" (Snow, 2004, p. 384) in mediating the relationship between meaning and movement (for general discussions on framing, see Benford & Snow, 2000; Snow, 2004).

The term "frame" comes from Goffman and refers to the "schemata of interpretations" (Goffman, 1974, p. 21) that "enable individuals to locate, perceive, identify and label occurrences" (Snow et al., 1986, p. 464) and that "selectively punctuate and encode objects, situations, events, experiences and sequences of actions within one's present and past environment" (Snow & Benford, 1992, p. 137). Effective frames are critical in investigating collective action in a specific context insofar as they render occurrences meaningful, organize experience, and guide action within the heterogeneity of groups and interests for mobilization. Notably, beyond mere interpretation of experience, whether individual or collective, Snow and Benford emphasize collective action frames as "action-oriented sets of beliefs and meanings" (2000, p. 614). As Snow further elucidates,

> collective action frames not only perform an interpretive function in the sense of providing answers to the question "What is going on here?", but they also are decidedly more *agentic* and *contentious* in the sense of calling for action that problematizes and challenges existing authoritative views and framings of reality. (Snow, 2004, p. 385, emphasis added)

As we see from the above-cited rumor cases, the "call for rumoring" rises as a significant collective action frame in contemporary China.

First, such a call draws people's attention toward the unjust authority of the regime. To the public, the term "rumor" denotes censorship and social control. So-called rumor in the official narrative has thus been perceived as either the initiation of censorship to wipe out what the authorities sees as inappropriate content or, even worse, the attempt of an overarching control and suppression of communicative practices in society. In such a way, for one thing, the call for forwarding rumors invites people to pay attention to the content of the so-called rumor for questioning and further contesting the "official" truth. In the Xiamen case, the officially accused rumor about massive toxic petrochemical production draws public attention to the previously less known PX project. The public concern over the PX project consequently aggregates. From that, the public further reveals the censorship over controversial issues and argues for greater civil engagement in the decision-making process. For another, the call for rumoring turns the spotlight on the arbitrary, problematic way that authorities allege certain messages to be rumors. This way, as one Weibo user wrote, is "against the Constitution and is robbing people of their freedom of speech" (Kaiman, 2013). The call itself hence brings attention to the injustice of the overuse of the accusation of rumor and thereby compromises the legitimacy of the official rumor crackdown.

Second, the call for rumoring articulates diverse experiences and emotions from the heterogeneous population into a coherent outlook. It connects the pervasive, repressed feeling of uncertainty, fear, anger, disgust, and dissatisfaction toward the government's tough suppression and punishment in the process of rumor allegation to reach a consensus. This created consensus exists against the expansion of the government's powers to police everyday communication in the name of rumor control. Take the chemical explosion rumor in Xiangshui as an example. According to a report from *China Youth Daily*, a villager received an emergency voice call around midnight, warning him about "the explosion." He left his house with his family immediately while forwarding the message to his friends. When the reporter asked this villager whether he had verified this message, the villager asked in reply, "To verify it? If someone tells me about an explosion a hundred times, it works every time! Does it need to be verified?" (Lin, 2011, p. 9). This conversation, in particular the last rhetorical question, shows strong discontent and outrage regarding government policies. More specifically, it reflects that people make and justify their decisions based on their lived experiences. These experiences, most of which revolve around the reality that the authorities often arbitrarily replaced rumors with their own contrived facts regardless of people' feelings, leaves them to live in great uncertainty and anxiety with frustration, resentment, and a complete lack of trust of the government. Rumoring and subsequent actions following the content of the rumor consequently embody the release of such locked-in emotions including distrust, frustration, and resentment toward the government.

Moreover, while the large majority of interviewees had experienced the phenomenon of rumor spreading even after the government and mass media deny the rumor's content, about half of the interviewees also agreed that they "would continue to pass on those messages after [the] government toss[es] out the accusation of a 'rumor.'" In other words, the (vigorous) accusations and rebuttals from the authorities to blast the growing rumors are in fact counterproductive—undermining their attempts to stop the rumor, they instead inflame and multiply it. This is because the accusations and rebuttals now rather easily ignite an enduring grievance: the belief that the government routinely invents haphazard accusations that frequently leave people believing they live in an unjust society where freedom and legitimate speech and communication are automatically curtailed by the official goal of eliminating rumor. Under such circumstances, rumors are instead accelerated and accredited—again, whether the message is true or not is of little importance. The dynamic driving the phenomenon of rumor flooding is the expressive dimension of contention (Goodwin & Jasper, 2006; Jasper, 1998, 2011): rumoring, embodying contentious agency, is laden with emotional discontentment against the authorities. The more severe the repression is, the more likely more severe forms of dissenting rumor communication become.

Third, as a collective action frame, the call performs a transformative function by reconstituting the understanding and meaning of "rumor" and "rumoring." In the public eye, a rumor is not just any false, fabricated, or defamatory message, as portrayed in the official narrative. Furthermore, rumoring is not just a morally problematic and politically dangerous communicative practice. Rather, the call for rumoring exemplifies a struggle against censorship, as well as disobedience against social control, and the generation of mobilization opportunities for further contention. Taken together, the call for rumoring epitomizes, to requote Kapferer, "a spontaneous vie for the right to speak" (2013, p. 7).

An innovative way of exploiting the political interpretation of the term "rumor" develops especially on digital platforms to facilitate unofficial communication. People add some rumor-related phases at the beginning of a message to call for circulation to as wide a circle as possible: "to spread the message before it has been censored," or "to circulate the information before it becomes a 'rumor.'" These notes motivate people to pass on certain pieces of a message or other information as a consensus by activating the agency and components of contention within the collective action frame. The consensus among the public is the following maxim: "to circulate [information] is to support [the suppressed voice] and to communicate [such information] is to popularize [the truth] (转发即是救援，传播便是普及)."[6]

- 6. A similar phenomenon can be observed on Weibo, China's microblogging platform, for instance, see http://www.weibo.com/1700757973/ylpTW3vqi.

In this way, the call for rumoring turns into a tactic (De Certeau, 1984) that is "deliberative, utilitarian, and goal directed . . . to achieve a specific purpose—to recruit new members, to mobilize adherents, to acquire resources, and so on" (Benford & Snow, 2000, p. 624). This consensus further demonstrates that rumoring may be an individual action, but this is not to say that it is uncoordinated. Even though nobody knows where and when a "rumor" will come up again, participants position themselves emotionally or prepare themselves cognitively in order to forward it through their personal digital devices. Rumoring consequently grows as a means of contention that is not just local but can easily be spread throughout the country and "require[s] little coordination" (Scott, 1985, p. 297) in contemporary China. It demonstrates an aggressive collective action that embeds, as Kapferer (1990, p. 14) describes, "a counter-power" behind its proliferation.

Rumoring, Resistance Identity, and Solidarity

Rumoring further constructs a resistant identity with "bounded solidarity" (Portes & Sensenbrenner, 1993, pp. 1324–1327) in the rumoring situation. In his elaboration of the concept of identity in networked society, Castells (2010, pp. 8–9) divides the forms and origins of identity into three types: legitimizing identity, resistance identity, and project identity. "Resistance identity," according to Castells, is

> generated by those actors who are in positions/conditions devalued and/or stigmatized by the logic of domination, thus building trenches of resistance and survival on the basis of principles different from, or opposed to, those permeating the institutions of society. (2010, p. 8)

Whereas Castells uses this concept to describe, in principle, "forms of collective resistance against otherwise *unbearable oppression*," he limits his examples to those "usually" excluded or oppressed identities that are defined by "history, geography, or biology" (Castells, 2010, p. 9, emphasis added). This approach, nevertheless, fails to take into account the reality of the complex, ever-changing strategy of exclusion and oppression in different social and political contexts. In the case of rumor in China, the repeated allegation of reactionary ("ulterior motives" [别有用心]) and irrational ("ignorant of the truth" [不明真相]) motivations in official anti-rumor rhetoric to crack down on public communication grows into a specific kind of "unbearable oppression." This unbearable oppression, in turn, galvanizes people into rumoring as contention against the official allegation. As one interviewee argues:

> [We] are [considered by authorities to be] "irrational" and "ignorant of the truth" only because we worry about our living environment and try to figure out the truth. On the contrary, people are "rational" insofar as we obey the rules and do not question the government. What kind of logic is that? . . . We are not "the many being ignorant of the truth"! (35-year-old resident in Xiamen, September 18, 2010, personal communication)[7]

The misused and overused political charges of "rumormongering" and "the many being ignorant of the truth" therefore have been widely regarded as inferior excuses for the government "to avoid responsibility for related public panic," "to ban people's discussions of hidden truths," or "to forbid people's opposition [against the government's decision]." Against this backdrop, rumoring generates an emergent sentiment of "we-ness," a "bounded solidarity" (Portes & Sensenbrenner, 1993, pp. 1324–1327) among the population resentful toward the authorities' abusive use of the accusation that certain information is a mere rumor and, in particular, against the very label of "the many [as] being ignorant of the truth." By forwarding officially alleged "rumors," people show each other that they are not alone, and they enact emergent sentiments of loyalty toward others like themselves.

Here, different from the discussion of endogenous exchanges of reciprocity in *guanxi* networks in the previous chapter, bounded solidarity comes from exogenous situations that excite group-oriented behaviors (Portes & Sensenbrenner, 1993). In the discussion of rumor, rumoring is considered a *situational* reaction with a counter-authoritarian nature borne out of an awareness of political suppression. In other words, rumoring expresses the feeling of injustice suffered by a collectivity. It comes from the public, who find themselves faced with a common adversary that pathologizes their ordinary communicative activities as irrational and malicious to ensure its suppressive governance. To go against this kind of governance, rumoring forms a public. It involves a participatory quality against the authorities: Anyone can join in by simply forwarding the so-called rumor, and anyone can make a contribution to the contention against the political accusation of rumormongering.

7. Also see "Chinese people are always 'being ignorant of the truth,' not because we are stupid but because the truth is quite unclear," retrieved from http://club.cul.sohu.com/r-history-771501-0-2-900.html.

According to Dewey, a public "consists of people who regard themselves as likely to become involved in the consequences of an event and are sufficiently concerned to interest themselves in the possibility of control" (1927, cited from Shibutani, 1966, p. 38, emphasis in original). Rumor communication, as Peterson and Gist point out, "tends to reduce the divergence in attitudes and to produce a common definition of the situation and a common feeling or mood" (1951, p. 160). In case of the appearance of rumors in China, people, by using their mobile phones, move together as a "rumor public" not just because they have a direct line to the event, such as an earthquake or chemical pollution (what Dewey calls "the consequences of an event," cited from Shibutani, 1966, p. 38), but, more importantly, because they reach a consensus that they feel insulted, stigmatized, and incriminated by what authorities are doing—demonizing and denigrating the public's concerns as mere "rumors" and accusing them of being "rumormongers" or "the many being ignorant of the truth"—and they manage to fight back through the communicative act of rumoring via their mobile phones (what Dewey calls the people "interest[ing] themselves in the possibility of control," cited from Shibutani, 1966, p. 38). People spontaneously and actively join the contention in slamming arbitrary government action by disseminating rumors and, in this process, express their discontent and anger toward the hegemonic discourse on what constitutes a rumor. This explains why as one rumor grows and is stamped out, another one emerges; rumor and rumoring are almost impossible to eradicate in contemporary China.

People further appropriate the rhetoric of rumor in the official narrative. They either mockingly state that "emotions are always incited [by rumor], the truth is always unclear, and the [rumoring] mass is always a small bunch," while presenting the people who share rumors as being "the many [who are] ignorant of the truth" (Hu, 2009, p. 77), as such accusations appear frequently in official allegations. Or they self-mock themselves as being "ignorant of the truth," involving themselves in snowballing officially alleged rumors to voice their dissatisfaction and vent their fury over the government. By doing so, the antagonism between the government and its populace further sharpens.

Still, it is worth noting that, so far, both the identity of protest and resistance accompanied by rumor communication and hence the collectivity of the rumor public are *temporary* in a specific context. The contention through the act of rumoring remains a strong instrumental orientation—it is against official stigmatization of rumoring rather than the dominant ideology. In other words, even though the contention may be, to a large extent, against the logic of domination, the temporarily formed rumor public disassembles soon after the affiliated event has ended. Moreover, because of its transient nature, the resistance identity accompanied by rumor communication would hardly transform into, as Castells (2010, p. 8) proposes, a legitimizing identity. As a result, the emergence of a rumor public is more or less an event-driven (instead of an ideology-driven) occurrence, which accordingly restricts its long-run impact on Chinese society.

This, emphatically, is not to deny the political importance of rumoring. By all accounts, rumoring emerges in the process of collective struggle and is a form of political contention: It embodies a power that ordinary people can take back for themselves. The political function of rumoring is not only to reveal the truth, which has been covered-up (e.g., unusual deaths), or to embarrass those individuals or institutions (e.g., local government) in power, but also to mobilize people in a pervasively political controlled environment. The more people who join in the dissemination of rumors, the louder the clamor of those who are oppressed grows, and the more influential the unofficial, contentious, and emotionally loaded counter-power communication becomes. As Cheng Yizhong, the former chief editor of the *Southern Metropolis Daily*, once commented:

> Rumors are powerful weapons for the masses to oppose official propaganda and lies. Rumors are not facts, but they are much more real than facts; rumors do not stand up to scrutiny, but they are more convincing than truth; rumors are full of holes, but that does not stop the masses from firmly believing them. (Cheng, 2011)

THE TACTICS OF MOBILE RUMORING: THE EMBEDDING OF THE MOBILE PHONE IN EVERYDAY RESISTANCE

The emerging political significance of rumoring and rumor communication cannot be separated from the embedding of mobile phones into everyday life in China. Such embedding enables the ordinary person to exercise rumoring as an everyday tactic (de Certeau, 1984) in an easy, low-cost, low-profile but contagious and influential way—it's just a flick of a finger that allows one to circulate officially alleged rumors to fight against the strategy of social control from the authorities. By doing so, people not only free themselves from the internalized oppression that the regime attempts to impose, but they also gain more and diverse political leverage.

The distinction—and further contention—between strategy and tactics, in de Certeau's (1984) work, is relevant to understand the political significance of mobile-enabled rumoring as everyday resistance in contemporary China. On the one hand, as the hegemonic structure organized by "the postulation of power" (de Certeau, 1984, p. 38), strategies function like overarching mechanisms of discipline that aim to capture all moments in daily life—very much like the rumor control and crackdown prevalent in authoritarian contexts.

On the other hand, tactics, or the individual actions in everyday activities that are determined by the "absence of power" (de Certeau, 1984, p. 38), are a technique for poaching influence or eroding existing mechanisms of power. These tactics develop as crucial practices that distort existing power structures and are "the ingenious ways in which the weak make use of the strong" (de Certeau, 1984, p. xvii). In the case of rumor communication, the strategy of control in the guises of rumor crackdown or rumor rebuttal starts to cripple when hundreds of people, with their mobile phones, frequently, deliberately, and collectively (but without top-down coordination) join the process of diffusing the messages that the authorities have labeled as rumors. Those who ricochet rumors via their mobile phones are not only demonstrating their worry about the lack of information, transparency, and formal channels for discussing demands and grievances, but they are also showing their dissatisfaction with official suppression and criminalization of their legitimate right to communicate. In turn, people appropriate the official rhetoric, i.e., the very term "rumor," and, with the affordances of the mobile phone, facilitate unofficial communication and further proliferate censored information. Furthermore, rumor rebuttal from the authorities in this context is no longer a way of stopping rumor circulation but rather becomes a full-fledged accomplice in rumor proliferation. Authorities in charge of cracking down on rumors have thus been delegitimized and have steadily lost their sanctioning power.

In this process, the mobile phone provides a simple yet effective way for people to take advantage of rumoring, as such tactics facilitate (rumor) communication as contention. In my view, benefiting from the low-cost and user-friendly operation, people with all levels of literacy have been empowered by their mobile phones, a mundane communication technology (Nielsen, 2011; also see Liu, 2017), to actively resist the regime. In fact, mobile technologies bring an unprecedented opportunity for ordinary people, even those without complicated communication skills (e.g., tweeting, online chatting, or special techniques for circumventing censorship), to voice and amplify their suspicions about authoritarian dominance, to resist and disregard authorities' directives, to show and share their disobedient attitudes toward the hegemonic discourse, and to carry out uncooperative activities. Strategies of control are undermined by the unpredictability of contention facilitated by the tactics of rumoring via mobile communication as a personal means of communication. Rather than the overt, observable insurgence, or what Scott (1990) calls the "public transcript," this kind of contention, afforded by mobile technologies, epitomizes the "hidden transcript"—the subtle, covert, low-profile but powerful forms of "everyday resistance" (Scott, 1985) that are "often oblique, symbolic, and too indefinite to incur prosecution" (Scott, 1990, p. 138). This phenomenon lowers the threshold of contention in everyday life—contention does not always mean organizing or joining a protest—with a mobile phone and a flick of a finger, one can send or forward those messages that are dubbed rumors by the authorities. Mobile-facilitated rumor communication, in such a way, expands the boundary of politics, with the mobile phone as a mundane, effective means for people to facilitate communication as contention and engage in politics in innovative ways. It is in this sense that mobile rumoring not just produces a rumor public with situational solidarity, but it also contests power by "challenging the normal channels of challenging power and revealing the truth" (Žižek, 2011, p. 10).

Beyond "Slacktivism"

Slacktivism or clicktivism are terms that describe a common critique toward ICT-mediated political participation. In contradistinction to the optimistic perspective that easy-to-use ICTs encourage relatively convenient forms of political participation from a broad strata of the population, studies have contended that these kind of low-risk forms of protest behavior, such as passively mouse clicking "like" on social media, forwarding letters or videos, or signing online petitions, and other "low effort activities . . . are considered incapable of furthering political goals as effectively as traditional forms of participation" (H. Christensen, 2011). Rather, as the "ideal type of activism for a lazy generation," in Morozov's (2009) critique, slacktivism leads to "feel-good online activism that has zero political or social impact . . . an illusion of having a meaningful impact on the world without demanding anything more than joining a Facebook group" (for similar critiques, see Halupka, 2014; White, 2010).

Is mobile rumoring—flicking a finger to forward a rumor via mobile phones—a kind of slacktivism? The answer is certainly no. First, as we have seen earlier, at least in the highly repressive Chinese context, the engagement of rumor circulation is a high-risk form of activism (McAdam, 1986) with political and legal dangers. Rumoring is an example of one way in which people, with the help of their ever-present mobile phones, can become active and critical political agents in their own right contesting prevailing dominance and shaping the boundary of (contentious) politics in a repressive context. Second, as a political action, rumoring contains rich implications with profound effects in reality. Rumoring represents a backlash against the all-embracing authoritarian rule, an undermining of the authority of the regime, and a disobedience that allows for the gestation and formation of further contentious actions. Furthermore, in practice, rumors frequently trigger follow-up confrontational conflicts and outright violence (e.g., G. Li, 2014; R. Li, 2005; Liu & Huang, 2014; Yu, 2010). In this sense, rumoring is rather a "difference-in-kind" (Karpf, 2010) of political action, as it can exist independently and of its potential for triggering further political engagement. Third, it is further in this sense that rumoring becomes a symbolic action—clicking "forward" or retweeting a rumor—it turns out that the widespread adoption of such symbolic micro-action (re) shapes the ways in which people make sense of their political agency and metacommunicate their emotion and political efficacy (Thoits, 1989).

More importantly, the engagement of rumoring via mobile phone allows people to free themselves from internalized oppression. To criminalize rumors and rumoring, the regime has tried to impose its own definitions of what constitutes a "rumor" and what a "rumormonger" might be. This affects not only the behavior of subordinate classes but their consciousness as well. In this vein, Scott warns: "[T]he critical implication for hegemony is that class rule is effected not so much by sanctions and coercion as by the consent and passive compliance of subordinate classes" (1985, pp. 315–316). As discussed earlier regarding the rule of fear and uncertainty—i.e. the ambiguity of the limits of political tolerance—, by dubbing certain messages as rumors, or as unauthenticated information, the authorities utilize rumor control as an effective means of fear control, whereas society remains in an unsure situation, failing to question authority as self-censorship is deeply ingrained into people's practices, and crackdowns on rumoring and rumors is pervasively legitimized. The official accusation of a piece of information as being a rumor aims to not only obliterate this information but also to deprive people of their legitimate rights to free speech and information flow, and further, to silence people's comments, doubts, and questions about the official story by establishing deterrence. The constraint and suppression of communication has many negative repercussions for the cohesiveness of a citizenry who lack an effective means of expression and interaction, leaving the general population at the mercy of a government-controlled media sphere with the dominant framing of acceptable political action.

The situation starts to change when hundreds of citizens frequently and enthusiastically join the process of sharing government-labeled rumor messages. Obviously, the action of mobile rumoring as such displays a gesture of political confrontation against a government call that people should "resolutely resist online rumor" (*People's Daily*, 2011), that people should be "firmly against online rumor," and that people should "not trust rumors, not spread rumors, and not give rumormongers with ulterior motives more room to operate" (Ren, 2011). In this sense, the use of mobile phones facilitates rumoring, and this activity releases people from the fearful silence that comes from the self-censorship that the authorities want to impose on the population.

In short, the embedding of mobile communication expands the limited freedoms allowed by the framework of strategies and further advocates the interrogation of "micropolitics"—and the resistance against such politics—in the sense of Deleuze and Guattari's (1987) detailed, supple movements of power and subversion that complement the rigid centralization of macropolitics (pp. 208–231). Rumor communication thereby calls for an appreciation of the multilayered and complex dimensions of digitally mediated, contentious "micropolitics" (Deleuze & Guattari, 1987, pp. 208–231) to establish a widening focus of both the scope and level of interrogation by including the more routinized, informal, and inconspicuous forms and contextualized aspects of everyday practices as a form of political disruption, disobedience, or resistance as significant to the processes of contention.

BEYOND RUMORING, BEYOND CHINA

Considering how prevalent rumors are in digital platforms in Chinese society today, there is a dearth of research on how rumors thrive and why people spread them. This chapter addresses the contentious nature of rumor with a special focus on the spread of rumors or "rumoring" through mobile communication. It tracks the frame of rumors in the official discourse in contemporary China, where the terms "rumor" and "rumoring" have been adopted by the authorities extensively in everyday practices in an attempt to ensure political stability. Meanwhile, the punishment for rumormongering and the vague or even unknowable threshold of what actually constitutes a rumor remains a significant part of the controlling strategy—with people uncertain about how much they can speak out on a given topic, the government maintains the status quo by ensuring a certain level of self-censorship.

By carefully analyzing a rumor's dissemination, interpretation, and implication in the cases I present here, I observe that mobile-phone-facilitated rumor communication has evolved into a special form of contentious politics. Rumor control and crackdown galvanize citizen concern, leading to politically salient expressions of protest and to the formation of a "rumor public" focused on the threats. The embedding of mobile phones into everyday life enables rumoring to be a key part of "everyday resistance" (Scott, 1985) at the grassroots level. With the click of a button, people engage in rumoring through their mobile phones, whereby they show their suspicions about, distrust of, and challenges toward the government, or in other ways involve themselves in struggles against authorities. The prevalence of mobile phones and synchronous mobile communication accumulates and collects various rumors into large-scale resistance over a very short time. The emergence, circulation, and proliferation of mobile phone rumors—while they sometimes lead to panic and mass incidents—serve to compromise the legitimacy of the regime. When the regime tries to call some piece of information a mere rumor to stifle any different voices and ordinary communicative activities, the opposite result tends to occur. Meanwhile, the emotions involved in political resistance and disobedience, beyond the specific content per se, tend to spread very quickly through mobile rumoring. Mobile technologies thus lower the average protest threshold and can function as a vent for long pent-up resentments against the entrenched authoritarian regime. This chapter hence suggests that ongoing interdisciplinary work is needed to understand the dynamics of ICT-mediated rumors in a highly complex culture of technological convergence.

The chapter furthers a broader research agenda beyond China and beyond the case of rumor. The observation on mobile rumoring as contention in contemporary China is hardly unique. Such an understanding, or similar ones, can also be observed in other parts of the world. In peasant resistance in Southeast Asia, rumor, among other tactics, has become a significant part of disguised, muted, and veiled resistance (Scott, 1990). In the former Soviet Union, rumor functioned as "a kind of offstage social space for the articulation of peasant dissent" (Viola, 1999, p. 65). To reformulate rumoring as contention hence opens new research initiatives into comparative studies of covert and overt forms of contentious politics across national, political, or historical contexts. Meanwhile, of greater importance is a similar, ongoing political tendency around the world that utilizes the term "fake news" as a rhetorical tool—the same as the way Chinese government uses the term "rumor"—to deliberately undermine dissident views, attack opponents, or discredit media scrutiny (Blake, 2017; Brummette, DiStaso, Vafeiadis, & Messner, 2018; Erlanger, 2017). Similar to the deliberation on rumors here, addressing the communication aspect of fake news may facilitate alternative interpretations on its diffusion beyond the narrow focus on the truth or falsity of the content.

CHAPTER 6

Conclusion

Beyond China, Moving Mobile

The sociological imagination enables us to grasp history and biography and the relations between the two within society. . . . No social study that does not come back to the problems of biography, of history and of their intersections within a society has completed its intellectual journey. (Mills, 2000, p. 6)

The understanding of the political use and influence of the mobile phone in the Chinese context epitomizes, in Mills's words (2000, p. 7), "the intersections of biography and history within society." *Biography*, here, entails "personal experience" (Mills, 2000, p. 8), exemplified through protesters' tactical or strategic appropriations of what would otherwise be the routine use of their mobile phones, instead, deploying them as part of their repertoires of protest as they confront inaction or suppression from the ruling regime, or seek support and solidarity from their social networks. *History*, for our purposes, then, encompasses the structure of a particular society as a whole, its essential components and their relations, and the meanings generated within it (Mills, 2000, p. 6). This notion of history is illustrated through the ways in which certain uses of the mobile phone have been modularized and legitimized by official mass media as a part of citizens' repertoire of protest, as well as in the sense in which the social norms within relationships and networking have encouraged mobile-mediated micromobilization as a result of reciprocity, and the manner in which mobile rumoring grows into a practice of everyday resistance. The relevance of communication lies in the fact that it establishes and shapes the interplay of biography and history in our discussions of contentious politics—as we can see from the sharing and articulation of individuals' personal experiences; the construction of specific meanings and interpretations as structured opportunities; the accumulation and activation of network resources in social ties as mobilizing structures; and the galvanization of widespread grievances, distrust, and anger toward the authorities as a "collective action frame" that incites people to further action. Before we move to summarizing the political relevance of mobile phones in China, it is appropriate to first return to the importance of communication in facilitating interdisciplinary dialogue regarding ICTs and contentious collective action, as I began this book by addressing this issue.

CONTENTIOUS POLITICS FROM THE PERSPECTIVE OF COMMUNICATION

Few topics across disciplines, including communication studies, political science, and sociology, have grown as much over the past two decades as the study of ICTs and contentious politics. Yet, disparate interests and divergent focuses still hinder mutually beneficial dialogue and reciprocal learning across these disciplines (e.g., Earl & Garrett, 2017; Earl, Hunt, & Garrett, 2014; Garrett, 2006). Over the last decade, the emergence and increasing influence of a perspective based in communication in the study of movements and actions has expounded communication as a key mechanism that structures, shapes, and drives unfolding episodes of contention in an era of the growing ubiquity of digital communication technologies (e.g., Bennett & Segerberg, 2012, 2013; Bimber, 2017; Bimber et.al, 2012; Castells, 2009; Ganesh & Stohl, 2013). The current book joins this effort and adds an important contribution to the current literature. It proposes a synthetic framework across a multitude of disciplines with an emphasis on various forms of communication and metacommunication that articulate different elements in contentious politics, including political opportunities, mobilizing structures, and framing processes. This framework presents a nuanced picture of various communication flows— face-to-face, mass, and networked communication—and their respective influences on elements of contentious politics. This, in consequence, helps pinpoint the contributions and the (r)evolution, if any, from ICTs and their mediated, networked communication into contentious politics.

The discussion developed at the beginning of this book asserted that, although communication, in either explicit or implicit ways, has drawn extensive attention to its relevance in movements and actions, few studies have tried to engage it to bridge the gap to overcome the "incommensurability" (Kuhn, 1963) among different disciplines. To situate communication at the center of political contention not only allows us to connect disparate works across disciplines, but, more importantly, avoids the highly contested techno- or media-centric approach that easily risks the danger of widely criticized technological determinism. Furthermore, as illustrated in the three chapters that follow the Introduction, an interrogation of contentious politics through the lens of communication, and further, together with an examination of metacommunication, help reveal at least three significant issues that fail to draw sufficient attention in the extant studies.

First, the question at the heart of most scholarship on ICTs and political activism maintains the "how" question: How do people use ICTs in acts of contention like riots, protests, and demonstrations? The basic assumption underlying this question is the attempt to understand ICT use through the moment of confrontation *alone*. Nevertheless, as McAdam (1986, p. 67) cautions, "[m]ovements are much more ephemeral." The assumption above apparently detaches and even isolates "moments of madness" (Zolberg, 1972) from their broader contexts, leaving out a great deal of what is politically significant that sets the scene for a contentious moment (for a general critique, see Staggenborg & Taylor, 2005, pp. 38–41). To advance the topic, what I emphasize is the importance of asking the "why" and "what" questions. Why and wherefore do people get involved with certain (functions of) ICTs but not others? What accounts for the variations in protest repertoires that emerge in different cases? A careful investigation of the perception and use of mobile phones as part of a repertoire of contention in the case of China in Chapter 3 serves as an example to throw light on these questions. Not just delving into the use alone, the term "repertoire of contention" cuts to the heart of the issue of agency in contention (Jasper, 2004)—people's situational understanding and strategic choice to adopt the mobile phone, or, more precisely, its specific function(s) out of affordance(s) as part of the protest repertoire in a given context. The discussion attributes such understanding and choice to *both* habitus in relation to media use in everyday life, and the effect of multiple flows of communication and their corresponding metacommunications in a long run beyond the contentious moment. For one thing, the current discussion is distinguished from the extant literature, which, too often, treats the issue as if activists have a unanimous understanding of digital communication technologies and thereby use them in the same way under all circumstances. Whereas, in practice, a significant difference in maneuvering and appropriating specific functions of mobile phones epitomizes a distinctive habitus for each user that represents divergent affordances out of the same mobile technology, in disparate social groups, and in diverse contexts. Hence, a link from affordances to repertoires of contention positions ICT uses in the contentious moment as a relational existence specific to social groups, along with their everyday practices. The analysis reminds us to tease out the complexity and diversity of the *meanings* of mobile phones for each user, that is, is it a device just to make voice calls or send texts, or is it a vessel for WeChat use only? This can further be extended to ICTs uses in political contention in a broad sense, which are derived from but not determined by affordances. For another, the discussion further illuminates the coexistence of face-to-face, mass, and networked communications in political contention. For the emergence of political activism in authoritarian regimes such as China, it is not enough to have an ICT and its networked communication alone. While networked and interpersonal communications proliferate information about the logistics of a protest, the coverage in official, mass communication and its metacommunication not least binds specific mobile phone use and protests together as a modularized uprising, inspires people to take their mobile phones as part of a legitimate protest repertoire, and contributes to opening up political opportunity for later struggles. This resonates with Tarrow's (1993, p. 85) argument that "it was in the shadow of the national state that social movements developed their characteristic modular forms of collective action."

Second, despite the fact that the body of literature about ICTs and political contention is becoming impressive, it may appear indiscriminate with respect to the distinction among digital communication technologies and their corresponding influences on collective actions with the use of umbrella terms such as "digital media" or "ICTs." To advance this understanding, Chapter 4 dissects the uniqueness of the mobile phone as a reciprocal technology and its specific influence on movement emergence. In the cases of mobile-mediated mobilization in the absence of movement organization in China, mobile *communication* entails and activates reciprocity in well-connected interpersonal relationships that are behind the decision for participation and recruitment to activism. Hence, consistent with the argument in social movement studies that objective structural availability (Schussman & Soule, 2005, p. 1086) acts as a necessary if not sufficient condition to an account of the rise of movement phenomenon,[1] my examination attributes mobile-mediated pattern of mobilization to the

---

1. For instance, see the relevance of cognitive liberation against "structural potential" (McAdam, 1982, p. 48) like political opportunities and established organizations, or the significance of framing as an actively interactive meaning construction process beyond structural arrangements (Benford & Snow, 2000).

decisive role of communication in encouraging interpersonal mobilization and driving peer-to-peer recruitment as part of protesters' fulfillment of reciprocal obligation.

Third, communication not just mobilizes social network resources for movements but also communication itself, by virtue of mobile phones, grows into contentious practice in some circumstances. Chapter 5 offers such an insight by looking at the communicative practice of forwarding "rumor," a pervasive, difficult-to-eradicate, but less-noted phenomenon that nowadays evolves even more on mobile platforms. A combination of scholarship mainly from psychology and sociology of rumor studies, I believe, offers a comprehensive understanding of rumor diffusion not only in terms of its content but also in respect with its ritual aspect (Carey, 2008). The chapter looks into the very communicative practice of rumoring that articulates insurgents' identity, metacommunicates collective resistance, and engenders a Durkheimian "collective effervescence" (Goodwin, Jasper, & Polletta, 2009) with long-suppressed grievances, anger, and discontent toward political suppression and preposterous accusations about rumors. By taking advantage of their mobile phones, Chinese people establish "the politics of rumoring" as part of everyday resistance.

Empirically and theoretically, these three chapters center on the political relevance of *communication* that institutes the mobile phone as a part of contentious repertoire (Chapter 3), mobilizes mobile-based network resources for movements (Chapter 4), and develops into a special form of contention (Chapter 5). As the mobile phone is playing an increasingly significant part in affording, structuring, and facilitating communication—and further contention—in the repressive Chinese context in which the regime controls the media and manipulates other means of communication, this process sees the mobile phone as being a notable part of politics in contemporary China.

MOBILE DEMOCRACY, OR THE EMBEDDING OF MOBILE PHONES IN POLITICS IN CHINA

The advancement and popularity of digital communication technologies has often boosted the expectation, advocacy, and deliberation of democratization (e.g., Barlow, 1996; Eisenstein, 1980; McChesney, 1999). Likewise, the advent of mobile technology, along with its widespread adoption in political activism across the global, brings about the hope and hype of "mobile democracy" (Hermanns, 2008; Nyíri, 2003; Suárez, 2006). Despite that, a closer look at the reality, together with these discussions about mobile democracy, suggest a more complicated reality. For one thing, even among studies that favor or embrace the term "mobile democracy," mobile phones are never the sole technology that promotes democracy and political participation. Rather, contends Hermanns (2008, p. 79), "mobile phones are not a revolutionising, independent tool. . . . Mobile phone use should therefore be included in the research on the effects of new ICTs on politics and democracy." For another, scholars clearly endorse not mobile technology by and of itself but rather the *communication* the technology facilitates (Suárez, 2006) for possible outcome of democratization. The term "mobile democracy" hence deflects attention from the fact that mobile phone use, despite its current prevalence in everyday life, remains a mere fraction of our life.

On a similar note, I avoid using the term "mobile democracy" as an exaggeration of the *one and only* role of mobile phones in the process of democratization. Nor do I reduce or oversimplify the contingent outcome or consequence of the political use of mobile phones to either the success or failure of democratization. Furthermore, democratization, the same as the outcome of political contention, depends on various contextual differences, involving, but not limited to, technology. The cases in China examined in this book hence rather demonstrate that mobile phones may play distinguishing roles in (contentious) politics in authoritarian regimes. On the whole, it is the embedding of mobile phones into a specific socio-political context and the increasing adoption of mobile phones in political-related activities that drives potential changes.

The point here is twofold. For one thing, the embedding of mobile phones in politics refers not to the eventual but rather the *procedural* influence of mobile tech on politics, which shapes and is shaped by the very society the mobile phone embeds in concurrently. Just as I elaborate in the methodological part (see details in Chapter 2 and the Appendix), the criteria of case selection is concerned less with the success or failure of political contention but rather with the use of mobile phones in the insurgent process. For instance, embedding the use of mobile phones in a widely acknowledged repertoire of contention in protests and demonstrations in contemporary China cannot exist without its context, in which the ubiquity of the mobile phone and its habituated use establish its availability to be improvised in actions and movements. Meanwhile, mass media coverage, given its relevant mouthpiece function, renders mobile phones as a means of contentious politics. Then, the embedding of mobile phones in politics introduces the significance of reciprocity in *guanxi* networks, which drives the process of micromobilization and recruitment. Furthermore, out of various uses of the mobile phone for political activism, mobile rumoring arises as a remarkable type of contentious collective action, with the mobile phone as an essential part of it.

For another, a better understanding of the influence of the embedding of the mobile phone in politics and, further, processes of democratization, if any, necessitate specific cultural codes as well as (implicit) social and political values in different societies. In our case, as the studies characterize, the Chinese people own a totally different understanding than the West of the definitions and implementation of democracy (e.g., Naisbitt & Naisbitt, 2010; Nathan, 1986; Shi, 1997, 2010). Based on the survey he conducted in China regarding the Chinese people's perception of democracy, Shi (2010) differentiates two separate definitions of democracy between the West and Asia: procedural democracy and substantive democracy. The former, which corresponds to Western democracy (e.g., Dahl, 1998; Schumpeter, 2010),

> determines the legitimacy of state governments based on democratic procedures such as election, lobbying, etc., while the latter believes the definition of democracy is mainly based on how well policies from the governments reflect the interests of the public (Pei & Shi, 2007).

As an alternative, argues Shi (2010), people in Asia in general, and in China in particular, associate themselves more with substantive democracy. Namely, making the government listen to the "voice" of people, whether through nonviolent resistance, popular protest, or even mass incidents, is a minimal, basic, but key condition to ensure substantive democracy, as it is impossible for the government to take your interests into account—in particular in a regime with stern controls of expression and communication— unless it hears your appeal. Against this backdrop, the embedding of mobile phones in politics affords an alternative approach to political participation beyond existing institutions, such as the People's Congress, the existing political system of representative democracy through which, by principle, the Chinese people exercise state power by democratically elected representatives. This system, as Nathan criticizes, "the regime admits, and everyone knows, that its authority has never been subject to popular review and is never intended to be" (Nathan, 2009, p. 38). In practice, mobile phone use contributes to a direct way to participate in and influence politics by accumulating people's resources, articulating their experiences, reflecting their wishes, and expressing their grievances. In this way, the use of mobile phones makes it possible for ordinary people to project their interests into the political agenda, thus enhancing their ability to influence politics and promoting the process of *substantial* democratization in the context of China.

CENSORSHIP AND STRUGGLE OVER MOBILE COMMUNICATION

One of the key questions regarding politics and digital communication technologies involves the issue of control from the regime, including censorship and not least the suppression of offline mobilization (e.g., King, Pan, & Roberts, 2013). What is the regime's response to the use of mobile phones for political purposes, and what are the implications of its attempt to restrain such use?

I by no means believe that the mobile phone, or mobile communication, is an artifact or a sphere that would be immune to government intervention. As illustrated in various points in the discussion, the regime has exploited different ways to try to sustain or to strengthen its existing control, just like it does in other spheres—in a similar way to the regulation imposed by the authorities against rumor diffusion. Clearly, the authorities struggle, in various ways, to prevent people from adapting their mobile phones for political purposes, including the real-name registration system that monitors VPN usage on mobile phones (Chai, 2011), "web cleansing" (净网) actions that erase officially alleged "harmful information" (Lam, 2017; Palmer, 2017), and even a complete shutdown of mobile services, when necessary, to stop riots (Anonymous, 2010; Branigan, 2012). If we consider these interventions in terms of the communication perspective, the essential intent undoubtedly aims at eradicating or at least discouraging politically precarious behaviors through impeding communication, which is the key *connective tissue* for these collective initiatives. In this sense, to cut off communication between members of its population acts as an effective means to prevent mobilization and recruitment by the regime.

For another thing, insurgents are aware of potential monitoring or possible intervention from the authorities. Against remarkable censorship, the Chinese people are magnificently skilled in maneuvering various techniques to disseminate forbidden topics in political discourse, such as code words, homophones, spoofing, parodies, and satires, just to mention a few (e.g., Tang & Yang, 2011; Wang, 2012; Xiao, 2011, 2014; Yang, 2011). In mobile-mediated mobilization, residents adopted the terms "(collective) stroll" (集体散步) or "taking a walk" (散步), rather than "parade" (游行) or "demonstration" (示威), as euphemisms for street protest mobilization (*China Digital Times*, 2014; Davies, 2012, pp. 126–127; Liu, 2013, p. 1004). Shanghai residents employed the term "shopping" (购物) as they disseminated mobilizing messages via bulletin board systems (BBS), internet forums, and mobile phones to organize and facilitate protests in one of the city's most crowded shopping streets against a proposed magnetic levitation train line (Zeng, 2015, p. 110). Taxi drivers in our cases borrowed the phrase "drink tea" (喝茶) to mobilize strikes in response to long-standing grievances over taxi company charges, government regulation, and competition from unlicensed taxis. The tactics people use in reaction to censorship complicates the struggle between the authorities and its population.

The interviews further display the fact that people are conscious of advantages that different affordances embody, for instance, in the mobilization and recruitment of political contention. For instance, in the taxi drivers' eyes, voice calls may leave fewer traces of their content than text-based communications, consequently reducing the risk of government censors or surveillance agencies identifying participants who disseminate politically sensitive information.[2] They believe that a large amount of manpower and data is necessary to carry out this kind of surveillance, which makes the intervention extremely difficult to be executed quickly. This is the case unless the authorities shut down the entire telecommunications network, a necessary part of daily lives nowadays, which will result in even larger scale discontent. Hence, voice calls enable people to catch the authorities unawares during the mobilization of contention.

To summarize, the strength of mobile phones as a potential political resource derives largely from the following two points. For one thing, as a mundane communication tool, the mobile phone's political relevance borne out of, and is based on, its ubiquity and significance in people's everyday lives. Put differently, as one of the taken-for-granted necessities nowadays (Ling, 2013) for always-on, always available communication and networking practice, the mobile phone is easily being manipulated and improvised (Tilly, 1986, p. 390) for other purposes, notwithstanding its different meanings to divergent social groups against various contexts. For another, even with the existence of control and censorship, people always work hard to explore possible ways to circumvent censorship and work against suppression, as we can see along the history of China (e.g., Cohen & Townsend, 1997; Yang & Jiang, 2015). Diverse and creative tactics grow and evolve in response to differing degrees of censorship and policies of control and governance.

2. Technologically, it is not difficult for the government to identify participants if it decides to intervene because all mobile information has to travel through state-owned networks.

FROM LOCAL EXPERIENCE TO GLOBAL APPLICATION: AN ILLUSTRATED COMPARATIVE STUDY

As I promised to explicate at the beginning of this book, one of the strengths of the communication-centered framework rests on its potential to draw a comparison across different cases in an effort to pinpoint and hence schematize contributions from ICTs to contentious politics. Comparison, in this sense, can take place both across time (i.e., contention before and after the popularity of ICTs) and place (i.e., contention involving the use of ICTs in different contexts). The subsequent comparative case study (Yin, 2009), with the second-hand data mainly from news and scholarly sources, is offered here to briefly illustrate the analytic power of the framework in the schematization of the change, if any, brought by ICTs to contention in different contexts.

The cases include the Mississippi Summer Project of 1964, also known as "Freedom Summer," which was a grassroots nonviolent movement to expand black voting in the US South (Andrews, 2004; McAdam, 1988); the Wukan protest in 2011, one of the landmark cases of political protest in China since Tian'anmen (Benney & Marolt, 2015, p. 88; Wines, 2011); and the Egyptian Uprising, also in 2011, part of a revolutionary wave in the Arab world with protesters from a range of socioeconomic and religious backgrounds demanding the overthrow of Egyptian President Hosni Mubarak (e.g., Allagui, 2014; Howard & Hussain, 2013; Ketchley, 2017; Lynch, 2012; Wilson & Dunn, 2011).

The richness of the literature on the cases available prevents me from going into great detail about them, but I can instead offer a brief description here. As a major statewide mobilization unfolded during the summer of 1964, the Freedom Summer civil rights project brought hundreds of civil rights activists to Mississippi, the majority of them white, Northern college students, to try to end the long-time political disenfranchisement of African Americans in the region. In this arduous and eventually bloody political campaign, Freedom Summer volunteers and participants established temporary Freedom Schools and community centers that educated black citizens and helped them register to vote in the face of death threats, kidnappings, beatings, bombings, and unjust arrests (Andrews, 2004; McAdam, 1988). In late 2011, around 4,000 residents of Wukan in Guangdong Province protested land-grab issues in front of a government building, before eventually attacking this building, clashing with police, and blocking roads. ICTs and mobile-phone-captured videos, photos, and tweets showing the clashes between the villagers and police proliferated across BBS, online forums, the instant messaging platform QQ, and social media like Weibo (Hess, 2015; Reporter, 2012; Tong & Zuo, 2014). The Wukan protest has hence been portrayed as "a victory for . . . the power of the Internet" (Mooney, 2012). Similarly, news coverage and some of the literature on the Egyptian Uprising have addressed the role of ICTs,[3] as the contention was characterized by the following statement: "we [participants] use Facebook to schedule the protests, Twitter to coordinate, and YouTube to tell the world" (Khondker, 2011, p. 667).

The criteria of case selection for this study involved three considerations. First, despite different time periods, geographical locations, and regime contexts in which these cases emerged and developed, they more or less belong to what McAdam (1986, p. 67) defines as "high-risk activism," i.e., collective action that involves "the anticipated dangers—whether legal, social, physical, financial and so forth—of engaging in a particular type of activity." For Freedom Summer volunteers and participants, they were facing constant threats of intimidation, retaliation, violence, and legal strategies perpetuated by white supremacists and segregationists in the highly repressive political context of the American South of the 1960s (Andrews, 2002, p. 920; also see Colby, 1987; McMillen, 1971). Comparably, insurgents in Wukan and Egypt confronted repression, punishment, and oppression from authoritarian regimes for their political action.

Second, the cases of Wukan and the Egyptian Uprising have been picked up largely in light of the reportedly focus on ICTs in contention. Meanwhile, Freedom Summer serves as a classic movement case *before* the rise of ICTs. As I have underscored, a comparison of movements *before* and *after* the popularity and adoption of ICTs helps nail down the specific contribution, if any, from the use of digital communication technologies.

Third, without denying individual characteristics of the cases on their own, a further key reason for case selection largely depends on the availability of rich data and proper descriptions of these three contentions.

Before the move to a close look at communications and metacommunication in cases, I should address that I make no claim to deny the relevance of existing models and frameworks in interpreting the cases, such as the classic political process model of social movements (McAdam, 1982) or the seminal connective action logic for digitally networked action (Bennett & Segerberg, 2012, 2013). Preferably, the effort aims to illustrate how the communication-centered framework in this book would take steps

---

3. The discussion of ICTs in the Egyptian Uprising has reflected prudential considerations on the impact of digital communication technologies (e.g., Howard & Hussain, 2013; Howard & Parks, 2012; Lynch, 2012; Rinke & Röder, 2011).

to tackle some of existing, highly debatable problems like the role of ICTs in contention, or what kinds of changes ICTs may introduce to contentious movements. In this vein, the idea of the nature of the comparative analysis goes the same as in McAdam's (1982, p. 63) work on the black protest movement, i.e., a comparative study here is not "a rigorous scientific test" of the proposed framework. Rather, the comparative study serves as "an assessment of the general fit" (McAdam, 1982, p. 63) of the framework in order to tease out the impact of ICTs by dissecting various communication and metacommunication issues in these cases. In view of this, the focus follows the proposed theoretical framework and centers on two issues. First, how various forms of communication and metacommunication shape the rise, development, or decline of movements in different contexts. Second, given the specific impact from digitally mediated networked communication, whether the role of ICTs, beyond mobile technologies, in political contention in different contexts is the same and if so, to what extent we could generalize what kind of conclusion about the ICTs influence on different contentious elements across cases. I continue with a detailed examination of communication and metacommunication, along with control over communication, if any, in relation to political opportunities, mobilizing structures, and the framing process. The last part brings us to the conclusion as well as its implications.

Three cases encompass a wide range of communication and metacommunication issues, albeit not always mediated by ICTs, that shape and articulate contentious elements. As shown in Table 6.1, for the first dimension of the framework, changes in political opportunity structure remain crucial to an understanding of conditions under which the Freedom Summer rose as part of black insurgency in the 1960s (for a detailed discussion, see McAdam, 1982, Chapter 7). Two out of the four sets of factors that contribute to a favorable structure of political opportunities—i.e., a supportive political context and the sense of optimism and political efficacy among black citizens (McAdam, 1982, pp. 179–180)—necessitate communication.[4] For one thing, as Funkhouser (1973, pp. 66–67) points out, the amount of news coverage about black people, race relations, and civil rights takes the second-place ranking, leading to its concomitant rank of No. 2 of

---

4. In line with my framework to include various forms of communication into analysis, Funkhouser also acknowledges the relevance of "a comprehensive analysis of *the total range of communications* which play a role in forming and influencing nationwide public opinion." Yet, to him, this kind of analysis then is "probably impossible and certainly beyond the capabilities of any single research effort" (1973, p. 62, emphasis added).

Table 6.1 A COMPARATIVE STUDY OF (TECHNOLOGICALLY MEDIATED) COMMUNICATION AND CONTENTION

	Freedom Summer	The Wukan Protest	The Egyptian Uprising
Political Opportunities	*Mass communication* on issues of black citizens, race relations, civil rights and the political significance of the black electorate *metacommunicates* and establishes the salience of these events, generating the sense of optimism among black citizens for favorable change and encouraging their collective action to achieve this improvement.	*Face-to-face communication* between returning migrants and local residents about protest experiences, strategies, and repertoires.	*Mass communication* from transnational media outlets delivers the idea of anti-authoritarian protests in other parts of the Arab world. *Many-to-many, networked communication,* and *one-to-one mobile communication* about Tunisian Ben Ali's exile and the death of Khaled Said, which had been ignored by state-controlled media.
Mobilizing Structure	*Face-to-face communication* in civil rights communities and SMOs, the Freedom Schools, flyers dissemination, door-to-door canvassing, and other mass meetings forge the mobilizing structure, spread repertoires of contention, and draw movement participation. Music and songs in mass meetings and the Freedom School engender a strong bond of solidarity through *metacommunication*.	*Face-to-face communication* and social network based on the clan system, *metacommunicating* a cultural and psychological supporting foundation.	*Networked communication* for mobilization within the young, tech-savvy population with solidarity through digital media. *Mobile communication* via social networks of family, friends, etc. and *face-to-face communication* via flyers, pamphlets, word-of-mouth *metacommunicates* trust and emotional resonance; fraternization performance like hugging, kissing, and shaking hands *metacommunicates* the feeling of solidarity.
Framing	*Mass communication* split, with local media expressing resistance to the civil rights activities while national media praises such activities and consequently consolidates the commitment among volunteers, establishing a sense of self-efficacy for the changes the volunteers were bringing to Mississippi.	Both *mass communication* and *networked communication* matter, as they generate the visibility of protest and promote the protest diffusion, maintaining the specific framing (i.e., not against the Party-state) against state-controlled media.	Both *mass communication* and *networked communication* matter, as they sustain the visibility of the uprising, lead to "international buy-in" (Howard and Hussain 2011, p. 42), and facilitate the protest diffusion.

the "most important problem facing America" in the public opinion survey during the period of 1960s. The correspondence between news coverage and public opinion here delineates that mass media not only distribute news but, more importantly, also metacommunicates the news event's salience (McCombs & Shaw, 1972), or, to use Funkhouser's words, "the only way that people could estimate the most important problem facing America would be to take their cues from the media" (Funkhouser, 1973, p. 69). Against this backdrop, the media attention through mass communication produces a growing public salience of civil rights issues and the subsequent public support as the most important issue facing the country. For another, in addition to the salience of the "Negro Question" or civil rights issues, the media coverage over the outcome of the presidential contests regarding the political significance of the black electorate (McAdam, 1988, pp. 157–158) further shapes political awareness in black communities. Again, it is mass communication that (not surprisingly) produces the sense of optimism among black citizens for favorable change and encourages their collective action to achieve this improvement.

For the other two cases, without denying the value of ICTs, a closer look at them in terms of the communication-centered framework sheds relevant light on the nuanced development of contention, the dynamics of communication, and the precise role of ICTs, if any. The Wukan protest exemplifies the significance of one-to-one, face-to-face interpersonal communication between returning migrants and local residents about protest experiences and strategies from elsewhere that underpin political opportunity and their contentious repertoires (Lu, Zheng, & Wang, 2017). The returnees later became the new village leaders and, given their experiences, organized protests against governance injustices in new ways, including keeping the outside world informed via social media (Lu et al., 2017, p. 10). Being a unique channel to circulate information on the contention what would normally be censored in both traditional and digital media (King, Pan, & Roberts, 2013b), interpersonal communication was hence "critical to the success of the Wukan protest" (Lu et al., 2017, p. 9) *without* the engagement of ICTs.

Meanwhile, in the Egyptian Uprising, as Rinke and Röder (2011, p. 1274) put it, the totality of communication—including digital, mass, and face-to-face forms of communication—drove the unfolding of these uprisings. As studies have identified, both mass communication and networked communication became critical to the perception of the sufficient openness of political opportunities for contention. Benefiting from the autonomy against local authorities' interference, transnational mass media outlets like Al Jazeera confronted the fabricated news from state-run channels in favor of the regime and delivered the idea of anti-authoritarian protests in other parts of the Arab world (Rinke & Röder, 2011, pp. 1279–1281). The near-total adoption of mobile phones (Howard & Hussain, 2011, p. 38) proliferated news of, for instance, Tunisian Ben Ali's exile, which allowed disaffected Egyptian citizens to learn from a nearby country about how to participate in similar protests in their own country (Howard & Hussain, 2013, pp. 56–57). Networked communication further facilitated the memorialization of events ignored by state-controlled media—i.e., the death of Khaled Said, which was exposed by social media—and subsequently galvanized long-standing grievances and outrage on Twitter and Facebook that later spilled out into the streets (Howard & Hussain, 2013, pp. 22–23; Lim, 2012, pp. 234–243). Clearly, mass communication and, especially, ICT-mediated communication could bring changes to the social construction of political opportunity *insofar as* the regime is incapable of tightly controlling them, which in turn encourages the emergence of political dissent and that puts the regime in a vulnerable position.[5]

For the second dimension of the framework, mobilizing structures vary but also share remarkable similarities in all three cases. For Freedom Summer, of significant relevance is face-to-face communication. This form of communication was first established in the movement organizations of the aggrieved population. "As the dominant organizational force in the movement" (McAdam, 1988, p. 156), established (civil rights) communities and well-developed social organizations fundamentally serve "an important communication function" (Fernandez & McAdam, 1988, p. 380) for recruitment and mobilization. According to McAdam's statistics (1988, p. 147), 53% of movement-generated events in 1964 were attributed to formal movement organizations, almost double from the period between 1955 and 1960 (29%). The dominant role of organizations in the movement hence indicates the relevance of interpersonal communication within organizations in mobilization, as interpersonal network functions as "communication channels that can be activated in helping social movement organizations mobilize resources . . . interpersonal relations . . . imply face-to-face encounters that are likely to be crucial in micromobilization" (Fernandez & McAdam, 1988, p. 364).

One such form of face-to-face encounter prevailed in the Freedom Schools, which functioned as a mobilizing structure that directed its students to be involved in influencing local policies and electoral politics

5. Arguably, China is home to the world's largest mobile phone and internet user base, with around 96% mobile phone penetration rate, all of which, however, remain under strict control of the regime.

and sustained the movement at the local level (Hale, 2011). Through educational efforts at the Freedom Schools, students learned nonviolent tactics and contentious repertories, cultivated a political consciousness committed to destroying the legalized oppression of segregation, and got involved in in-person demonstrations (Hale, 2011, pp. 325, 336). The following description recounts various forms of face-to-face communication during everyday life at the Freedom School:

> They [the students] began the school day by singing "freedom songs" such as "We Shall Overcome," or "Keep Your Eyes on the Prize." Rather than regularly assigned seating, students sat where they chose and in a way that *facilitated dialogue*. Students and teachers earnestly *discussed* issues and questions related to the civil rights campaigns such as: "Why are we (students and teachers) in Freedom Schools? What is the freedom movement? What alternatives does the freedom movement offer us?" (Hale, 2011, p. 335, emphasis added)

Face-to-face communication also occurs in other circumstance, such as when passing out flyers or through word-of-mouth and canvassing. The last item is worth discussing at some length, because, as Rachal (2000, pp. 178–179) notes, "nothing could substitute for the door-to-door canvassing" (also see McAdam, 1988, pp. 77–83). In practice, it refers to "the slow and patient work of going door to door to talk to neighbors about the opportunity to participate in the movement by registering to vote or attending an upcoming mass meeting" (Hale, 2011, pp. 335–336). Obviously, interpersonal persuasion processes exert a determining influence on community organizing. Canvassing work further invites people to face-to-face mass meetings, which, usually held at a church, compounded education, politics, prayer, song, and exhortation, with the goal to inspire, persuade, and encourage black people to register to vote through interpersonal communication (Rachal, 2000, p. 181).

While various forms of face-to-face interaction forge a mobilizing structure, spread repertoires of contention, and draw movement participation, music and song, as specific types of communication, engender a strong bond of solidarity among volunteers and students through metacommunication. Music and songs not just suffused mass meetings and the Freedom School—as we just read from the everyday routine in the school—but also permeated the movement, including recruiting, teaching, giving courage, and inspiring (Rachal, 2000, p. 182).

> At mass meetings, songs inspired normally unconvinced residents to commit to making the attempt to register, transcending the common sense reasons

and natural fears that argued otherwise. Even in temporary defeat, the songs consoled and strengthened; several staffers and volunteers have given testimony to the spiritual uplift gained from singing while in jail or on the way to or from the courthouse . . . Cobb (1996) remembers a silent group of locals returning by bus from an unsuccessful trip to the courthouse in 1962, when the then-unknown Hamer started singing in a strong voice, changing the mood on the bus and foreshadowing her leadership in the movement. Clemson (1995), the only White face in a crowd of marchers to the Biloxi courthouse, thought his time was up as he and a lady who had just given a speech led the group two abreast straight into a White mob; she took him by the arm and said, "Walk slow and sing loud.". . . Songs also recruited. SNCC staffer and Mississippi native Sam Block "began to see the music itself as an important organizing tool" after people would approach him on the street, remembering the songs at a mass meeting more vividly than even the oratory, and asking him, "when were we going to have another meeting and sing those songs?" (Dittmer, 1994, p. 131, cited from Rachal, 2000, pp. 181–182)

In short, the following quotation vividly testifies to the influence of music and songs: "Music has been the backbone of the Freedom Movement. I dare say that freedom songs have done as much for inspiring our students . . . as all the teaching and preaching" (cited from Rachal, 2000, p. 181). Above and beyond, it is not music or songs per se, but rather the way in which people interpret them and the communicative relationships among singers or listeners that generates pertinent spiritual resonance for the movement.

Face-to-face communication preserves its political relevance in the Wukan protest, as well. Studies about protest engagement in Wukan underscore the relevance of "communal resistance" that is based upon the traditional clan or kin system, or "a relatively small-scale and enclosed social network" (He & Xue, 2014, p. S132) in China. The powerful, established social network of personal connection in the clan system embodies a collective identity, mutual trust, group norms and pressure, and cohesion and solidarity that, put together, exert significant influence on successful protest mobilization and engagement. Especially in the mobilization process, it is face-to-face communication rather than the use of ICTs that occupied a crucial role. The village leaders openly discussed their protest plans with residents. Beyond information itself, the discussion metacommunicated mutual trust, dependence, and reliability on the basis of the long-term established kin relationship, which in turn built confidence among the villagers (for detailed information, see He & Xue, 2014, p. S134; Zeng, 2013). Similar to canvassing in Freedom Summer, local women paid personal visits, household by household, to spread the decision to protest once it has been made. Again, the active engagement of women metacommunicated a strong belief in the village leadership, which consequently eliminated doubt and united the whole village (He & Xue, 2014, p. S134). Noticeably, protest organizers deliberatively avoided the use of digital media to ensure the authorities had "no way of getting their hands on any information, and they ha[d] no way of intercepting" it (Zeng, 2013, p. 35). In short, interpersonal communication within the established social network ensures the facilitation of mobilizing structures.

The Egyptian Uprising, by contrast, involves diversified forms of mobilization for different segments of the population, with one-to-one communication as the prominent channel for mobilization. Social mobilization among the young, computer-literate, like-minded population on the basis of networked, horizontal connectivity establishes solidarity through various forms of digital media (Howard & Hussain, 2013, p. 22). In this process, emotions, including frustration with, resentment toward, and anger over the regime, permeate political mobilization and unify both strong and weak network ties with a collective identity of "shared victimization" (Lim, 2012, p. 242). Still, as several scholars, especially with on-the-ground ethnographical observation, recognize, social media played "little role" (Ketchley, 2017, p. 158) in shaping the dynamics of mobilization on the ground (also see same arguments in Lynch, 2011, 2012). Above all, for the poor, the lack of sufficient digital-literate, digital media like Twitter and Facebook were the last things on their minds (Nunns & Idle, 2011, p. 22). For them, one-to-one communication, either face-to-face or via mediated means like SMS that substantially advances mobilization and recruitment among non-tech-savvy populations were of particular relevance (Rinke & Röder, 2011, p. 1279). In actuality, on the basis of trust-embedded personal networks, this kind of communication turns out to be more effective for assembling people than anonymous, fluid, and dispersed online social networks like Facebook (Rinke & Röder, 2011, p. 1278). One-to-one mobile communication via social networks of family, friends, and colleagues (Howard & Hussain, 2013, p. 22), and face-to-face communications at local mosques, churches, major squares (Aman & Jayroe, 2013, p. 321), cabs, and coffee shops, together with flyers and pamphlets (Lim, 2012, pp. 243–244), fueled the uproar on the ground. Empirical data not least illustrates the political significance of word-of-mouth and pamphlet dissemination during the Friday sermon as "an ancillary mobilizing ground" (Rinke & Röder, 2011, p. 1279) after network communications were severely hampered by the regime.

In the Arab high-context culture (Hall, 1976), the meaning lies "not in the message, but in the *relationship* between the speaker and his audience"

(Zaharna, 1995, p. 251, emphasis added) through metacommunication. In view of that, oral exchange, as the long-established, preferred Arab communication pattern, bears not so much on information transmission per se but rather acts as "a social conduit in which emotional resonance is stressed" (Zaharna, 1995, p. 246) in terms of the relationship between communicators (also see Cohen, 1987, p. 31). Consequently, the uprising implicates the process of one-to-one, *oral* communication as a key driving force of mobilization in view of "the source of trust" and emotional resonance from the spoken word (Zaharna, 1995).

Metacommunication resides not just in orality but also through protesters' physical movements and performances. During uprisings, as Ketchley observes, interpersonal fraternization performances by protestors like hugging, kissing, and shaking hands with security forces are deployed to overcome social and political heterogeneity and stimulate feelings of solidarity toward further participation even in the face of regime oppression. These exceptional intimate gestures metacommunicate messages such as "You, we have nothing against," "You, we won't attack," or "Let's be one hand [against the regime]" (Ketchley, 2017, pp. 46–77), strategically aiming to soften the antagonistic relationship between the protesters and security forces.

For the third dimension, the strategic use of media resources, including the framing of the contention, can both legitimize or de-legitimize the event, maintain its visibility, and further contribute to the diffusion of the contention that enables later struggles to learn from the experience. The case of Freedom Summer illustrates a contested picture, with mass communication being the dominate role. The Freedom School published newspapers by the students to motivate, activate, and reinforce their connections to the larger movement (Hale, 2011, p. 326). Meanwhile, the coverage and diffusion of Freedom Summer was reported mostly via national and local news agencies, with distinctive frames toward it. On the one hand, the majority of Mississippi daily newspapers expressed resistance to the civil rights activities and voiced opposition to forced desegregation as well as federal control (Weill, 2001, p. 551). This kind of impediment existed not only among white-owned newspapers but also in the only black newspaper, *The Mississippi Enterprise*, which discouraged its readers to become involved with the civil rights activities of Freedom Summer (Weill, 2001, p. 552). While few local daily newspapers covered the violence, even the deaths, that the volunteers suffered from in the campaign, most of the reporting instead adopted a hostile attitude toward the activists, virulently denouncing them as "meddlers, misfits, nitwits, and mongrels," "tramps, homosexuals and warped Communists," and "race agitators and integration zealots" (Weill, 2001, p. 555), and they characterized the project as an "invasion" of "intruders," "left-wing agitators," "carpetbaggers," "trouble makers," "integrationists," "ideological manipulators," (Rachal, 2000, p. 185), just to mention a few. The bilious frames deepened the hostility and facilitated resistance from the local populations.

On the other hand, the coverage by national media offered a marked contrast to that given by local media, which significantly consolidated the commitment among volunteers, strengthening their solidarity and (re-) establishing a sense of self-efficacy for the changes they were bringing to Mississippi. For instance, one of interviewees in McAdam's work (1988, p. 71) underscored the encouragement they have gained through national TV's coverage in a general assembly after the disappearance of Andrew Goodman, James Chaney, and Michael Schwerner, all of whom were later found to have been kidnapped and killed:

> We [volunteers] were all watching the CBS TV show . . . Walter Cronkite told how the whole country was watching Mississippi. And then the television was singing out the freedom song, "We shall overcome, we shall overcome." So we all joined hands and sang with the television. We sang with all our hearts—"justice shall be done . . . we shall vote together . . . we shall live in freedom." (McAdam, 1988, p. 71)

Just quoting part of the interview here, it still exemplifies how different frames from one-to-many mass communication, TV in this case, can motivate volunteers to devote themselves further to Freedom Summer.

To the (success of) the latter two cases, Wukan and the Egyptian Uprising, the use of ICTs as communication resources is crucial. While none of the newspapers in the Chinese mainland covered the Wukan protest due to the propaganda directive, local villagers uninterruptedly distributed their own messages and real-time records of the situation via QQ and Weibo. These distributions secured the visibility of the protest by allowing both the overseas media and the domestic population to maintain their attention to it. The villagers also established their own media center that catered to journalists (Lagerkvist, 2015, p. 142). The villagers spoke with their own voices beyond official reports, even after the police force besieged the village and took over control of its connections to the outside world. Most importantly, they kept the framing of the protest from being misled by government accounts: Villagers emphasized that they were "only protesting about the [illegal] land[-grabbing] issues" instead of the leadership of the communist party (Zeng, 2013, pp. 76, 62). These communications not only broke the censorship by authorities but also won moral support from the domestic public and international media (Hess, 2015; Lagerkvist, 2015). Furthermore, the information on social media and the coverage by overseas media generated a long-term impact on later contention, as several protests replicated the strategies in the Wukan protest (Hess, 2015, p. 24).

A similar situation occurred, but with a much more complicated picture, in the Egyptian Uprising. For one thing, mass communication and networked communication joined the struggle over framing the uprising in order to shape public opinion (Hamdy & Gomaa, 2012). State-run official and semiofficial mass media, for instance, portrayed the protesters as "incapable, misguided youths who were helpless to resist foreign influences or to formulate a strategy," described the uprising as chaotic, and attributing it to a conspiracy coming from the United States (Hamdy & Gomaa, 2012, pp. 199, 201–203). In contrast, a distinctive picture emerged from social media, which acknowledged human suffering under Mubarak's repressive policy, associated the deaths that occurred during the riots to police brutality, and placed responsibility for the uprising on the corruption, injustice, and so forth of the dictatorial regime (Hamdy & Gomaa, 2012, pp. 198–204). With a substantial sense of credibility toward its content, communication via social media fundamentally molded public opinion in society. Moreover, networked communications via Facebook, YouTube, Flickr, Twitter, to mention a few, helped sustain the visibility of the event and drew global attention—the "international buy-in" (Howard & Hussain, 2011, p. 42)—to the uprising as a revolution against authoritarianism (Howard & Hussain, 2013, pp. 57–63; Lim, 2012, pp. 243–244), despite the fact that, as studies disclose, communication on social media was used less by protesters on the ground and was predominated by English-language tweets (around 96%, see Aday et al., 2013; Wilson & Dunn, 2011) from a restricted amount of overseas accounts.

Apart from communications that structure, shape, or encourage contention in different ways, it comes as no surprise to see the control over communication asserted against the emergence of political movements in these cases. In the Egyptian Uprising, for instance, after realizing that Facebook and blogs were integral parts of the street protest, the regime almost completely shut off the internet and telecommunication services to cripple the communications and subsequent organization of its challengers (Ketchley, 2017, p. 28; Lynch, 2012, p. 90). The cutoff of "the communicative foundations of the protest movement" (Rinke & Röder, 2011, p. 1280), however, produced the opposite effect. Street protests were escalated in order to sustain communication and to meet their friends, relatives, and counterparts *face-to-face* (Lynch, 2012, pp. 90–91). Again, the clear move from online to offline exemplifies the relevance of communication, instead of technology per se, in promoting mobilization.

What we can draw from this comparative study? And, specifically, what kinds of conclusion we may draw in relation to the changes that ICTs have introduced to contentious politics? For political opportunities (see Table 6.1), ICTs—the same as mass media outlets, such as Al Jazeera in the Egyptian Uprising—would bring about changes that communicate about the opening up of political structures and opportunities, *only if* the regime fails to keep them under extensive and constrictive control. The Freedom Summer case more or less represents the situation in an open, democratic context, where information about political opportunities enjoys a certain degree of free flow, either through mass media or social movement organizations—and nowadays definitely via ICT-mediated communication. The Wukan case evidently illustrates an extreme example, in which the authoritarian regime (still) manages to suppress information about political opportunities in the digital age through its repressive policies toward mass media and sophisticated censorship of both the internet and mobile communication. Against this backdrop, face-to-face communication continues to be relevant when sharing information about political opportunities and repertoires of contention. The Egyptian Uprising, then, exemplifies a prime example of the widespread perception of the opening up of political opportunities due to the regime's lack of control over ICTs and (transnational) mass media.

As for mobilizing structures, given the embedding of trust, reliability, and reciprocity from strong-tie relationships, interpersonal and face-to-face communications sustain their remarkable roles in mobilization and recruitment in all three cases. This suggests a marked contrast to most existing studies about ICTs and political contention that acknowledge the advantage of ICTs in building ties among activists and ordinary citizens, as well as the strength of weak-tie connections from socially distant groups that are brought together for network building and the establishment of solidarity (e.g., the preparation phase in Howard & Hussain, 2011; also see Bennett & Segerberg, 2012, 2013). A plausible explanation for this contrast is that specific social and political contexts matter much more than ICTs in the consideration of the adoption and appropriation of certain kinds of communication(s) for movement emergence. For one thing, keep in mind that all three cases, as I underline already, are forms of high-risk activism. Protesters living under authoritarian regimes tend to rely upon intimate, interpersonal communication in order to draw strength from the strong ties (McAdam, 1986) of their close-knit social networks. That is to say, in the face of potential repression against mobilization, the credibility, reliability, and reciprocity from strong-tie connections would be much more efficient than anonymity (from ICT-mediated communication) to encourage participation and recruitment. For another, interpersonal communication, face-to-face interactions in particular, embodies rich cues via metacommunication in high-context cultures like China and Egypt and hence exerts a specific influence on micromobilization. This suggests the need for a careful examination of the mobilization potential of ICTs against different contexts. Future study may explore and compare, for instance, other contentions such as the Spanish "Indignado" movement or the Occupy Wallstreet movement in different contexts in terms of the high-/low-risk/cost activism frameworks.

For the framing process, ICTs do indeed bring changes. Although it would be difficult—and dangerous—to claim any revolutionary change that ICTs may bring into contentious politics, the cases do bear witness to a structural difference that is introduced by the ubiquity of ICTs: The significant change in the capacity for personal communication. As we can see it, what makes the cases of Wukan and the Egyptian Uprising different from Freedom Summer in this regard is that many-to-many communication by ICTs have had relevant roles in the last two cases. The availability and accessibility of digital devices enable ordinary people to broadcast information (in multiple forms) concerning the protests to the world with remarkable speed and with a personalized frame (Bennett, 2012; Bennett & Segerberg, 2012). This brought inevitable and irresistible attention from the public at large, the regime, and overseas media, which in turn empowered people in these two cases in ways they had not even envisioned at the outset of the protests. In a broader sense, in democratic regimes, this change may mean an advantage for the articulation of weak ties for collective or connective action (Bennett & Segerberg, 2012, 2013); while in authoritarian regimes, it signifies an expanding opportunity to facilitate communication, be it one-to-one like the voice call, or many-to-many, such as the interaction via Facebook or Twitter, which would create a better chance, either to increase the perception of political opportunities, to call up available social network resources for mobilization and recruitment, or to frame political upheaval in favor of certain aspects if it is politically expedient to do so.

By comparing Freedom Summer, the Wukan protest, and the Egyptian Uprising, this section has presented a nuanced analysis of communication and metacommunication, along with their respective contributions to political opportunities, mobilizing structures, and the framing process. The analysis demonstrates the significance of communication in political contention, or, as Benney and Marolt underlined, "citizens who have . . . communicative talents can play novel roles in social change" (2015, p. 95). It further exemplifies the analytical power of the communication-centered framework that allows us to avoid the exaggeration of the role of ICTs and to pin down their exact contributions in political contention. We may therefore conclude that the result here seems slightly divergent from some of the extant scholarship in the field. All in all, ICTs do not promise people the ability to quickly organize, but rather, they afford opportunities to frame and disseminate issues however they see fit. As Bimber (2003, p. 213) holds, "sociotechnological developments do not determine political outcomes, but instead simply alter the matrix of opportunities and costs associated with political intermediation, mobilization, and the organization of politics." To this end, it is people that take different contexts into consideration, then strategically leverage new advantages while minimizing disadvantages from ICTs for communicative, collective purpose.

Furthermore, the preliminary comparative study once again reminds us of a general issue in studying ICTs and contentious politics. In line with the suggestion in Chapter 3, even though ICTs may seem to be critical for the cascade of contentious moments nowadays, a better understanding of their use and influence necessitates a connection between contentious moments and everyday life. As we draw from all three cases, the specific, short-term manifestation of contention should not be isolated from, but rather situated back into, its everyday context for an appropriate understanding. For instance, it is "the sheer everydayness and familiarity of mobile phones" (Howard & Hussain, 2011, p. 42) among Egyptians that underlies its use in the moment of political turbulence. No matter how the perception of political opportunity changes, or the ways in which the activation of social networks for mobilization evolves, or the interpretation or manipulation of frames for influencing public opinion are enhanced, a comprehensive understanding of ICTs and contentious elements requires that ICT use be situated in its everyday context. By delving into ICT use in everyday life, we may position ourselves in a better place to envision how potential uses of mobile phones in contentions might be different in accord with different contexts.

TAKING STOCK AND MOVING MOBILE

The Danish Nobel laureate Niels Bohr reminds us that "prediction is very difficult, especially if it's about the future." So, what can we draw from the discussion so far? As the mobile phone is becoming more and more "smart," with the integration of more multifunctional and diversified applications into a single device, mobile phones are in the process of replacing other digital devices like desktops, laptops, or tablets in everyday life (Bonnington, 2015; Elgan, 2017). Given the current speed at which the mobile industry is moving forward, more and more people will become mobile-phone-first or even mobile-phone-only, a phenomenon that is already happening in some parts of the world today, such as in the migrant population in China (e.g., Qiu, 2009; Wallis, 2013) and certain African populations where their cell phones are used for almost everything in their everyday lives. The understanding of the political impact of mobile phones will certainly need to connect mobile phone users' "biographies" with their larger "histories," or institutional contexts (Mills, 2000). Meanwhile, mobile apps with multiple functions, like WeChat, further complicate the potential role in voicing dissent, as mobile phone users may—or will only need to—engage in diversified degrees of communication via the single device. As the mobile phone has been engrained into everyday life as a taken-for-granted element, the prediction we would develop concerns the mobile phone, in that it will no doubt be further embedded in politics in the near future. That is to say, communication, networking, organization, and mobilization will become ever more "mobile." Without doubt, both the government and its people evolve along the way with the ubiquity of mobile communication technology. As its pervasive use expands, compatible multiple functions develop, and ubiquitous surveillance expands, for better or worse, mobile communication is, like all other communication spheres, becoming a space in which various political interests compete for influence.

Methodological Reflections

The sensitive nature of movements and contention leaves researchers with difficulties in determining what is really happening during protest events (Archer, 2000, pp. 6–7). Most notably, "individual acts of protest" (Archer, 2000, p. 7) in movement studies are particularly lacking. To overcome this problem, what we should not neglect is that the individual's perception, choice, and action constitute an essential means by which to analyze and understand the initiation, progress, success, or failure of protest movements and contention (Jasper, 2004). Therefore, by conducting a fieldwork-based study and taking an "emic" perspective (Headland, Pike, & Harris, 1990), I explore how Chinese people perceive and use mobile phones for expression, mobilization, and coordination, thereby facilitating political contention and engagement. Furthermore, by finding out what people actually do with their mobile phones and how they actually think and behave both at the level of everyday life and at that of political contention, I am able to produce a fine-grained account of the emerging role and the political potential of the mobile phone in contemporary China.

Equally important, to maintain a neutral position as a researcher, I do not put myself into any resistant or protest activity, even if I have also received calls and text messages about some protests and demonstrations. As a Chinese researcher, for one thing, I have the advantage of already knowing how people perceive and interpret their social-political contexts, and I have been able to easily access the people I want to interview. For another, this identity reminds me to distance myself from this familiar environment in order to learn to be an "outsider." To keep an "etic" perspective in this research, I regularly question any practice that seems normal while using mobile phones. In this way, I collect as much potentially relevant data as possible and consider it in context in order to accurately describe a behavior (e.g., under what circumstances—and how—do people distribute rumors via mobile phones?) or belief (why do people distribute rumors via their mobile phones?) as an observer. In general, in my data-collection process, I keep in mind that the emic-etic concept is a dialectical interaction.

Interviewees were recruited first by identifying possible initial candidates as "seeds"; second by proceeding through snowball sampling; and third by gaining permission to interview. To foreground ethical practices, I obtained permission from interviewees in all cases. Specifically, each participant involved in data collection, focus groups, or interviews was given information on this research, including the background of the researcher, the purpose of this study, information on anonymity and confidentiality, and his or her right to withdraw from the process at any time. Because participation in contentious activities against the authorities is a politically sensitive issue in China, this study also wanted participants to be safe after participating in this research. In other words, this research actively tried not to disrupt participants' lives or cause harm. Most interviewees asked to have only their careers used as illustrated by the list of interviewees. For the rest, all individuals' names have been changed to protest their identities.

The interview guide includes (1) basic demographic information, (2) the availability of different types of media and communications, including face-to-face interactions, during contention (e.g., how did interviewees hear about the event, if they received messages from several channels of communication, which was the most important one and why), (3) the use of mobile phones in contentions, (4) the interpretation of both communication practices and information via mobile phones (e.g., do interviewees send or receive the mobilizing message via their mobile devices; if so, how do they perceive the mobilizing message on their mobiles; whether they follow it to join offline contention or not; and why), (5) how interviewees deal with mobile messages (e.g., do they disseminate the message or respond to it, to whom do they forward the message, via which channels, and why), and (6) how they perceived the role of mobile phones in general in these events.

All interviews were conducted face-to-face in friendly environments, or in socio-mental spaces that the interviewees would often inhabit or visit, and lasted between one hour and one-and-a-half hours. In all cases, the promise of anonymity was essential. In addition, I documented interviews only when the interviewee was comfortable with this. If documenting was seen as too intrusive for a candid conversation, I instead summarized the interview immediately after each session and later clarified points from interviewees. Interviewees were also assured that the information collected would be securely stored and would only be available to the researcher.

Given the complexity of relevant issues in the Chinese context, the question of validity is addressed in this research by three considerations: (a) combining historical, observational, and interview methods to gain a comprehensive picture of political activism, and (b) eliciting views from different social groups of mobile phone users in various cases to ensure that the research has integrity and adequately examines what it is intended to examine. In other words, the collection of data from multiple groups of mobile phone users in different cases allows me to replicate findings across cases and generalize conclusions in a theoretical sense.

The interviews were initially coded with an open-coding method, through which a series of key themes and sub-themes were progressively identified.

REFERENCES

Abul-Fottouh, D., & Fetner, T. (2018). Solidarity or schism: Ideological congruence and the Egyptian activists' Twitter networks. *Mobilization: An International Quarterly*, 23(1), 23–44.

Aday, S., Farrell, H., Freelon, D., Lynch, M., Sides, J., & Dewar, M. (2013). Watching from afar: Media consumption patterns around the Arab Spring. *American Behavioral Scientist*, 57(7), 899–919.

AG Reporter. (2015, March 18). Social media in the Arab world. Retrieved from https://arabiangazette.com/social-media-in-the-arab-world-2015-report/

Allagui, I. (2014). Waiting for spring: Arab resistance and change. *International Journal of Communication*, 8, 983–1007.

Allagui, I., & Kuebler, J. (2011). The Arab Spring and the role of ICTs. *International Journal of Communication*, 5, 1435–1442.

Allport, G. W., & Postman, L. J. (1947). *The psychology of rumor*. New York: Henry Holt.

Almanzar, N. P., Sullivan-Catlin, H., & Deane, G. (1998). Is the political personal? Everyday behaviors as forms of environmental movement participation. *Mobilization: An International Quarterly*, 3(2), 185–205.

Aman, M. M., & Jayroe, T. J. (2013). ICT, social media, and the Arab transition to democracy: From venting to acting. *Digest of Middle East Studies*, 22(2), 317–347.

Aminzade, R., & McAdam, D. (2002). Emotions and contentious politics. *Mobilization: An International Quarterly*, 7(2), 107–109.

Ampuja, M. (2012). Globalization theory, media-centrism and neoliberalism: A critique of recent intellectual trends. *Critical Sociology*, 38(2), 281–301.

Andrews, K. T. (2002). Movement-countermovement dynamics and the emergence of new institutions: The case of "white flight" schools in Mississippi. *Social Forces*, 80(3), 911–936.

Andrews, K. T. (2004). *Freedom is a constant struggle: The Mississippi civil rights movement and its legacy*. Chicago: University of Chicago Press.

Andrews, K. T., & Biggs, M. (2006). The dynamics of protest diffusion: Movement organizations, social networks, and news media in the 1960 sit-ins. *American Sociological Review*, 71(5), 752–777.

Anduiza, E., Cristancho, C., & Sabucedo, J. M. (2014). Mobilization through online social networks: The political protest of the indignados in Spain. *Information, Communication & Society*, 17(6), 750–764.

Anduiza, E., Jensen, M. J., & Jorba, L. (2012). *Digital media and political engagement worldwide: A comparative study.* New York: Cambridge University Press.

Anonymous. (2010). Xinjiang Internet restored after 10 months. Retrieved from http://www.farwestchina.com/2010/05/xinjiang-internet-restored-after-10-months.html

Antonucci, T. C., Fuhrer, R., & Jackson, J. S. (1990). Social support and reciprocity: A cross-ethnic and cross-national perspective. *Journal of Social and Personal Relationships, 7*(4), 519–530.

Archer, J. E. (2000). *Social unrest and popular protest in England, 1780–1840.* Cambridge: Cambridge University Press.

Arthur, C. (2014, April 27). How to keep on selling smartphones when we've nearly all got one already. *The Guardian.* Retrieved from https://www.theguardian.com/technology/2014/apr/27/smartphone-market-saturation-apple-samsung

Ayres, J. M. (1999). From the streets to the Internet: The cyber-diffusion of contention. *The Annals of the American Academy of Political and Social Science, 566*(1), 132–143.

Bai, Y. (2010). An analysis of the spread of internet rumors from the apporach of dynamics (网络流言传播的动力学机制分析). *Journalism & Communication (新闻与传播研究), 5,* 91–96.

Ball, J., & Brown, S. (2011, 7 Dec). Why BlackBerry Messenger was rioters' communication method of choice. *The Guardian.* Retrieved from https://www.theguardian.com/uk/2011/dec/07/bbm-rioters-communication-method-choice

Banerjee, A. V. (1993). The economics of rumours. *The Review of Economic Studies, 60*(2), 309–327.

Barbalet, J. (2014). The structure of *guanxi*: Resolving problems of network assurance. *Theory and Society, 43*(1), 51–69.

Barbalet, J. (2015). *Guanxi,* tie strength, and network attributes. *American Behavioral Scientist, 59*(8), 1038–1050.

Barboza, D., & Bradsher, K. (2010, June 16). In China, labor movement enabled by technology. *The New York Times,* p. B1.

Barlow, J. P. (1996). A declaration of the independence of cyberspace. Retrieved from https://www.eff.org/cyberspace-independence

Baumgarten, B., Daphi, P., & Ullrich, P. (Eds.). (2014). *Conceptualizing culture in social movement Research.* London: Palgrave Macmillan.

BBC. (2014, April 4). China Maoming environmental protest violence condemned. Retrieved from http://www.bbc.com/news/world-asia-china-26849814

Bedford, O., & Hwang, K. K. (2003). Guilt and shame in Chinese culture: A cross-cultural framework from the perspective of morality and identity. *Journal for the Theory of Social Behaviour, 33*(2), 127–144.

Beinin, J., & Vairel, F. (Eds.). (2013). *Social movements, mobilization, and contestation in the Middle East and North Africa.* Stanford: Stanford University Press.

Bekkers, V., Beunders, H., Edwards, A., & Moody, R. (2011). New media, micromobilization, and political agenda setting: Crossover effects in political mobilization and media usage. *The Information Society, 27*(4), 209–219.

Bekkers, V., Moody, R., & Edwards, A. (2011). Micro-mobilization, social media and coping strategies: Some Dutch experiences. *Policy & Internet, 3*(4), 1–29.

Benford, R. D. (1993a). Frame disputes within the nuclear disarmament movement. *Social Forces, 71*(3), 677–701.

Benford, R. D. (1993b). You could be the hundredth monkey. *The Sociological Quarterly, 34*(2), 195–216.

Benford, R. D. (1997). An insider's critique of the social movement framing perspective. *Sociological Inquiry, 67*(4), 409–430.

Benford, R. D., & Snow, D. A. (2000). Framing processes and social movements: An overview and assessment. *Annual Review of Sociology, 26*, 611–639.

Bennett, W. L. (2003). Communicating global activism: Strengths and vulnerabilities of networked politics. *Information, Communication & Society, 6*(2), 143–168.

Bennett, W. L. (2005). Social movements beyond borders: Understanding two eras of transnational activism. In D. della Porta & S. Tarrow (Eds.), *Transnational protest and global activism* (pp. 203–226). Lanham, MD: Rowman & Littlefield.

Bennett, W. L. (2012). The personalization of politics: Political identity, social media, and changing patterns of participation. *The Annals of the American Academy of Political and Social Science, 644*(1), 20–39.

Bennett, W. L., Breunig, C., & Givens, T. (2008). Communication and political mobilization: Digital media and the organization of anti-Iraq war demonstrations in the U.S. *Political Communication, 25*(3), 269–289.

Bennett, W. L., & Segerberg, A. (2012). The logic of connective action: Digital media and the personalization of contentious politics. *Information, Communication & Society, 15*(5), 739–768.

Bennett, W. L., & Segerberg, A. (2013). *The logic of connective action: Digital media and the personalization of contentious politics.* Cambridge: Cambridge University Press.

Bennett, W. L., & Segerberg, A. (2015). Communication in movements. In D. Della Porta & M. Diani (Eds.), *The Oxford Handbook of Social Movements* (pp. 367–383). Oxford: Oxford University Press.

Benney, J., & Marolt, P. (2015). Introduction: Modes of activism and engagement in the Chinese public sphere. *Asian Studies Review, 39*(1), 88–99.

Berenson, B. (1952). *Rumor and reflection.* New York: Simon and Schuster.

Berinsky, A. J. (2015). Rumors and health care reform: Experiments in political misinformation. *British Journal of Political Science, 47*(2) 1–22.

Bian, Y. (1994). *Guanxi* and the allocation of jobs in urban China. *The China Quarterly, 140*, 971–999.

Bian, Y. (1997). Bringing strong ties back in: Indirect ties, network bridges, and job searches in China. *American Sociological Review, 62*(3), 366–385.

Bian, Y. (2017). The comparative significance of guanxi. *Management and Organization Review, 13*(2), 261–267.

Bian, Y. (2018). The prevalence and the increasing significance of guanxi. *The China Quarterly, 235*, 597–621.

Bian, Y., & Ang, S. (1997). Guanxi networks and job mobility in China and Singapore. *Social Forces, 75*(3), 981–1005.

Bimber, B. (2003). *Information and American democracy: Technology in the evolution of political power.* Cambridge: Cambridge University Press.

Bimber, B. (2017). Three prompts for collective action in the context of digital media. *Political Communication, 34*(1), 6–20.

Bimber, B., Flanagin, A., & Stohl, C. (2012). *Collective action in organizations: Interaction and engagement in an era of technological change.* Cambridge: Cambridge University Press.

Bimber, B., Flanagin, A. J., & Stohl, C. (2005). Reconceptualizing collective action in the contemporary media environment. *Communication Theory, 15*(4), 365–388.

Blake, A. (2017, February 24). Donald Trump's fake case against the "fake news media." *The Washington Post.* Retrieved from https://www.washingtonpost.

com/news/the-fix/wp/2017/02/24/donald-trumps-fake-case-against-the-fake-news-media/?noredirect=on&utm_term=.36e8aba21853

Blumer, H. (1954). What is wrong with social theory? *American Sociological Review*, *19*(1), 3–10.

Boekkooi, M., & Klandermans, B. (2013). Micro-meso mobilization. In D. A. Snow, D. della Porta, B. Klandermans, & D. McAdam (Eds.), *The Wiley-Blackwell encyclopedia of social and political movements.* Retrieved from: https://onlinelibrary.wiley.com/doi/abs/10.1002/9780470674871.wbespm129

Bommel, J. V. (2003). Rumors. *The Journal of Finance, 58*(4), 1499–1520.

Bond, M. H., & Hwang, K.-k. (1986). The social psychology of Chinese people. In M. H. Bond (Ed.), *The Psychology of the Chinese people* (pp. 213–266). New York: Oxford University Press.

Bond, R. M., Fariss, C. J., Jones, J. J., Kramer, A. D., Marlow, C., Settle, J. E., & Fowler, J. H. (2012). A 61-million-person experiment in social influence and political mobilization. *Nature, 489*(7415), 295.

Bonnell, V. E. (1983). *Roots of rebellion: Workers' politics and organizations in St. Petersburg and Moscow, 1900–1914.* California: University of California Press.

Bonnington, C. (2015, 2 October). In less than two years, a smartphone could be your only computer. *Wired.* Retrieved from https://www.wired.com/2015/02/smartphone-only-computer/

Bordia, P., & DiFonzo, N. (2002). When social psychology became less social: Prasad and the history of rumor research. *Asian Journal of Social Psychology, 5*(1), 49–61.

Bordia, P., & DiFonzo, N. (2004). Problem solving in social interactions on the Internet: Rumor as social cognition. *Social Psychology Quarterly, 67*(1), 33–49.

Bourdieu, P. (1984). *Distinction: A social critique of the judgement of taste* (R. Nice, Trans.). Cambridge, MA: Harvard University Press.

Bourdieu, P. (2000). The politics of protest. An interview by Kevin Ovenden. *Socialist Review, 242,* 18–20.

Boyle, M. P., & Schmierbach, M. (2009). Media use and protest: The role of mainstream and alternative media use in predicting traditional and protest participation. *Communication Quarterly, 57*(1), 1–17.

Brady, A.-M. (2009). Mass persuasion as a means of legitimation and China's popular authoritarianism. *American Behavioral Scientist, 53*(3), 434–457.

Branigan, T. (2008, November 24). China taxi drivers strike as economic unrest spreads. *The Guardian.* Retrieved from http://www.guardian.co.uk/world/2008/nov/24/china-taxis

Branigan, T. (2012). China cut off Internet in area of Tibetan unrest. *The Guardian.* Retrieved from http://www.guardian.co.uk/world/2012/feb/03/china-internet-links-tibetan-unrest

Brummette, J., DiStaso, M., Vafeiadis, M., & Messner, M. (2018). Read all about it: The Politicization of "fake news" on Twitter. *Journalism & Mass Communication Quarterly, 95*(2), 497–517.

Buckley, C. (2018, June 26). Marching across China, army veterans join ranks of protesters. *The New York Times,* p. A11.

Buckner, H. T. (1965). A theory of rumor transmission. *Public Opinion Quarterly, 29*(1), 54–70.

Buechler, S. M. (2000). *Social movements in advanced capitalism: The political economy and cultural construction of social activism.* Oxford: Oxford University Press.

Buxi. (2008). Weng'an riots: How the state media hurts China. Retrieved from http://blog.foolsmountain.com/2008/07/02/wengan-how-the-state-media-hurts-china/

Cammaerts, B. (2012). Protest logics and the mediation opportunity structure. *European Journal of Communication, 27*(2), 117–134.

Cammaerts, B., Mattoni, A., & McCurdy, P. (2013). *Mediation and protest movements*. Bristol: Intellect Books.

Campbell, S. W., & Kwak, N. (2010). Mobile communication and civic life: Linking patterns of use to civic and political engagement. *Journal of Communication, 60*(3), 536–555.

Campbell, S. W., & Kwak, N. (2011). Political involvement in "mobilized" society: The interactive relationships among mobile communication, network characteristics, and political participation. *Journal of Communication, 61*(6), 1005–1024.

Campbell, S. W., & Kwak, N. (2012). Mobile communication and strong network ties: Shrinking or expanding spheres of public discourse? *New Media & Society, 14*(2), 262–280.

Campbell, S. W., & Park, Y. J. (2008). Social implications of mobile telephony: The rise of personal communication society. *Sociology Compass, 2*(2), 371–387.

Campbell, S. W., & Russo, T. C. (2003). The social construction of mobile telephony: An application of the social influence model to perceptions and uses of mobile phones within personal communication networks. *Communication Monographs, 70*(4), 317–334.

Cao, Y. (2014, April 17). 3 years in jail for online rumors. *China Daily*. Retrieved from http://www.chinadaily.com.cn/china/2014-04/17/content_17440561.htm

Caplow, T. (1947). Rumors in war. *Social Forces, 25*(3), 298–302.

Carey, J. W. (2008). *Communication as culture: Essays on media and society (revised edition)*. London: Routledge.

Castells, M. (2007). Communication, power and counter-power in the network society. *International Journal of Communication, 1*, 238–266.

Castells, M. (2009). *Communication power*. Oxford: Oxford University Press.

Castells, M. (2010). *The power of identity* (2rd ed.). Malden, Mass.: Blackwell.

Castells, M. (2012). *Networks of outrage and hope: Social movements in the internet age*. Cambridge: Polity.

Castells, M., Fernandez-Ardevol, M., Qiu, J. L., & Sey, A. (2007). *Mobile communication and society: A global perspective*. Cambridge, MA: The MIT Press.

Center for Public Opinion Monitor. (2014). To guide the public opion toward PX project in the Maoming protest. *Public Opinion on Politics and Law, 114*(14), 3–8.

Chadwick, A. (2013). *The Hybrid Media System: Politics and power*. Oxford: Oxford University Press.

Chai, Y. (2011). Speech up the Internet and mobile phone real-name registration system (加快推行网络手机实名制). Retrieved from http://www.china.com.cn/2011/2011-03/05/content_22074147.htm

Chan, C. S.-c. (2009). Invigorating the content in social embeddedness: An ethnography of life insurance transactions in China. *American Journal of Sociology, 115*(3), 712–754.

Chang, M. (2013, May 17). Thousands protest Kunming PX plan. *Global Times*. Retrieved from http://www.globaltimes.cn/content/782252.shtml#.UvvahOJdVW4

Chang, T.-K., Wang, J., & Chen, C.-H. (1994). News as social knowledge in China: The changing worldview of Chinese national media. *Journal of Communication*, 44(3), 52–69.

Chen, H., & Jiang, H. (2003, February 13). Guangzhou against unknown viruses. *Southern Weekend*, p. A1.

Chen, H., Lu, Y. K., & Suen, W. (2016). The power of whispers: A theory of rumor, communication, and revolution. *International Economic Review*, 57(1), 89–116.

Chen, L. (2011, June 25). China's Weibo fever needs to be checked. *China Daily*, p. 6.

Chen, T. (2015). 2.1 million WeChat "false rumors" deleted daily. Retrieved from https://walkthechat.com/centership-of-wechat-rumors-on-wechat-2-1million-rumors-deleated-daily/

Chen, Y. (2011). Give online rumor spreaders a fierce head-on attack. Retrieved from http://opinion.people.com.cn/GB/16456190.html

Cheng, L., & Rosett, A. (1991). Contract with a Chinese face: Socially embedded factors in the transformation from hierarchy to market, 1978–1989. *Journal of Chinese Law*, 5(2), 143–244.

Cheng, Y. (2011). The rumor debate. Retrieved from http://zonaeuropa.com/201107a.brief.htm

China Daily. (2009, July 29). Another mass incident? *China Daily*, p. 8.

China Daily. (2010a, April 23). Around China: Taxi drivers go on strike. *China Daily*, p. 7.

China Daily. (2010b). Special issue on earthquake bureau refusing the earthquake rumors. *China Daily*. Retrieved from http://www.chinadaily.com.cn/micro-reading/mfeed/hotwords/20100415902.html

China Daily. (2014). Stop rumors spreading via WeChat. *China Daily*. Retrieved from http://europe.chinadaily.com.cn/opinion/2014-08/08/content_18270359.htm

China Digital Times. (2014, April 4). "Taking a walk" to protest chemical plant in Guangdong. *Huffington Post*. Retrieved from http://www.huffingtonpost.com/2014/04/14/china-chemical-protest_n_5143790.html

China in Pictures. (2009). The taxi strike in Yueyang. Retrieved from http://chinapic.people.com.cn/frame.php?frameon=yes&referer=http%3A//chinapic.people.com.cn/viewthread.php%3Ftid%3D41378

China Internet Network Information Center (CNNIC). (2014). *The 33nd Statistical Report on Internet Development*. Retrieved from http://www.cnnic.net.cn/hlwfzyj/hlwxzbg/hlwtjbg/201401/P020140116395418429515.pdf

China Mobile. (2007, September). Construction of information society. Retrieved from http://www.chinamobile.com/aboutus/res/2007cr_cn/09/090201.htm

China Radio International. (2010). *The Peoples's Daily* calls for resisting online rumor. Retrieved from http://www.scio.gov.cn/ztk/hlwxx/07/4/Document/1022277/1022277.htm

China Youth Daily. (2012). Online rumor proliferates, how can we look on and do nothing. *China Youth Daily*. Retrieved from http://www.chinanews.com/it/2012/12-30/4448400.shtml

China Youth International. (2011). Surfling online *jianghu* (江湖), be careful not to on board the pirate ship of "rumor." Retrieved from http://news.youth.cn/jrht/201112/t20111221_1823183.htm

Christensen, C. (2011). Twitter revolutions? Addressing social media and dissent. *The Communication Review*, 14(3), 155–157.

Christensen, H. S. (2011). Political activities on the Internet: Slacktivism or political participation by other means? *First Monday*, *16*(2), Retrieved from https://firstmonday.org/ojs/index.php/fm/article/view/3336/2767

Christensen, K., & Levinson, D. (2003). Guanxi. In K. Christensen & D. Levinson (Eds.), *Encyclopedia of community: From the village to the virtual world* (pp. 572–574). London: Sage.

Chu, R. W.-c., Fortunati, L., Law, P.-l., & Yang, S. (2012). *Mobile communication and greater China*. London: Routledge.

Chu, W.-c., & Yang, S. (2006). Mobile phones and new migrant workers in a south China village: An initial analysis of the interplay between the "social" and the "technological." In P. Luo, L. Fortunati, & S. Yang (Eds.), *New technologies in global societies* (pp. 221–244). Singapore: World Scientific Publishing.

Clark, D. (2018). China: Mobile usage will overtake TV this year. *eMarketer*. Retrieved from https://newsroom.emarketer.com/newsroom/index.php/2018/04/

Cody, F. (2016). The obligation to act: Gender and reciprocity in political mobilization. *HAU: Journal of Ethnographic Theory*, *6*(3), 179–199.

Cohen, P. A., & Townsend, P. A. (1997). *History in three keys: The Boxers as event, experience, and myth*. New York: Columbia University Press.

Cohen, R. (1987). Problems of intercultural communication in Egyptian-American diplomatic relations. *International Journal of Intercultural Relations*, *11*(1), 29–47.

Colby, D. (1987). White violence and the civil rights movement. In T. A. Baker, L. W. Moreland, & R. P. Steed (Eds.), *Blacks in southern politics* (pp. 31–48). Santa Barbara, CA: Praeger.

Corcoran, K. E., Pettinicchio, D., & Young, J. T. (2011). The context of control: A cross-national investigation of the link between political institutions, efficacy, and collective action. *British Journal of Social Psychology*, *50*(4), 575–605.

Costanza-Chock, S. (2003). Mapping the repertoire of electronic contention. In A. Opel & D. Pompper (Eds.), *Representing resistance: Media, civil disobedience and the global justice movement* (pp. 173–191). Greenwood, NJ: Greenwood.

Costanza-Chock, S. (2012). Mic check! Media cultures and the Occupy movement. *Social Movement Studies*, *11*(3–4), 375–385.

Couldry, N., Rodriguez, C., Bolin, G., Cohen, J., Volkmer, I., Goggin, G., . . . Wasserman, H. (2018). Media, communication and the struggle for social progress. *Global Media and Communication*, *14*(2), 173–191.

Craig, R. T. (1999). Communication theory as a field. *Communication Theory*, *9*(2), 119–161.

Crossley, N. (2002a). *Making sense of social movements*. Buckingham: Open University Press.

Crossley, N. (2002b). Repertoires of contention and tactical diversity in the UK psychiatric survivors movement: The question of appropriation. *Social Movement Studies*, *1*(1), 47–71.

Crossley, N. (2003). From reproduction to transformation: Social movement fields and the radical habitus. *Theory, Culture & Society*, *20*(6), 43–68.

Custer, C. (2014, Feburary 4). The demise of Sina Weibo: Censorship or evolution? *Forbes*. Retrieved from https://www.forbes.com/sites/ccuster/2014/02/04/the-demise-of-sina-weibo-censorship-or-evolution/

Dahl, R. A. (1998). *On democracy*. New Haven: Yale University Press.

Dahlberg, L. (2011). Re-constructing digital democracy: An outline of four "positions." *New Media & Society*, *13*(6), 855–872.

Dalton, R., Van Sickle, A., & Weldon, S. (2010). The individual-institutional nexus of protest behaviour. *British Journal of Political Science, 40*(1), 51–73.

Dalziel, G. (Ed.) (2013). *Rumor and communication in Asia in the Internet age.* London: Routledge.

Davies, G. (2012). Discontent in digital China. In G. R. Barmé, J. Goldkorn, C. Cartier, & G. Davies (Eds.), *China Story Yearbook 2012* (pp. 126–145). Canberra: The Australian National University.

Davis, J. L., & Chouinard, J. B. (2016). Theorizing affordances: From request to refuse. *Bulletin of Science, Technology & Society, 36*(4), 241–248.

Davies, H., Leung, T. K., Luk, S. T., & Wong, Y.-h. (1995). The benefits of "Guanxi": The value of relationships in developing the Chinese market. *Industrial Marketing Management, 24*(3), 207–214.

de Certeau, M. (1984). *The practice of everyday life.* Berkeley: University of California Press.

De Fleub, M. L. (1962). Mass communication and the study of rumor. *Sociological Inquiry, 32*(1), 51–70.

Deacon, D., & Stanyer, J. (2014). Mediatization: Key concept or conceptual bandwagon? *Media, Culture & Society, 36*(7), 1032–1044.

Deleuze, G., & Guattari, F. (1987). A thousand plateaus (Brian Massumi, Trans.). Minneapolis: University of Minnesota Press.

Della Porta, D. (2011). Communications in movements: Social movement as agents of participatory democracy. *Information, Comunication & Society, 14*(6), 800–819.

Della Porta, D. (2013). Repertoires of contention. In D. A. Snow, D. della Porta, B. Klandermans, & D. McAdam (Eds.), *The Wiley-Blackwell Encyclopedia of Social and Political Movements.* Retrieved from https://onlinelibrary.wiley.com/doi/10.1002/9780470674871.wbespm178

Della Porta, D., & Mosca, L. (2005). Global-net for global movements? A network of networks for a movement of movements. *Journal of Public Policy, 25*(1), 165–190.

Deng, Y., & O'Brien, K. J. (2013). Relational repression in China: Using social ties to demobilize protesters. *The China Quarterly, 215,* 533–552.

Dewey, J. (2004). *Democracy and education.* New York: Courier Corporation.

Diamond, L. (2010). Liberation technology. *Journal of Democracy, 21*(3), 69–83.

Diamond, L., & Plattner, M. F. (2012). *Liberation technology: Social media and the struggle for democracy.* Baltimore: Johns Hopkins University Press.

Diani, M. (1992). The concept of social movement. *The Sociological Review, 40*(1), 1–25.

Diani, M. (2000). Social movement networks: Virtual and real. *Information, Communication & Society, 3*(3), 386–401.

Diani, M., & McAdam, D. (Eds.). (2003). *Social movements and networks: Relational approaches to collective action.* New York: Oxford University Press.

DiFonzo, N., & Bordia, P. (2007a). Rumor, gossip and urban legends. *Diogenes, 54*(1), 19–35.

DiFonzo, N., & Bordia, P. (2007b). Trust and organizational rumor transmission. In N. DiFonzo & P. Bordia (Eds.), *Rumor psychology: Social and organizational approaches* (pp. 185–204). Washington, DC: American Psychological Association.

DiFonzo, N., & Bordia, P. (Eds.). (2007c). *Rumor psychology: Social and organizational approaches.* Washington, DC: American Psychological Association.

Ding, B. (2008, July 10). Weng'an, an unpeaceful county city. *Southern Weekend,* p. A1.

Dong, D., Chang, T.-K., & Chen, D. (2008). Reporting AIDS and the invisible victims in China: Official knowledge as news in *the People's Daily*, 1986–2002. *Journal of Health Communication*, *13*(4), 357–374.

Dong, S. (2017). The Cybersecurity Law launched yesterday, targeting at phishing websites, telecommunication fraud, and rumor diffusion, etc. *Yanzhao Evening News*. Retrieved from http://he.xinhuanet.com/hbGongyi/20170602/3718284_c.html

Donovan, P. (2007). How idle is idle talk? One hundred years of rumor research. *Diogenes*, *54*(1), 59–82.

Downing, J. (2008). Social movement theories and alternative media: An evaluation and critique. *Communication, Culture & Critique*, *1*(1), 40–50.

Dresner, E., & Herring, S. C. (2010). Functions of the nonverbal in CMC: Emoticons and illocutionary force. *Communication Theory*, *20*(3), 249–268.

Earl, J. (2010). The dynamics of protest-related diffusion on the Web. *Information, Communication & Society*, *13*(2), 209–225.

Earl, J., & Garrett, R. K. (2017). The new information frontier: Toward a more nuanced view of social movement communication. *Social Movement Studies*, *16*(4), 479–493.

Earl, J., Hunt, J., & Garrett, R. K. (2014). Social movements and the ICT revolution. In H.-A. van der Heijden (Ed.), *Handbook of political citizenship and social movements* (pp. 359–386). Cheltenham: Edward Elgar.

Earl, J., & Kimport, K. (2011). *Digitally enabled social change: Activism in the Internet age*. Cambridge, MA: The MIT Press.

Earl, J., Kimport, K., Prieto, G., Rush, C., & Reynoso, K. (2010). Changing the world one webpage at a time: Conceptualizing and explaining Internet activism. *Mobilization: An International Quarterly*, *15*(4), 425–446.

EChinacities.com. (2010). Taxis go on strike in Shenzhen. Retrieved from http://www.echinacities.com/shenzhen/city-in-pulse/taxis-go-on-strike-in-shenzhen.html

Economist. (2014, Jannary 18). From Weibo to WeChat. *Economist*. Retrieved from https://www.economist.com/china/2014/01/18/from-weibo-to-wechat

Economist. (2016, August 6). WeChat's world. *Economist*. Retrieved from https://www.economist.com/business/2016/08/06/wechats-world

Egros, A. (2011). *Social media usage across cultures*. Retrieved from https://www.compukol.com/social-media-usage-across-cultures/

Eisenstein, E. L. (1980). *The printing press as an agent of change*. Cambridge: Cambridge University Press.

Eisinger, P. K. (1973). The conditions of protest behavior in American cities. *American Political Science Review*, *67*(1), 11–28.

Elegant, S. (2008). China's taxi strikes: A test for the government. *Time*. Retrieved from http://www.time.com/time/world/article/0,8599,1862718,00.html

Elgan, M. (2017, Dec. 9). With smartphones like these, why do we need laptops? *Computer World*. Retrieved from https://www.computerworld.com/article/3241233/smartphones/with-smartphones-like-these-why-do-we-need-laptops.html

Ellingson, S. (1995). Understanding the dialectic of discourse and collective action: Public debate and rioting in antebellum Cincinnati. *American Journal of Sociology*, *101*(1), 100–144.

Eltantawy, N., & Wiest, J. B. (2011). Social media in the Egyptian revolution: Reconsidering resource mobilization theory. *International Journal of Communication, 5,* 1207–1224.

Enjolras, B., Steen-Johnsen, K., & Wollebæk, D. (2013). Social media and mobilization to offline demonstrations: Transcending participatory divides? *New Media & Society, 15*(6), 890–908.

Entman, R. M. (1993). Framing: Toward clarification of a fractured paradigm. *Journal of Communication, 43*(4), 51–58.

Erlanger, S. (2017, December 13). Globe's autocrats echo Trump's "fake news cry." *The New York Times,* p. A1.

Evans, S. K., Pearce, K. E., Vitak, J., & Treem, J. W. (2017). Explicating affordances: A conceptual framework for understanding affordances in communication research. *Journal of Computer-Mediated Communication, 22*(1), 35–52.

Farh, J.-L., Tsui, A. S., Xin, K., & Cheng, B.-S. (1998). The influence of relational demography and guanxi: The Chinese case. *Organization Science, 9*(4), 471–488.

Fei, X. (1992). *From the soil: The foundations of Chinese society.* Berkeley: University of California Press.

Fenton, N., & Barassi, V. (2011). Alternative media and social networking sites: The politics of individuation and political participation. *The Communication Review, 14*(3), 179–196.

Fernandez, R., & McAdam, D. (1989). Multiorganizational fields and recruitment to social movements. In B. Klandermans (Ed.), *Organizing for change: Social movement organizations in Europe and the United States* (pp. 315–343). Greenwich, CT: JAI Press.

Fernandez, R. M., & McAdam, D. (1988). Social networks and social movements: Multiorganizational fields and recruitment to Mississippi Freedom Summer. *Sociological Forum, 3*(3), 357–382.

Festinger, L., Cartwright, D., Barber, K., Fleischl, J., Gottsdanker, J., Keysen, A., & Leavitt, G. (1948). A study of a rumor: Its origin and spread. *Human Relations, 1,* 464–485.

Fitzpatrick, S. (1996). *Stalin's peasants: Resistance and survival in the Russian village after collectivization.* Oxford: Oxford University Press.

Flam, H. (2015). Micromobilization and emotions. In D. della Porta & M. Diani (Eds.), *The Oxford handbook of social movements* (pp. 264–276). Oxford: Oxford University Press.

Flam, H., & King, D. (2005). Introduction. In H. Flam & D. King (Eds.), *Emotions and social movements* (pp. 1–18). London: Routledge.

Flanagin, A. J., Stohl, C., & Bimber, B. (2006). Modeling the structure of collective action. *Communication Monographs, 73*(1), 29–54.

Forsythe, M. (2011). China calls for Internet crackdown after "prostitute diary" shut. Retrieved from http://www.bloomberg.com/news/2011-10-01/china-calls-for-internet-crackdown-after-prostitute-diary-blog-is-shut.html

Freelon, D., McIlwain, C., & Clark, M. (2018). Quantifying the power and consequences of social media protest. *New Media & Society, 20*(3), 990–1011.

Friedman, D., & McAdam, D. (1992). Collective identity and activism: Networks, choices, and the life of a social movement. In A. D. Morris & C. M. Mueller (Eds.), *Frontiers in social movement theory* (pp. 156–173). New Haven: Yale University Press.

Funkhouser, G. R. (1973). The issues of the sixties: An exploratory study in the dynamics of public opinion. *Public Opinion Quarterly, 37*(1), 62–75.

Garrison, W. A. (1992). The social psychology of collective action. In A. D. Morris & C. M. Mueller (Eds.), *Frontiers in social movement theory* (pp. 53–76). New Haven: Yale University Press.

Gamson, W. A., & Meyer, D. S. (1996). Framing political opportunity. In D. McAdam, J. D. McCarthy, & M. N. Zald (Eds.), *Comparative perspectives on social movements, political opportunities, mobilizing structures, and cultural framings* (pp. 275–290). Cambridge: Cambridge University Press.

Gamson, W. A., & Wolfsfeld, G. (1993). Movements and media as interacting systems. *The Annals of the American Academy of Political and Social Science, 528*, 114–125.

Ganesh, S., & Stohl, C. (2013). From Wall Street to Wellington: Protests in an era of digital ubiquity. *Communication Monographs, 80*(4), 425–451.

Garrett, R. K. (2006). Protest in an information society: A review of literature on social movements and new ICTs. *Information, Communication and Society, 9*(2), 202–224.

Garrett, R. K. (2011). Troubling consequences of online political rumoring. *Human Communication Research, 37*(2), 255–274.

Garrison, W. A. (1992). The social psychology of collective action. In A. D. Morris & C. M. Mueller (Eds.), *Frontiers in social movement theory* (pp. 53–76). New Haven: Yale University Press.

Geertz, C. (1983). *Further essays in interpretive anthropology*. New York: Basic Books.

Gerbaudo, P. (2012). *Tweets and the streets: Social media and contemporary activism*. London: Pluto Press.

Gerbaudo, P. (2014). The persistence of collectivity in digital protest. *Information, Communication & Society, 17*(2), 264–268.

Gergen, K. J. (2002). The challenge of absent presence. In J. E. Katz & M. Aakhus (Eds.), *Perpetual Contact: Mobile communication, private talk, public performance* (pp. 227–241). Cambridge: Cambridge University Press.

Gergen, K. J. (2008). Mobile communication and the transformation of the democratic process. In J. E. Katz (Ed.), *Handbook of mobile communication studies* (pp. 297–310). Cambridge, MA: The MIT Press.

Gerhards, J., & Rucht, D. (1992). Mesomobilization: Organizing and framing in two protest campaigns in West Germany. *American Journal of Sociology, 98*(3), 555–596.

Gershon, I. (2010). Media ideologies: An introduction. *Journal of Linguistic Anthropology, 20*(2), 283–293.

Gibson, J. J. (1966). *The senses considered as perceptual systems*. Boston: Houghton Mifflin.

Gibson, J. J. (1977). The theory of affordances. In R. Shaw & J. Bransford (Eds.), *Perceiving, acting, and knowing: Toward an ecological psychology* (pp. 67–82). Hillsdale, NJ: Lawrence Erlbaum.

Gil de Zúñiga, H., & Valenzuela, S. (2011). The mediating path to a stronger citizenship: Online and offline networks, weak ties, and civic engagement. *Communication Research, 38*(3), 397–421.

Givan, R. K., Roberts, K. M., & Soule, S. A. (2010). *The diffusion of social movements: Actors, mechanisms, and political effects*. Cambridge: Cambridge University Press.

Gladwell, M. (2010). Small change. *The New Yorker, 4*, 42–49.

Gladwell, M., & Shirky, C. (2011). From innovation to revolution: Do social media make protests possible? *Foreign Affairs, 90*(2), 153–154.

Gleason, B. (2013). # Occupy Wall Street: Exploring informal learning about a social movement on Twitter. *American Behavioral Scientist*, 57(7), 966–982.

Goffman, E. (1974). *Frame analysis: An essay on the organization of experience.* Cambridge: Harvard University Press.

Goffman, E. (2008). *Interaction ritual: Essays in face to face behavior.* New Brunswick, NJ: Aldine Transaction.

Goggin, G. (2013). Democratic affordances: Politics, media, and digital technology after WikiLeaks. *Ethical Space*, 10(2/3), 6–14.

Gold, T., Guthrie, D., & Wank, D. (2002a). An introduction to the study of guanxi. In T. Gold, D. Guthrie, & D. Wank (Eds.), *Social connections in China: Institutions, culture, and the changing nature of guanxi* (pp. 3–20). Cambridge: Cambridge University Press.

Gold, T., Guthrie, D., & Wank, D. (2002b). *Social connections in China: Institutions, culture, and the changing nature of guanxi.* Cambridge: Cambridge University Press.

Goldstone, J. A. (1991). Ideology, cultural frameworks, and the process of revolution. *Theory and Society*, 20(4), 405–453.

Goldstone, J. A. (2004). More social movements or fewer? Beyond political opportunity structures to relational fields. *Theory and Society*, 33(3–4), 333–365.

González-Bailón, S., Borge-Holthoefer, J., Rivero, A., & Moreno, Y. (2011). The dynamics of protest recruitment through an online network. *Scientific Reports*, 1, 197.

Goodwin, J., & Jasper, J. M. (1999). Caught in a winding, snarling vine: The structural bias of political process theory. *Sociological Forum*, 14(1), 27–54.

Goodwin, J., & Jasper, J. M. (2004). *Rethinking social movements: Structure, meaning, and emotion.* London: Rowman & Littlefield.

Goodwin, J., & Jasper, J. (2006). Emotions and social movements. In J. E. Stets & J. H. Turner (Eds.), *Handbook of the Sociology of Emotions* (pp. 611–635). New York: Springer.

Goodwin, J., Jasper, J. M., & Polletta, F. (Eds.). (2009). *Passionate politics, emotions and social movements.* Chicago: University of Chicago Press.

Google. (2018). Consumer barometer. Retrieved from https://www.consumerbarometer.com/en/trending/ ?countryCode=CN&category=TRN-NOFILTER-ALL

Gould, R. V. (1991). Multiple networks and mobilization in the Paris Commune, 1871. *American Sociological Review*, 56(6), 716–729.

Gould, R. V. (1993). Collective action and network structure. *American Sociological Review*, 58(2), 182–196.

Gould, R. V. (1995). *Insurgent identities: Class, community, and protest in Paris from 1848 to the Commune.* Chicago: University of Chicago Press.

Gould, R. V. (2003). Why do networks matter? Rationalist and structuralist interpretations. In M. Diani & D. McAdam (Eds.), *Social movements and networks: Relational approaches to collective action* (pp. 234–257). Oxford; New York: Oxford University Press.

Gouldner, A. W. (1960). The norm of reciprocity: A preliminary statement. *American Sociological Review*, 25(2), 161–178.

Granovetter, M. (1973). The strength of weak ties. *American Journal of Sociology*, 78(6), 1360–1380.

Graves, L. (2007). The affordances of blogging: A case study in culture and technological effects. *Journal of Communication Inquiry, 31*(4), 331–346.

Grof, S. (1981). Nature, mind, and consciousness: Gregory Bateson and the new paradigm. *Journal of Transpersonal Psychology, 5/2/31, 72.*

Gudykunst, W. B. (1997). Cultural variability in communication: An introduction. *Communication Research, 24*(4), 327–348.

Gudykunst, W. B., & Lee, C. M. (2005). Theorizing about intercultural communication. In W. B. Gudykunst & B. Mody (Eds.), *Handbook of international and intercultural communication* (pp. 25–50). Thousand Oaks, CA: Sage.

Hachigian, N., & Wu, L. (2003). The information revolution in Asia. Retrieved from http://www.rand.org/pubs/monograph_reports/MR1719.html

Hale, J. (2011). "The student as a force for social change": The Mississippi freedom schools and student engagement. *The Journal of African American History, 96*(3), 325–347.

Hall, E. T. (1976). *Beyond culture.* New York: Doubleday.

Halupka, M. (2014). Clicktivism: A systematic heuristic. *Policy & Internet, 6*(2), 115–132.

Hamdy, N., & Gomaa, E. H. (2012). Framing the Egyptian uprising in Arabic language newspapers and social media. *Journal of Communication, 62*(2), 195–211.

Han, F., & Lu, H. (2007, June 2). Xiamen bureau of public security urges residents to distrust rumors. *Southern Metropolis Daily.* p.1.

Hands, J. (2011). *@ is for activism: Dissent, resistance and rebellion in a digital culture.* London: Pluto Press.

Hargittai, E., & Hinnant, A. (2008). Digital inequality: Differences in young adults' use of the Internet. *Communication Research, 35*(5), 602–621.

Harney, A., Sanchanta, M., & Yeh, A. (2005, April 9). Japanese businesses feel heat of Chinese fury. *Financial Times.* Retrieved from http://www.ft.com/cms/s/0/18d01e86-a894-11d9-87a9-00000e2511c8.html#axzz343atmRgX

Harsin, J. (2006). The rumour bomb: Theorising the convergence of new and old trends in mediated US politics. *Southern Review: Communication, Politics & Culture, 39*(1), 84–110.

He, S., & Xue, D. (2014). Identity building and communal resistance against landgrabs in Wukan Village, China. *Current Anthropology, 55*(S9), S126–S137.

Headland, T. N., Pike, K. L., & Harris, M. (1990). *Emics and etics: The insider/outsider debate.* London: Sage.

Hermanns, H. (2008). Mobile democracy: Mobile phones as democratic tools. *Politics, 28*(2), 74–82.

Hermeking, M. (2005). Culture and Internet consumption: Contributions from cross-cultural marketing and advertising research. *Journal of Computer-Mediated Communication, 11*(1), 192–216.

Hermida, A., Lewis, S. C., & Zamith, R. (2014). Sourcing the Arab Spring: A case study of Andy Carvin's sources on Twitter during the Tunisian and Egyptian revolutions. *Journal of Computer-Mediated Communication, 19*(3), 479–499.

Hess, S. (2015). Foreign media coverage and protest outcomes in China: The case of the 2011 Wukan rebellion. *Modern Asian Studies, 49*(1), 177–203.

Hille, K. (2013). China detains well-known blogger in social media crackdown. *Financial Times.* Retrieved from https://www.ft.com/content/4bf5b3e8-0d6c-11e3-ba82-00144feabdc0

Hofheinz, A. (2011). Nextopia? Beyond Revolution 2.0. *Oriente Moderno,* *91*(1), 23–39.

Howard, P. N., & Hussain, M. M. (2011). The role of digital media. *Journal of Democracy, 22*(3), 35–48.

Howard, P. N., & Hussain, M. M. (2013). *Democracy's fourth wave? Digital media and the Arab Spring.* New York: Oxford University Press.

Howard, P. N., & Parks, M. R. (2012). Social media and political change: Capacity, constraint, and consequence. *Journal of Communication, 62*(2), 359–362.

Hu, Y. (2009). Rumor as social protest. *The Chinese Journal of Communication and Society, 9,* 67–94.

Huang, C. (2011). *Facebook and Twitter key to Arab Spring uprisings: Report.* Retrieved from https://www.thenational.ae/uae/facebook-and-twitter-key-to-arab-spring-uprisings-report-1.428773

Huang, H. (2015). A war of (mis) information: The political effects of rumors and rumor rebuttals in an authoritarian country. *British Journal of Political Science, 47*(2), 283–311.

Huang, L. (2005). Rumor and revolution—An analysis about the Wuchang Revolt of 1911 from the angle of political communication. *Journal of Huangzhong Normal University (Humainites and Social Science), 44*(6), 141–145.

Huang, P. C. C. (1993). "Public sphere"/"civil society" in China? The third realm between state and society. *Modern China, 19*(2), 216–240.

Human Rights Watch. (2015). China: New ban on "spreading rumors" about disasters. Retrieved from https://www.hrw.org/news/2015/11/02/china-new-ban-spreading-rumors-about-disasters

Hwang, K.-k. (1987). Face and favor: The Chinese power game. *American Journal of Sociology, 92*(4), 945–947.

Ibahrine, M. (2008). Mobile communication and sociopolitical change in the Arab World. In J. E. Katz (Ed.), *Handbook of mobile communication studies* (pp. 257–272). Cambridge, MA: The MIT Press.

ITU. (2016). Press Release: ITU releases 2016 ICT figures. Retrieved from https://www.itu.int/en/mediacentre/Pages/2016-PR30.aspx

Jackson, M. H. (1996). The meaning of "communication technology": The technology-context scheme. *Annals of the International Communication Association, 19*(1), 229–267.

Jacobs, A., & Buckley, C. (2015, February 27). In China, civic groups' freedom, and followers, are vanishing. *New York Times,* p. A4.

Jacobson, J., & Mascaro, C. (2016). Movember: Twitter conversations of a hairy social movement. *Social Media+ Society,* April–June, 1–12.

Jasper, J. (2004). A strategic approach to collective action: Looking for agency in social-movement choices. *Mobilization: An International Quarterly, 9*(1), 1–16.

Jasper, J. M. (1998). The emotions of protest: Affective and reactive emotions in and around social movements. *Sociological Forum, 13*(3), 397–424.

Jasper, J. M. (2008). *The art of moral protest: Culture, biography, and creativity in social movements.* Chicago: University of Chicago Press.

Jasper, J. M. (2011). Emotions and social movements: Twenty years of theory and research. *Annual Review of Sociology, 37,* 285–303.

Jasper, J. M., & Poulsen, J. D. (1995). Recruiting strangers and friends: Moral shocks and social networks in animal rights and anti-nuclear protests. *Social Problems, 42*(4), 493–512.

Jensen, K. B. (2010). *Media convergence: The three degrees of network, mass, and interpersonal communication*. London: Routledge.

Jensen, K. B. (2013). Definitive and sensitizing conceptualizations of mediatization. *Communication Theory, 23*(3), 203–222.

Jensen, K. B., & Helles, R. (2011). The internet as a cultural forum: Implications for research. *New Media & Society, 13*(4), 517–533.

Jing, L. (2012, October 30). Ningbo residents doubt pledge to halt chemical plant expansion. Retrieved from https://www.scmp.com/news/china/article/1072760/ningbo-residents-doubt-pledge-halt-chemical-plant-expansion.

Jinling Evening News. (2003, April 30). Special reports on anti-SARS: Over 2 million rumor-message spread. *Jinling Evening News*, p. A20.

Johnsen, T. E. (2003). The social context of the mobile phone use of Norwegian teens. In J. E. Katz (Ed.), *Machines that become us: The social context of personal communication technology* (pp. 161–169). New Brunswick, NJ: Transaction Publishers.

Johnston, H., & Klandermans, B. (Eds.). (1995). *Social movements and culture*. Minneapolis: University of Minnesota Press.

Johnston, H., & Noakes, J. A. (2005). *Frames of protest: Social movements and the framing perspective*. Lanham, MD: Rowman & Littlefield.

Juris, J. S. (2005). The new digital media and activist networking within anti-corporate globalization movements. *The Annals of the American Academy of Political and Social Science, 597*(1), 189–208.

Juris, J. S. (2008). *Networking futures: The movements against corporate globalization*. Durham, NC: Duke University Press.

Juris, J. S. (2012). Reflections on # Occupy Everywhere: Social media, public space, and emerging logics of aggregation. *American Ethnologist, 39*(2), 259–279.

Kaiman, J. (2013, September 10). China cracks down on social media with threat of jail for "online rumours." *The Guardian*. Retrieved from https://www.theguardian.com/world/2013/sep/10/china-social-media-jail-rumours

Kan, M. (2011). China detains Internet users for spreading rumors. PC World. Retrieved from http://www.pcworld.com/article/242589/china_detains_internet_users_for_spreading_rumors.html

Kapferer, J.-N. (1990). *Rumors: Uses, interpretations, and images*. New Brunswick, NJ: Transaction Publishers.

Kapferer, J.-N. (2013). *Rumors: Uses, interpretations, and images*. New Brunswick, NY: Transaction Publishers.

Karpf, D. (2010). Online political mobilization from the advocacy group's perspective: Looking beyond clicktivism. *Policy & Internet, 2*(4), 7–41.

Katz, J. E. (2003a). *Connections: Social and cultural studies of the telephone in American life*. New Brunswick, NJ: Transaction Publishers.

Katz, J. E. (2003b). Introduction. In J. E. Katz (Ed.), *Machines that become us: The social context of personal communication technology* (pp. 1–25). New Brunswick, NJ: Transaction Publishers.

Katz, J. E. (2006). *Magic in the air: Mobile communication and the transformation of social life*. New Brunswick, NJ: Transaction Publishers.

Katz, J. E. (2008). *Handbook of mobile communication studies*. Cambridge, MA: The MIT Press.

Katz, J. E., & Aakhus, M. (2002). *Perpetual contact: Mobile communication, private talk, public performance*. Cambridge; New York: Cambridge University Press.

Kaun, A., & Stiernstedt, F. (2014). Facebook time: Technological and institutional affordances for media memories. *New Media & Society, 16*(7), 1154–1168.

Kavada, A. (2010). Email lists and participatory democracy in the European Social Forum. *Media, Culture & Society, 32*(3), 355–372.

Kavada, A. (2016). Social movements and political agency in the digital age: A communication approach. *Media and Communication, 4*(4), 8–12.

Ketchley, N. (2017). *Egypt in a time of revolution.* Cambridge: Cambridge University Press.

Khondker, H. H. (2011). Role of the new media in the Arab Spring. *Globalizations, 8*(5), 675–679.

Kim, Y., Chen, H.-T., & Gil de Zúñiga, H. G. (2013). Stumbling upon news on the Internet: Effects of incidental news exposure and relative entertainment use on political engagement. *Computers in Human Behavior, 29*(6), 2607–2614.

King, G., Pan, J., & Roberts, M. E. (2013). How censorship in China allows government criticism but silences collective expression. *American Political Science Review, 107*(2), 1–18.

King, G., Pan, J., & Roberts, M. E. (2014). Reverse-engineering censorship in China: Randomized experimentation and participant observation. *Science, 345*(6199), 891.

Kipnis, A. B. (1997). *Producing guanxi: Sentiment, self, and subculture in a North China village.* Durham, NC: Duke University Press.

Kitts, J. A. (2000). Mobilizing in black boxes: Social networks and social movement organizations. *Mobilization: An International Journal, 5*(2), 241–257.

Klandermans, B. (2013). Consensus and action mobilization. In D. A. Snow, D. della Porta, B. Klandermans, & D. McAdam (Eds.), *The Wiley-Blackwell encyclopedia of social and political movements.* Retrieved from https://onlinelibrary.wiley.com/doi/abs/10.1002/9780470674871.wbespm048

Klandermans, B., & Tarrow, S. (1988). Mobilization into social movements: Synthesizing European and American approaches. *International Social Movement Research, 1*(1), 1–38.

Kleinman, A., & Watson, J. L. (2006). *SARS in China: Prelude to pandemic?* Stanford, CA: Stanford University Press.

Knapp, R. H. (1944). A psychology of rumor. *Public Opinion Quarterly, 8*(1), 22–37.

Knopf, T. A. (1975). *Rumors, race, and riots.* New Brunswick, NJ: Transaction Publishers.

Kolbert, E. (2009, November 2). The things people say: Rumors in an age of unreason. *The New Yorker.* Retrieved from https://www.newyorker.com/magazine/2009/11/02/the-things-people-say

Koskinen, I. (2008). Mobile multimedia: Uses and social consequences. In J. E. Katz (Ed.), *Handbook of mobile communication studies* (pp. 241–255). Cambridge MA: The MIT Press.

Kobayashi, T., Ikeda, K. i., & Miyata, K. (2006). Social capital online: Collective use of the Internet and reciprocity as lubricants of democracy. *Information, Community & Society, 9*(5), 582–611.

Koopmans, R. (1999). Political opportunity structure: Some splitting to balance the lumping. *Sociological Forum, 14*(1), 93–105.

Koopmans, R. (2004). Protest in time and space: The evolution of waves of contention. In D. A. Snow, S. A. Soule, & H. Kriesi (Eds.), *The Blackwell companion to social movements* (pp. 19–46). Malden, MA: Blackwell.

Kuang, X., & Wei, R. (2017). How framing of nationally and locally sensitive issues varies: A content analysis of news from party and nonparty newspapers in China. *Journalism*, http://journals.sagepub.com/doi/abs/10.1177/1464884917731179.

Kuhn, T. S. (1963). *The structure of scientific revolutions*. Chicago: University of Chicago Press.

Kurzman, C. (1996). Structural opportunity and perceived opportunity in social-movement theory: The Iranian revolution of 1979. *American Sociological Review*, 61(1), 153–170.

Lagerkvist, J. (2015). The unknown terrain of social protests in China: "Exit," "Voice," "Loyalty," and "Shadow." *Journal of Civil Society*, 11(2), 137–153.

Lai, Y. (2010, February 24). 20 million SMS to stop earthquake rumor. *China Youth Daily*, p. 7.

Lam, O. (2013). Chinese social media users are rumor-happy, low-educated, report says. Retrieved from https://globalvoices.org/2013/07/07/chinese-social-media-users-are-rumor-happy-low-educated-report-says/

Lam, O. (2017). "Web cleansing": China's Xinjiang residents forced to install surveillance apps on their mobile phones. Retrieved from https://www.hongkongfp.com/2017/07/22/web-cleansing-chinas-xinjiang-residents-forced-install-surveillance-apps-mobile-phones/

Lan, Y., & Zhang, Y. (2007, May 29). Millions of Xiamen residents spread crazily the same SMS to against high-pollution project. *Southern Metropolis Daily*, p. 1.

Laraña, E. (1994). *New social movements, from ideology to identity*. Philadelphia: Temple University Press.

Larson, C. (2011, July 8). The People's Republic of rumors. *Foreign Policy*. Retrieved from https://foreignpolicy.com/2011/07/08/the-peoples-republic-of-rumors/

Larson, C. (2012, March 22). Still the People's Republic of rumors. *Foreign Policy*. Retrieved from http://foreignpolicy.com/2012/03/22/still-the-peoples-republic-of-rumors/

Law, P.-l., & Chu, W.-c. R. (2008). ICTs and migrant workers in contemporary China. *Knowledge, Technology & Policy*, 21(2), 43–45.

Law, P.-l., & Peng, Y. (2006). The use of mobile phones among migrant workers in southern China. In P.-L. Law, L. Fortunaiti, & S. Yang (Eds.), *New technology in global societies* (pp. 245–258). Singapore: World Scientific.

Layman, G. C., & Green, J. C. (2005). Wars and rumours of wars: The contexts of cultural conflict in American political behaviour. *British Journal of Political Science*, 36(1), 61–89.

Lazarsfeld, P. F., Berelson, B., & Gaudet, H. (1948). *The people's choice: How the voter makes up his mind in a presidential campaign* (2nd ed.). New York: Columbia University Press.

Le Bon, G. (1897). *The crowd: A study of the popular mind*. London: Unwin.

Lee, C.-C. (1990). Mass media: Of China, about China. In C.-C. Lee (Ed.), *Voices of China: The interplay of politics and journalism* (pp. 3–29). New York: The Guilford Press.

Lee, C.-C. (2000). *Power, money, and media communication patterns and bureaucratic control in cultural China*. Evanston, IL: Northwestern University Press.

Lee, C.-C. (2016). Involution and vacuum: Comments on mainstream US media studies. *International Communication Gazette*, 78(7), 657–662.

Lee, C.-C. (Ed.) (1994). *China's media, media's China*. Boulder, CO: Westview Press.

Lee, C.-C. (Ed.) (2003). *Chinese media, global contexts*. London: Routledge.

Lee, F. L., & Chan, J. M. (2018). *Media and protest logics in the digital era: The Umbrella movement in Hong Kong*. Oxford: Oxford University Press.

Lee, K., & Ho, M.-s. (2014). The Maoming anti-PX protest of 2014. *China Perspectives, 2014*(3), 33–39.

Lee, M. (2011). China taxi drivers strike, dismiss pledges to boost fares. *Reuters*. Retrieved from http://www.reuters.com/article/2011/08/02/china-strike-idUSL3E7J21TA20110802

Lei, Y.-W. (2017). *The contentious public sphere: Law, media, and authoritarian rule in China*. Princeton: Princeton University Press.

Lemert, J. B. (1984). News context and the elimination of mobilizing information: An experiment. *Journalism Quarterly, 61*(2), 243.

Leonardi, P. M. (2014). Social media, knowledge sharing, and innovation: Toward a theory of communication visibility. *Information Systems Research, 25*(4), 796–816.

Li, G. (2014, April 3). "15 deaths and 300 injured" in Maoming was a rumor. *The People's Daily*, p. 4.

Li, J., & Zhao, X. (2010, April 29). Why people trust the rumors about earthquake and acid rains? *Nanfang Daily*.

Li, P., & Liu, B. (2017, 20 February). Punch hard to eradicate online rumor. *The People's Daily (overseas)*, p. 8.

Li, R. (2005). The reflection of social change: A study of the rumor of "Hairy Man and Water Monster" in 1950s. *Sociological Studies, 5*, 182–201.

Li, R. (2011a). How does a rumor come about? A re-analysis of the rumor of "Hairy Men" and "Water Monsters." *Open Times, 3*, 105–125.

Li, R. (2011b). *Wandering between illusion and reality: The analysis of rumors in mainland China during 1950s*. Beijing: Social Science Academic Press.

Licoppe, C., & Smoreda, Z. (2005). Are social networks technologically embedded?: How networks are changing today with changes in communication technology. *Social Networks, 27*(4), 317–335.

Lievrouw, L. (2011). *Alternative and activist new media*. Malden, MA: Polity.

Lim, C. (2010). Mobilizing on the margin: How does interpersonal recruitment affect citizen participation in politics? *Social Science Research, 39*(2), 341–355.

Lim, L. (2004, July 2). China to censor text messages. *BBC*. Retrieved from http://news.bbc.co.uk/2/hi/asia-pacific/3859403.stm

Lim, M. (2012). Clicks, cabs, and coffee houses: Social media and oppositional movements in Egypt, 2004–2011. *Journal of Communication, 62*(2), 231–248.

Lim, S., & Soriano, C. (Eds.). (2016). *Asian perspectives on digital culture: Emerging phenomena, enduring concepts*. London: Routledge.

Lin, A., & Tong, A. (2008). Mobile cultures of migrant workers in southern China: Informal literacies in the negotiation of (new) social relations of the new working women. *Knowledge, Technology & Policy, 21*(2), 73–81.

Lin, F., & Zhang, X. (2018). Movement-press dynamics and news diffusion: A typology of activism in digital China. *China Review, 18*(2), 33–64.

Lin, N. (2001). *Social capital: A theory of social structure and action*. Cambridge: Cambridge University Press.

Lin, N. (2017). Advancing network analysis of Chinese businesses: Commentary on Burt and Burzynska. *Management and Organization Review, 13*(2), 269–274.

Lin, Y. (2011, February 16). First-hand accounts of "escape" in Xiangshui. *China Youth Daily*, p. 9.

Ling, R. (2004). *The mobile connection: The cell phone's impact on society*. San Francisco, CA: Morgan Kaufmann.

Ling, R. (2008). *New tech, new ties: How mobile communication is reshaping social cohesion*. Cambridge, MA: The MIT Press.

Ling, R. (2013). *Taken for grantedness: The embedding of mobile communication into society*. Cambridge, MA: The MIT Press.

Ling, R. (2016). Soft coercion: Reciprocal expectations of availability in the use of mobile communication. *First Monday*, *21*(9). Retrieved from http://firstmonday.org/ojs/index.php/fm/article/view/6814/5622

Ling, R., & Yttri, B. (2002). Hyper-coordination via mobile phones in Norway. In J. Katz & M. Aakhus (Eds.), *Perpetual contact: Mobile communication, private talk, public performance* (pp. 139–169). Cambridge: Cambridge University Press.

Liu, D., & Yan, S. (2012, October 29). Ningbo backs down from PX project. *Global Times*. Retrieved from http://www.globaltimes.cn/content/740943.shtml

Liu, H. (2015, 25 June). WeChat intercepts 2.1 million rumors daily; Tuesday is the peak propagation time. *Beijing Daily*. Retrieved from http://www.cssn.cn/xwcbx/xwcbx_rdjj/201506/t20150625_2047693_1.shtml

Liu, J. (2013). Mobile communication, popular protests and citizenship in China. *Modern Asian Studies*, *47*(3), 995–1018.

Liu, J. (2014). Calling for strikes: Mundane mobile calls, mobilizing practices, and collective action in China. *Georgetown Journal of International Affairs*, *XV*(1), 15–24.

Liu, J. (2015). Communicating beyond information: Mobile phones and mobilization to offline protests in China. *Television & New Media*, *16*(6), 503–520.

Liu, J. (2016). Digital media, cycle of contention, and sustainability of environmental activism—The case of anti-PX protests in China. *Mass Communication and Society*, *19*(5), 604–625.

Liu, J. (2017a). From "moments of madness" to "the politics of mundanity"—Researching digital media and contentious collective actions in China. *Social Movement Studies*, *16*(4), 418–432.

Liu, J. (2017b). Mobile phones, social ties, and collective action mobilization in China. *Acta Sociologica*, *60*(3), 213–227.

Liu, J., & Ju, J. (2013). Behind the scenes of "the crackdown on online rumor." *Nanfang Weekend*. Retrieved from http://www.infzm.com/content/93974/

Liu, K., & Zhang, Y. (2016, October 17). Scholars refute Falungong's organ rumor. *China Daily*. Retrieved from http://www.chinadaily.com.cn/china/2016-10/17/content_27079070.htm

Liu, L., & Huang, H. (2014, April 11). A review of "Qin Huohuo" event. Retrieved from http://news.sina.com.cn/c/2014-04-11/235629915363.shtml

Liu, X. (2016, May 12). China to launch platform to fight online rumors. *Global Times*. Retrieved from http://www.globaltimes.cn/content/982602.shtml

Lu, Y., Zheng, W., & Wang, W. (2017). Migration and popular resistance in rural China: Wukan and beyond. *The China Quarterly*, *229*, 1–22.

Lv, M., & Wang, N. (2010). Shanxi: Dispelling "earthquake rumors," wiping off public panic. Retrieved from http://news.xinhuanet.com/society/2010-02/21/content_13020662.htm

Lv, Z. (2003). Rumor and rumor-like utterance in the Han empire. *Historical Research*, *2*, 14–31.

Lynch, M. (2011). After Egypt: The limits and promise of online challenges to the authoritarian Arab state. *Perspectives on politics*, *9*(2), 301–310.

Lynch, M. (2012). *The Arab Uprising: The unfinished revolutions of the new Middle East.* New York: Public Affairs.

Ma, J. (2008, July 17). Weng'an officials organize teachers to dispel online rumors and provide "full company" during interviews. *Youth Weekend*, p. A12.

Ma, R. (2005). Media, crisis, and SARS: An introduction. *Asian Journal of Communication, 15*(3), 241–246.

Maher, T. V., & Earl, J. (2017). Pathways to contemporary youth protest: The continuing relevance of family, friends, and school for youth micromobilization. In J. S. Earl & D. A. Rohlinger (Eds.), *Social movements and media* (Vol. 14, pp. 55–87). Bingley: Emerald Publishing Limited.

Margetts, H., John, P., Hale, S., & Yasseri, T. (2015). *Political turbulence: How social media shape collective action.* Princeton: Princeton University Press.

Marwell, G., Oliver, P. E., & Prahl, R. (1988). Social networks and collective action: A theory of the critical mass. III. *American Journal of Sociology, 94*(3), 502–534.

Marx, G. T., & Wood, J. L. (1975). Strands of theory and research in collective behavior. *Annual Review of Sociology, 1*(1), 363–428.

Mattoni, A. (2016). *Media practices and protest politics: How precarious workers mobilise.* London: Routledge.

Mattoni, A., & Treré, E. (2014). Media practices, mediation processes, and mediatization in the study of social movements. *Communication Theory, 24*(3), 252–271.

McAdam, D. (1982). *Political process and the development of black insurgency, 1930–1970.* Chicago: University of Chicago Press.

McAdam, D. (1983). Tactical innovation and the pace of insurgency. *American Sociological Review, 48*(6), 735–754.

McAdam, D. (1986). Recruitment to high-risk activism: The case of Freedom Summer. *American Journal of Sociology, 92*(1), 64–90.

McAdam, D. (1988a). *Freedom Summer.* Oxford: Oxford University Press.

McAdam, D. (1988b). Micromobilization contexts and recruitment to activism. *International Social Movement Research, 1*, 125–154.

McAdam, D. (1995). "Initiator" and "spin-off" movements: Diffusion processes in protest cycles. In M. Traugott (Ed.), *Repertoires and cycles of collective action* (pp. 217–239). Durham NC; London: Duke University Press.

McAdam, D. (1996). Conceptual origins, current problems, future directions. In D. McAdam, J. D. McCarthy, & Mayer N. Zald (Eds.), *Comparative perspectives on social movements: Political opportunities, mobilizing structures, and cultural framings* (pp. 23–40). Cambridge: Cambridge University Press.

McAdam, D. (2013). Initiator and spin-off movements. In D. A. Snow, D. della Porta, B. Klandermans, & D. McAdam (Eds.), *The Wiley-Blackwell encyclopedia of social and political movements.* Retrieved from https://onlinelibrary.wiley.com/doi/abs/10.1002/9780470674871.wbespm109.

McAdam, D., McCarthy, J. D., & Zald, M. N. (1996a). *Comparative perspectives on social movements: Political opportunities, mobilizing structures, and cultural framings,* Cambridge: Cambridge University Press.

McAdam, D., McCarthy, J. D., & Zald, M. N. (1996b). Introduction: Opportunities, mobilizing structures and framing processes—Toward a synthetic, comparative perspective on social movements. In D. McAdam, J. D. McCarthy, & M. N. Zald (Eds.), *Comparative perspectives on social movements: Political opportunities, mobilizing structures, and cultural framings* (pp. 1–22). Cambridge: Cambridge University Press.

McAdam, D., & Paulsen, R. (1993). Specifying the relationship between social ties and activism. *American Journal of Sociology*, *99*(3), 640–667.

McAdam, D., & Rucht, D. (1993). The cross-national diffusion of movement ideas. *The Annals of the American Academy of Political and Social Science*, *528*(1), 56–74.

McAdam, D., & Schaffer Boudet, H. (2012). *Putting social movements in their place.* Cambridge: Cambridge University Press.

McAdam, D., Tarrow, S. G., & Tilly, C. (2001). *Dynamics of contention.* New York: Cambridge University Press.

McAdam, D., Tarrow, S., & Tilly, C. (2009). Comparative perspectives on contentious politics. In M. I. Lichbach & A. S. Zuckerman (Eds.), *Comparative politics: Rationality, culture, and structure* (pp. 260–290). Cambridge: Cambridge University Press.

McCaffrey, D., & Keys, J. (2000). Competitive framing processes in the abortion debate: Polarization-vilification, frame saving, and frame debunking. *Sociological Quarterly*, *41*(1), 41–61.

McCarthy, J. D. (1996). Constraints and opportunities in adopting, adapting, and inventing. In D. McAdam, J. D. McCarthy, & M. N. Zald (Eds.), *Comparative perspectives on social movements: Political opportunities, mobilizing structures, and cultural framings* (pp. 141–151). Cambridge: Cambridge University Press.

McCarthy, J. D., & Zald, M. N. (1973). *The trend of social movements in America: Professionalization and resource mobilization.* Retrieved from https://deepblue.lib.umich.edu/bitstream/handle/2027.42/50939/164. pdf?sequence=1&isAllowed=y

McCarthy, J. D., & Zald, M. N. (1977). Resource mobilization and social movements: A partial theory. *American Journal of Sociology*, *82*(6), 1212–1241.

McChesney, R. W. (1999). *Rich media, poor democracy: Communication politics in dubious times.* Urbana: University of Illinois Press.

McCombs, M. E., & Shaw, D. L. (1972). The agenda-setting function of mass media. *Public Opinion Quarterly*, *36*(2), 176–187.

McMillen, N. R. (1971). *The citizens' council.* Urbana: University of Illinois Press.

McPherson, M., Smith-Lovin, L., & Brashears, M. E. (2006). Social isolation in America: Changes in core discussion networks over two decades. *American Sociological Review*, *71*(3), 353–375.

Melucci, A. (1985). The symbolic challenge of contemporary movements. *Social Research*, *52*(4), 789–816.

Melucci, A. (1988). Getting involved: Identity and mobilization in social movements. *International Social Movement Research*, *1*, 329–348.

Melucci, A. (1989). *Nomads of the present: Social movements and individual needs in contemporary society.* Philadelphia: Temple University Press.

Melucci, A. (1996). *Challenging codes: Collective action in the information age.* Cambridge: Cambridge University Press.

Mercea, D. (2013). Probing the implications of Facebook use for the organizational form of social movement organizations. *Information, Communication & Society*, *16*(8), 1306–1327.

Merton, R. K. (1968). *Social theory and social structure.* New York: The Free Press.

Meyer, D. S. (1993). Protest cycles and political process: American peace movements in the nuclear age. *Political Research Quarterly*, *46*(3), 451–479.

Meyer, D. S. (2004). Protest and political opportunities. *Annual Review of Sociology*, *30*, 125–145.

Meyer, D. S., & Minkoff, D. C. (2004). Conceptualizing political opportunity. *Social Forces, 82*(4), 1457–1492.

Meyer, D. S., & Staggenborg, S. (1996). Movements, countermovements, and the structure of political opportunity. *American Journal of Sociology, 101*(6), 1628–1660.

Meyer, R. (2018, March 8). The grim conclusions of the largest-ever study of fake news. *The Atlantic.* Retrieved from https://www.theatlantic.com/technology/archive/2018/03/largest-study-ever-fake-news-mit-twitter/555104/

Michaels, C. F. (2003). Affordances: Four points of debate. *Ecological psychology, 15*(2), 135–148.

Minkoff, D. C. (1997). The sequencing of social movements. *American Sociological Review, 62*(5), 779–799.

Mische, A. (2003). Interventions: Dynamics of contention conversation with Charles Tilly about his recently published book, *Dynamics of Contention,* co-authored with Doug McAdam. *Social Movement Studies, 2*(1), 85–96.

Milkman, R. (2017). A new political generation: Millennials and the post-2008 wave of protest. *American Sociological Review, 82*(1), 1–31.

Miller, D. E. (2005). Rumor: An examination of some stereotypes. *Symbolic Interaction, 28*(4), 505–519.

Mills, C. W. (2000). *The sociological imagination.* Oxford: Oxford University Press.

Monterde, A., & Postill, J. (2014). Mobile ensembles: The uses of mobile phones for social protest by Spain's Indignados. In L. Hjorth & G. Goggin (Eds.), *The Routledge Companion to Mobile Media* (pp. 429–438). London: Routledge.

Mooney, P. (2012). *Wukan: Citizens fight to keep land.* Retrieved from http://www.hrichina.org/en/crf/article/6454

Morin, E. (1971). *Rumour in Orléans.* New York: Pantheon.

Morozov, E. (2009). The brave new world of slacktivism. *Foreign Policy, 19*(5). Retrieved from https://foreignpolicy.com/2009/05/19/the-brave-new-world-of-slacktivism/

Morozov, E. (2011). *The net delusion: How not to liberate the world.* London: Allen Lane.

Mortensen, M., Neumayer, C., & Poell, T. (Eds.). (2019). *Social media materialities and protest: Critical reflections.* London: Routledge.

Munson, Z. W. (2010). *The making of pro-life activists: How social movement mobilization works.* Chicago: University of Chicago Press.

Myers, D. J. (2000). The diffusion of collective violence: Infectiousness, susceptibility, and mass media networks. *American Journal of Sociology, 106*(1), 173–208.

Naisbitt, J., & Naisbitt, D. (2010). *China's megatrends: The 8 pillars of a new society.* New York: Harper Business.

Nathan, A. J. (1986). *Chinese democracy.* Berkeley: University of California Press.

Nathan, A. J. (2009). Authoritarian impermanence. *Journal of Democracy, 20*(3), 37–40.

Nekmat, E., Gower, K. K., Gonzenbach, W. J., & Flanagin, A. J. (2015). Source effects in the micro-mobilization of collective action via social media. *Information, Communication & Society, 18*(9), 1076–1091.

Neubauer, H.-J. (1999). *The rumour: A cultural history.* London: Free Association.

Ng, J. Q. (2015). China's rumor mill. *Foreign Affairs.* Retrieved from https://www.foreignaffairs.com/articles/china/2015-10-06/chinas-rumor-mill

Nielsen, R. K. (2011). Mundane internet tools, mobilizing practices, and the coproduction of citizenship in political campaigns. *New Media & Society, 13*(5), 755–771.

Nielsen, R. K. (2013). Mundane Internet tools, the risk of exclusion, and reflexive movements—Occupy Wall Street and political uses of digital networked technologies. *The Sociological Quarterly, 54*(2), 173–177.

Norman Donald, A. (1988). *The psychology of everyday things.* New York: Basic Books.

Norris, P. (2002). *Democratic phoenix: Reinventing political activism.* Cambridge: Cambridge University Press.

Nunns, A., & Idle, N. (Eds.). (2011). *Tweets from Tahrir: Egypt's revolution as it unfolded, in the words of the people who made it.* New York: OR Books.

Nyíri, K. (Ed.) (2003). *Mobile democracy. Essays on society, self and politics.* Vienna: Passagen Verlag.

O'Brien, K. J. (1996). Rightful resistance. *World Politics, 49*(1), 31–55.

O'Brien, K. J. (2009). *Popular protest in China.* Cambridge: Harvard University Press.

O'Brien, K. J., & Li, L. (2006). *Rightful resistance in rural China.* New York: Cambridge University Press.

Oberschall, A. (1973). *Social conflict and social movements.* Englewood Cliffs: Prentice Hall.

Ogan, C., & Varol, O. (2016). What is gained and what is left to be done when content analysis is added to network analysis in the study of a social movement: Twitter use during Gezi Park. *Information, Communication & Society, 20*(8), 1220–1238.

Oliver, P., & Johnston, H. (2000). What a good idea! Ideologies and frames in social movement research. *Mobilization: An International Quarterly, 5*(1), 37–54.

Oliver, P. E., & Marwell, G. (1988). The paradox of group size in collective action: A theory of the critical mass. II. *American Sociological Review, 53*(1), 1–8.

Oliver, P., Marwell, G., & Teixeira, R. (1985). A theory of the critical mass. I. Interdependence, group heterogeneity, and the production of collective action. *American Journal of Sociology, 91*(3), 522–556.

Oliver, P. E., & Maney, G. M. (2000). Political processes and local newspaper coverage of protest events: From selection bias to triadic interactions. *American Journal of Sociology, 106*(2), 463–505.

Oliver, P. E., & Myers, D. J. (1999). How events enter the public sphere: Conflict, location, and sponsorship in local newspaper coverage of public events. *American Journal of Sociology, 105*(1), 38–87.

Olson, M. (1975). *The logic of collective action* (5th ed.). Cambridge: Harvard University Press.

Olufowote, J. O. (2006). Rousing and redirecting a sleeping giant: Symbolic convergence theory and complexities in the communicative constitution of collective action. *Management Communication Quarterly, 19*(3), 451–492.

Palmer, J. (2017, August 25). China is trying to give the Internet a death blow. *Foreign Policy.* Retrieved from https://foreignpolicy.com/2017/08/25/china-is-trying-to-give-the-internet-a-death-blow-vpn-technology/

Pan, Z. (2016, July7). Key questions in the transformation of news media. *Chinese Social Sciences Today*, p. 3.

Papacharissi, Z. (2015). *Affective publics: Sentiment, technology, and politics.* Oxford: Oxford University Press.

Parchoma, G. (2014). The contested ontology of affordances: Implications for researching technological affordances for collaborative knowledge production. *Computers in Human Behavior, 37*, 360–368.

Parks, M. R., & Floyd, K. (1996). Making friends in cyberspace. *Journal of Computer-Mediated Communication, 1*(4). Retrieved from https://onlinelibrary.wiley.com/doi/full/10.1111/j.1083-6101.1996.tb00176.x

Park, S. H., & Luo, Y. (2001). Guanxi and organizational dynamics: Organizational networking in Chinese firms. *Strategic Management Journal, 22*(5), 455–477.

Passy, F. (2003). Social networks matter. But how? In M. Diani & D. McAdam (Eds.), *Social movements and networks: Relational approaches to collective action* (pp. 21–48). Oxford; New York: Oxford University Press.

Pavan, E. (2014). Embedding digital communications within collective action networks: A multidimensional network approach. *Mobilization: An International Quarterly, 19*(4), 441–455.

Payne, C. (1989). Ella Baker and models of social change. *Signs: Journal of Women in Culture and Society, 14*(4), 885–899.

Pei, M. (2016). China's rule of fear. Retrieved from https://www.project-syndicate.org/commentary/china-fear-bureaucratic-paralysis-by-minxin-pei-2016-02?barrier=true

Pei, M., & Shi, T. (2007). How do Asian people understand democracy? Retrieved from http://carnegieendowment.org/2007/11/28/how-do-asian-people-understand-democracy/fb3

Pendleton, C. (1998). Rumor research revisited and expanded. *Language & Communication, 1*(18), 69–86.

Penney, J., & Dadas, C. (2014). (Re)Tweeting in the service of protest: Digital composition and circulation in the Occupy Wall Street movement. *New Media & Society, 16*(1), 74–90.

People's Daily. (2011, October 2). Resolutely resist online rumor. *People's Daily.* Retrieved from http://cpc.people.com.cn/GB/64093/64099/15803501.html

Perry, E. J., & Selden, M. (Eds.). (2010). *Chinese society: Change, conflict and resistance* (3rd ed.). London: Routledge.

Peterson, W., & Gist, N. (1951). Rumor and public opinion. *American Journal of Sociology, 57*(2), 159–167.

Pew Research Center. (2015, April 15). *Cell phones in Africa: Communication lifeline.* Retrieved from http://www.pewglobal.org/2015/04/15/cell-phones-in-africa-communication-lifeline/

Pfau, M. (2008). Epistemological and disciplinary intersections. *Journal of Communication, 58*(4), 597–602.

Pierskalla, J. H., & Hollenbach, F. M. (2013). Technology and collective action: The effect of cell phone coverage on political violence in Africa. *American Political Science Review, 107*(2), 207–224.

Poell, T. (2014). Social media and the transformation of activist communication: Exploring the social media ecology of the 2010 Toronto G20 protests. *Information, Communication & Society, 17*(6), 716–731.

Polletta, F. (2012). *Freedom is an endless meeting: Democracy in American social movements.* Chicago: University of Chicago Press.

Polletta, F., Chen, P. C. B., Gardner, B. G., & Motes, A. (2013). Is the Internet creating new reasons to protest? In J. van Stekelenburg, C. Roggeband, & B. Klandermans (Eds.), *Dynamics, mechanisms, and processes: The future of social movement research* (pp. 17–36). Minneapolis: University of Minnesota Press.

Polletta, F., & Jasper, J. M. (2001). Collective identity and social movements. *Annual Review of Sociology, 27*(1), 283–305.

Portes, A., & Sensenbrenner, J. (1993). Embeddedness and immigration: Notes on the social determinants of economic action. *American Journal of Sociology, 98*(6), 1320–1350.

Postmes, T., & Brunsting, S. (2002). Collective action in the age of the Internet: Mass communication and online mobilization. *Social Science Computer Review, 20*(3), 290–301.

Prasad, J. (1935). The psychology of rumour: A study relating to the great Indian earthquake of 1934. *British Journal of Psychology. General Section, 26*(1), 1–15.

Putnam, R. D. (2000). *Bowling alone: The collapse and revival of American community.* London: Simon & Schuster.

Putnam, R. D., Leonardi, R., & Nanetti, R. Y. (1993). *Making democracy work: Civic traditions in modern Italy.* Princeton: Princeton University Press.

Qiu, J. L. (2008a). Mobile civil society in Asia: A comparative study of People power II and the Nosamo movement. *Javnost-The Public, 15*(3), 39–58.

Qiu, J. L. (2008b). Working-class ICTs, migrants, and empowerment in south China. *Asian Journal of Communication, 18*(4), 333–347.

Qiu, J. L. (2009). *Working-class network society: Communication technology and the information have-less in urban China.* Cambridge, MA: The MIT Press.

Qiu, J. L. (2017). *Goodbye iSlave: A manifesto for digital abolition.* Urbana: University of Illinois Press.

Qu, L. (2007, March 18). The controversy on the safety of the billion chemical F] factory complex project in Xiamen. *China Business Journal,* p. A1.

Rachal, J. R. (2000). We'll never turn back: Adult education and the struggle for citizenship in Mississippi's Freedom Summer. *Adult Education Quarterly, 50*(3), 166–196.

Rafael, V. L. (2003). The cell phone and the crowd: Messianic politics in the contemporary Philippines. *Popular Culture, 15*(3), 399–425.

Rainie, H., & Wellman, B. (2012). *Networked: The new social operating system.* Cambridge, MA: The MIT Press.

Rajagopalan, M., & Rose, A. (2013). China crackdown on online rumors seen as ploy to nail critics. *Reuters.* Retrieved from http://www.reuters.com/article/net-us-china-internet-idUSBRE98H07X20130918

Reardon, K. K., & Rogers, E. M. (1988). Interpersonal versus mass media communication: A false dichotomy. *Human Communication Research, 15*(2), 284–303.

Reed, T. V. (2005). *The art of protest: Culture and activism from the civil rights movement to the streets of Seattle.* Minnesota: University of Minnesota Press.

Ren, B. (2011). Online rumors are narcotics, please resist and stay away. Retrieved from http://opinion.people.com.cn/GB/16408972.html

Ren, S. (2011, March 6). Maintain stability by each person. *Beijing Daily,* p. 1.

Reporter. (2007, May 28). Haicang PX project has already been approved according to nationally recognized legal procedures and is under construction. *Xiamen Evening News,* pp. 2–3.

Reporter. (2012). Armed with cameras and the web, youth spurred Wukan protests. Retrieved from http://www.wantchinatimes.com/news-subclass-cnt.aspx?id=20120304000030&cid=1101

Reuters. (2014, February 20). China's mobile subscribers up 0.6 percent at 1.24 billion in January. *Reuters.* Retrieved from http://www.reuters.com/article/2014/02/20/us-china-mobilesubscribers-idUSBREA1J0JI20140220

Rheingold, H. (2002). *Smart mobs: The next social revolution.* Cambridge, MA: Perseus.

Rheingold, H. (2008). Mobile media and political collective action. In J. E. Katz (Ed.), *Handbook of mobile communication studies* (pp. 225–240). Cambridge, MA: The MIT Press.

Rinke, E. M., & Röder, M. (2011). Media ecologies, communication culture, and temporal-spatial unfolding: Three components in a communication model of the Egyptian regime change. *International Journal of Communication, 5,* 1273–1285.

Roberts, M. E. (2018). *Censored: Distraction and diversion inside Chinas Great Firewall.* Princeton: Princeton University Press.

Rodríguez, C. (2011). *Citizens' media against armed conflict: Disrupting violence in Colombia.* Minnesota: University of Minnesota Press.

Rodríguez, C., Ferron, B., & Shamas, K. (2014). Four challenges in the field of alternative, radical and citizens' media research. *Media, Culture & Society, 36*(2), 150–166.

Rogers, E. M. (1962). *Diffusion of innovations.* New York: Free Press of Glencoe.

Rogers, T., Goldstein, N. J., & Fox, C. R. (2018). Social mobilization. *Annual Review of Psychology, 69,* 357–381.

Rojecki, A., & Meraz, S. (2016). Rumors and factitious informational blends: The role of the web in speculative politics. *New Media & Society, 18*(1), 25–43.

Rolfe, B. (2005). Building an electronic repertoire of contention. *Social Movement Studies, 4*(1), 65–74.

Rosnow, R., & Kimmel, A. (2000). Rumors. In A. E. Kazdin (Ed.), *Encyclopedia of psychology* (pp. 122–123). Oxford: Oxford University Press.

Rosnow, R. L. (1974). On rumor. *Journal of Communication, 24*(3), 26–38.

Rosnow, R. L. (1980). Psychology of rumor reconsidered. *Psychological Bulletin, 87*(3), 578–591.

Rosnow, R. L. (1988). Rumor as communication: A contextualist approach. *Journal of Communication, 38*(1), 12–28.

Rosnow, R. L., & Fine, G. A. (1976). *Rumor and gossip: The social psychology of hearsay.* New York: Elsevier.

Rubin, V. L., Chen, Y., & Conroy, N. J. (2015). Deception detection for news: Three types of fakes. *Proceedings of the Association for Information Science and Technology, 52*(1), 1–4.

Ruesch, J., & Bateson, G. (1951). *Communication: The social matrix of psychiatry.* New York: Norton.

Russell, A. (2005). Myth and the Zapatista Movement: Exploring a network identity. *New Media & Society, 7*(4), 559–577.

Schachter, S., & Burdick, H. (1955). A field experiment on rumor transmission and distortion. *The Journal of Abnormal and Social Psychology, 50*(3), 363–371.

Scherer, K. R., Johnstone, T., & Klasmeyer, G. (2002). Vocal expression of emotion. In R. J. Davidson, K. R. Scherer, & H. H. Goldsmith (Eds.), *Handbook of affective sciences* (pp. 433–456). New York: Oxford University Press.

Schradie, J. (2018). Moral Monday is more than a hashtag: The strong ties of social movement emergence in the digital era. *Social Media+ Society,* January–March, 1–13. Retrieved from http://journals.sagepub.com/doi/pdf/10.1177/2056305117750719

Schrock, A. R. (2015). Communicative affordances of mobile media: Portability, availability, locatability, and multimediality. *International Journal of Communication, 9,* 1229–1246.

Schumpeter, J. A. (2010). *Capitalism, socialism and democracy.* London: Routledge.

Schussman, A., & Soule, S. A. (2005). Process and protest: Accounting for individual protest participation. *Social Forces, 84*(2), 1083–1108.

Scott, J. C. (1985). *Weapons of the Weak: Everyday forms of peasant resistance*. New Haven: Yale University Press.

Scott, J. C. (1990). *Domination and the arts of resistance: Hidden transcripts*. New Haven: Yale University Press.

Seawright, J., & Gerring, J. (2008). Case selection techniques in case study research: A menu of qualitative and quantitative options. *Political Research Quarterly, 61*(2), 294–308.

Segerberg, A., & Bennett, W. L. (2011). Social media and the organization of collective action: Using Twitter to explore the ecologies of two climate change protests. *The Communication Review, 14*(3), 197–215.

Selander, L., & Jarvenpaa, S. L. (2016). Digital action repertoires and transforming a social movement organization. *MIS Quarterly, 40*(2), 331–352.

Shah, A. (2013). The intimacy of insurgency: Beyond coercion, greed or grievance in Maoist India. *Economy and Society, 42*(3), 480–506.

Shan, G. (2010, February 4). A comprehensive analysis of mass incidents in 2009. *Southern Weekend*. Retrieved from http://www.infzm.com/content/41159/0

Shan, G., & Jiang, Z. (2009). The characteristics and conflicts of mass incidents at township level. *Leaders, 29*, 100–110.

Shao, C., Ciampaglia, G. L., Flammini, A., & Menczer, F. (2016). *Hoaxy: A platform for tracking online misinformation*. Paper presented at the Proceedings of the 25th International Conference Companion on World Wide Web.

Shapiro, J. N., & Weidmann, N. B. (2015). Is the phone mightier than the sword? Cellphones and insurgent violence in Iraq. *International Organization, 69*(2), 247–274.

Sherkat, D. E., & Blocker, T. J. (1994). The political development of sixties' activists: Identifying the influence of class, gender, and socialization on protest participation. *Social Forces, 72*(3), 821–842.

Shi, F., & Cai, Y. (2006). Disaggregating the state: Networks and collective resistance in Shanghai. *The China Quarterly, 186*, 314–332.

Shi, T. (1997). *Political participation in Beijing*. Cambridge, MA: Harvard University Press.

Shi, T. (2010). China: Democratic values supporting an authoritarian system. In Y.-H. Chu, L. Diamond, & A. J. Nathan (Eds.), *How East Asians view democracy* (pp. 210–237). New York: Columbia University Press.

Shibutani, T. (1966). *Improvised news: A sociological study of rumor*. Indianapolis: Bobbs-Merrill.

Shibutani, T. (1968). Rumor. In D. L. Sills (Ed.), *International encyclopedia of the social sciences* (volume 13) (pp. 576–580). New York: MacMillan & Free Press.

Shin, J., Jian, L., Driscoll, K., & Bar, F. (2017). Political rumoring on Twitter during the 2012 US presidential election: Rumor diffusion and correction. *New Media & Society, 19*(8), 1214–1235.

Shirk, S. L. (2011). Changing media, changing China. In S. L. Shirk (Ed.), *Changing media, changing China* (pp. 1–37). New York: Oxford University Press.

Shirky, C. (2008). *Here comes everybody: The power of organizing without organizations*. New York: Penguin Press.

Shirky, C. (2011). The political power of social media. *Foreign Affairs*. Retrieved from http://www.gpia.info/files/u1392/Shirky_Political_Poewr_of_Social_Media.pdf

Shu, T. (2009, March 23). Rethinking Weng'an incident. *Oriental Outlook*. Retrieved from http://news.sina.com.cn/c/sd/2009-03-23/143117464065.shtml.

Siles, I., & Boczkowski, P. (2012). At the intersection of content and materiality: A texto-material perspective on the use of media technologies. *Communication Theory*, 22(3), 227–249.

Simmel, G., & Hughes, E. C. (1949). The sociology of sociability. *American Journal of Sociology*, 55(3), 254–261.

Smart, A. (1993). Gifts, bribes, and guanxi: A reconsideration of Bourdieu's social capital. *Cultural Anthropology*, 8(3), 388–408.

Smith, B. L., & Lasswell, H. D. (2015). *Propaganda, communication and public opinion*. Princeton: Princeton University Press.

Smith, S. A. (2006). Talking toads and Chinless ghosts: The polities of "superstitious" rumors in the People's Republic of China, 1961–1965. *American Historical Review*, 111(2), 405–427.

Smith, S. A. (2008). Fear and rumour in the People's Republic of China in the 1950s. *Cultural and Social History*, 5(3), 269–288.

Snow, D. A. (2004). Framing processes, ideology, and discursive fields. In D. A. Snow, S. A. Soule, & H. Kriesi (Eds.), *The Blackwell companion to social movements* (pp. 380–412). Malden: Blackwell.

Snow, D. A., & Benford, R. D. (1992). Master frames and cycles of protest. In A. D. Morris & C. M. Mueller (Eds.), *Frontiers in social movement theory* (pp. 133–155). New Haven: Yale University Press.

Snow, D. A., Louis A. Zurcher, J., & Ekland-Olson, S. (1980). Social networks and social movements: A microstructural approach to differential recruitment. *American Sociological Review*, 45(5), 787–801.

Snow, D. A., Rochford, E. B., Jr., Worden, S. K., & Benford, R. D. (1986). Frame alignment processes, micromobilization, and movement participation. *American Sociological Review*, 51(4), 464–481.

So, Y. L., & Walker, A. (2006). *Explaining guanxi: The Chinese business network*. New York: Routledge.

Solove, D. J. (2007). *The future of reputation: Gossip, rumor, and privacy on the Internet*. New Haven: Yale University Press.

Soule, S. A. (1997). The student divestment movement in the United States and tactical diffusion: The shantytown protest. *Social Forces*, 75(3), 855–882.

South China Morning Post. (2013, May 1). Hundreds of Zhejiang taxi drivers strike on Labour Day. Retrieved from https://www.scmp.com/news/china/article/1227480/hundreds-zhejiang-taxi-drivers-strike-labour-day

Sreberny, A., & Mohammadi, A. (1994). *Small media, big revolution: Communication, culture, and the Iranian revolution*. Minnesota: University of Minnesota Press.

Staff Reporter. (2013). Governments toughen stance on environmental protesters amid Kunming, Chengdu actions. *South China Morning Post*. Retrieved from http://www.scmp.com/news/china/article/1241474/governments-toughen-their-stance-towards-environmental-protesters

Staggenborg, S. (2002). The "meso" in social movement research. In D. S. Meyer, N. Whittier, & B. Robnett (Eds.), *Social movements: Identity, culture, and the state* (pp. 124–139). Oxford: Oxford University Press.

Staggenborg, S., & Taylor, V. (2005). Whatever happened to the women's movement? *Mobilization: An International Quarterly*, 10(1), 37–52.

Stark, R., & Bainbridge, W. S. (1980). Networks of faith: Interpersonal bonds and recruitment to cults and sects. *American Journal of Sociology*, 85(6), 1376–1395.

Steinhardt, H. C. (2015). From blind spot to media spotlight: Propaganda policy, media activism and the emergence of protest events in the Chinese public sphere. *Asian Studies Review, 39*(1), 119–137.

Stern, R. E., & Hassid, J. (2012). Amplifying silence uncertainty and control parables in contemporary China. *Comparative Political Studies, 45*(10), 1230–1254.

Stockmann, D. (2013). *Media commercialization and authoritarian rule in China.* Cambridge: Cambridge University Press.

Stockmann, D., & Luo, T. (2017). Which social media facilitate online public opinion in China? *Problems of Post-Communism, 64*(3–4), 189–202.

Strang, D., & Soule, S. A. (1998). Diffusion in organizations and social movements: From hybrid corn to poison pills. *Annual Review of Sociology, 24*(1), 265–290.

Suárez, S. L. (2006). Mobile democracy: Text messages, voter turnout, and the 2004 Spanish general election. *Representation, 42*(2), 117–128.

Sunstein, C. R. (2009). *On rumors: How falsehoods spread, why we believe them, what can be done.* London: Allen Lane.

Supreme People's Court of PRC and the Supreme People's Procuratorate of PRC. (2013). SPC and SPP interpretation on internet speech crimes. Retrieved from http://www.spp.gov.cn/zdgz/201309/t20130910_62417.shtml

Tang, G., & Lee, F. L. (2013). Facebook use and political participation: The impact of exposure to shared political information, connections with public political actors, and network structural heterogeneity. *Social Science Computer Review, 31*(6), 763–773.

Tang, L., & Yang, P. (2011). Symbolic power and the internet: The power of a "horse." *Media, Culture & Society, 33*(5), 675–691.

Tarde, G. (1903). *The laws of imitation.* New York: Holt.

Tarrow, S. (1993a). Cycles of collective action: Between moments of madness and the repertoire of contention. *Social Science History, 17*(2), 281–307.

Tarrow, S. (1993b). Modular collective action and the rise of the social movement: Why the French Revolution was not enough. *Politics & Society, 21*(1), 69–90.

Tarrow, S. (1996). States and opportunities: The political structuring of social movements In D. McAdam, J. D. McCarthy, & M. N. Zald (Eds.), *Comparative perspectives on social movements: Political opportunities, mobilizing structures, and cultural framings* (pp. 41–61). Cambridge: Cambridge University Press.

Tarrow, S. (1998). Fishnets, internets, and catnets: Globalization and transnational collective action. In M. P. Hanagan, L. P. Moch, & W. P. T. Brake (Eds.), *Challenging authority: The historical study of contentious politics* (pp. 228–244). Minneapolis: University of Minnesota Press

Tarrow, S. (2001). Silence and voice in the study of contentious politics: Introduction. In R. R. Aminzade, J. A. Goldstone, D. McAdam, E. J. Perry, W. H. Sewell, S. Tarrow, & C. Tilley (Eds.), *Silence and voice in the study of contentious politics* (pp. 1–13). Cambridge: Cambridge University Press.

Tarrow, S. (2008). Charles Tilly and the practice of contentious politics. *Social Movement Studies, 7*(3), 225–246.

Tarrow, S. (2010). Dynamics of diffusion: Mechanisms, institutions, and scale shift. In R. K. Givan, K. M. Roberts, & S. A. Soule (Eds.), *The diffusion of social movements: Actors, mechanisms, and political effects* (pp. 204–219). Cambridge: Cambridge University Press.

Tarrow, S. (2011). *Power in Movement: Social movements and contentious politics* (Rev. & 3rd ed.). New York: Cambridge University Press.

Tarrow, S. (2013). *The language of contention: Revolutions in words, 1688–2012*. Cambridge: Cambridge University Press.

Theocharis, Y., Lowe, W., Van Deth, J. W., & García-Albacete, G. (2015). Using Twitter to mobilize protest action: Online mobilization patterns and action repertoires in the Occupy Wall Street, Indignados, and Aganaktismenoi movements. *Information, Communication & Society, 18*(2), 202–220.

Thoits, P. A. (1989). The sociology of emotions. *Annual Review of Sociology, 15*(1), 317–342.

Thireau, I., & Linshan, H. (2003). The moral universe of aggrieved Chinese workers: Workers' appeals to arbitration committees and letters and visits offices. *The China Journal, 50*, 83–103.

Thorson, K., Driscoll, K., Ekdale, B., Edgerly, S., Thompson, L. G., Schrock, A., . . . Wells, C. (2013). YouTube, Twitter and the Occupy movement: Connecting content and circulation practices. *Information, Communication & Society, 16*(3), 421–451.

Tilly, C. (1978). *From mobilization to revolution*. Reading: Addison-Wesley.

Tilly, C. (1986). *The contentious French*. Cambridge. MA: Harvard University Press.

Tilly, C. (1995). *Popular contention in Great Britain, 1758–1834*. Cambridge, MA: Harvard University Press.

Tilly, C. (2004). *Social movements, 1768–2004*. Boulder, CO: Paradigm Publishers.

Tilly, C. (2005). *Trust and rule*. Cambridge: Cambridge University Press.

Tilly, C. (2008). *Contentious performances*. Cambridge: Cambridge University Press.

Tilly, C. (2010). *Regimes and repertoires*. Chicago: University of Chicago Press.

Tilly, C., & Tarrow, S. G. (2006). *Contentious politics*. Oxford: Oxford University Press.

Tindall, D. B. (2004). Social movement participation over time: An ego-network approach to micro-mobilization. *Sociological Focus, 37*(2), 163–184.

Tong, J., & Zuo, L. (2014). Weibo communication and government legitimacy in China: A computer-assisted analysis of Weibo messages on two "mass incidents." *Information, Communication & Society, 17*(1), 66–85.

Touraine, A. (1988). *Return of the actor: Social theory in postindustrial society* (M. Godzich, Trans.). Minneapolis: University of Minnesota Press.

Traugott, M. (1993). Barricades as repertoire: Continuities and discontinuities in the history of French contention. *Social Science History, 17*(2), 309–323.

Traugott, M. (1995a). Recurrent patterns of collective action. In M. Traugott (Ed.), *Repertoires and cycles of collective action* (pp. 1–14). Durham; London: Duke University Press.

Traugott, M. (1995b). *Repertoires and cycles of collective action*. Durham; London: Duke University Press.

Tsang, E. W. (1998). Can guanxi be a source of sustained competitive advantage for doing business in China? *The Academy of Management Executive, 12*(2), 64–73.

Tseng, S.-F., & Hsieh, Y. P. (2015). The implications of networked individualism for social participation: How mobile phone, e-mail, and IM networks afford social participation for rural residents in Taiwan. *American Behavioral Scientist, 59*(9), 1157–1172.

Tufekci, Z. (2014). The medium and the movement: Digital tools, social movement politics, and the end of the free rider problem. *Policy & Internet, 6*(2), 202–208.

Tufekci, Z., & Wilson, C. (2012). Social media and the decision to participate in political protest: Observations from Tahrir square. *Journal of Communication*, *62*(2), 363–379.

Uehara, E. S. (1995). Reciprocity reconsidered: Gouldner's "moral norm of reciprocity" and social support. *Journal of Social and Personal Relationships*, *12*(4), 483–502.

Valdesolo, P. (2015). Scientists study nomophobia—Fear of being without a mobile phone. *Scientific American*. Retrieved from https://www.scientificamerican.com/article/scientists-study-nomophobia-mdash-fear-of-being-without-a-mobile-phone/

Valenzuela, S. (2013). Unpacking the use of social media for protest behavior: The roles of information, opinion expression, and activism. *American Behavioral Scientist*, *57*(7), 920–942.

Van Laer, J. (2010). Activists online and offline: The internet as an information channel for protest demonstrations. *Mobilization: An International Quarterly*, *15*(3), 347–366.

Van Laer, J., & Van Aelst, P. (2010). Internet and social movement action repertoires: Opportunities and limitations. *Information, Communication & Society*, *13*(8), 1146–1171.

Van Stekelenburg, J., & Klandermans, P. (2009). Social movement theory: Past, present and prospect. In I. van Kessel & S. Ellis (Eds.), *Movers and shakers: Social movements in Africa* (pp. 17–44). Leiden: Brill.

Van Stekelenburg, J., Roggeband, C., & Klandermans, B. (2013). *The future of social movement research: Dynamics, mechanisms, and processes*. Minnesota: University of Minnesota Press.

Viola, L. (1999). *Peasant rebels under Stalin: Collectivization and the culture of peasant resistance*. Oxford: Oxford University Press.

Vosoughi, S., Roy, D., & Aral, S. (2018). The spread of true and false news online. *Science*, *359*(6380), 1146–1151.

Vitak, J., Zube, P., Smock, A., Carr, C. T., Ellison, N., & Lampe, C. (2011). It's complicated: Facebook users' political participation in the 2008 election. *Cyberpsychology, Behavior, and Social Networking*, *14*(3), 107–114.

Wada, T. (2012). Modularity and transferability of repertoires of contention. *Social Problems*, *59*(4), 544–571.

Walder, A. G. (2009). Political sociology and social movements. *Annual Review of Sociology*, *35*, 393–412.

Walgrave, S., Bennett, W. L., Van Laer, J., & Breunig, C. (2011). Multiple engagements and network bridging in contentious politics: digital media use of protest participants. *Mobilization: An International Quarterly*, *16*(3), 325–349.

Walgrave, S., & Wouters, R. (2014). The missing link in the diffusion of protest: Asking others. *American Journal of Sociology*, *119*(6), 1670–1709.

Wall, M. A. (2007). Social movements and email: Expressions of online identity in the globalization protests. *New Media & Society*, *9*(2), 258–277.

Wallis, C. (2013). *Technomobility in China: Young migrant women and mobile phones*. New York: The New York University Press.

Walther, J. B. (1992). Interpersonal effects in computer-mediated interaction: A relational perspective. *Communication Research*, *19*(1), 52–90.

Wang, D. J., & Soule, S. A. (2012). Social movement organizational collaboration: Networks of learning and the diffusion of protest tactics, 1960–1995. *American Journal of Sociology*, *117*(6), 1674–1722.

Wang, Q., & Sun, R. (2010, February 22). Rumors lead to earthquake panic in Shanxi. *China Daily*. Retrieved from http://www.chinadaily.com.cn/china/2010-02/22/content_9481564.htm

Wang, S. S. (2012). China's Internet lexicon: The symbolic meaning and commoditization of Grass Mud Horse in the harmonious society. *First Monday*, 17(1–2).

Wank, D. L. (1996). The institutional process of market clientelism: Guanxi and private business in a South China city. *The China Quarterly*, 147, 820–838.

Ward, M. (2016). Rethinking social movement micromobilization: Multi-stage theory and the role of social ties. *Current Sociology*, 64(6), 853–874.

Washington Times. (2005, March 7). Cell-phone technology an explosive tool for insurgents. *Washington Times*. Retrieved from https://www.washingtontimes.com/news/2005/mar/7/20050307-121323-4533r/

Watts, J. (2010, June 11). Chinese workers strike at Honda Lock parts supplier. *The Guardian*. Retrieved from http://www.guardian.co.uk/business/2010/jun/11/honda-china

Weber, I. (2011). Mobile, online and angry: The rise of China's middle-class civil society? *Critical Arts: South-North Cultural and Media Studies*, 25(1), 25–45.

Weber, L. M., Loumakis, A., & Bergman, J. (2003). Who participates and why? An analysis of citizens on the Internet and the mass public. *Social Science Computer Review*, 21(1), 26–42.

Weeks, B., & Southwell, B. (2010). The symbiosis of news coverage and aggregate online search behavior: Obama, rumors, and presidential politics. *Mass Communication and Society*, 13(4), 341–360.

Weeks, B. E., & Garrett, R. K. (2014). Electoral consequences of political rumors: Motivated reasoning, candidate rumors, and vote choice during the 2008 US presidential election. *International Journal of Public Opinion Research*, 26(4), 401–422.

Wellman, B., & Hampton, K. (1999). Living networked on and offline. *Contemporary Sociology*, 28(6), 648–654.

Wellman, B., & Tindall, D. (1993). Reach out and touch some bodies: How social networks connect telephone networks. *Progress in Communication Sciences*, 12, 63–93.

Wei, R. (2006). Lifestyles and new media: Adoption and use of wireless communication technologies in China. *New Media & Society*, 8(6), 991–1008.

Wei, R. (Ed.) (2016). *Mobile media, political participation, and civic activism in Asia*. London: Springer.

Wei, R., Huang, J., & Zheng, P. (2018). Use of mobile social apps for public communication in China: Gratifications as antecedents of reposting articles from WeChat public accounts. *Mobile Media & Communication*, 6(1), 108–126.

Wei, R., & Lo, V.-H. (2006). Staying connected while on the move: Cell phone use and social connectedness. *New Media & Society*, 8(1), 53–72.

Weill, S. (2001). Hazel and the "Hacksaw": Freedom Summer coverage by the women of the Mississippi Press. *Journalism Studies*, 2(4), 545–561.

Weinberg, B. D., & Pehlivan, E. (2011). Social spending: Managing the social media mix. *Business Horizons*, 54(3), 275–282.

White, M. (2010). Clicktivism is ruining leftist activism. *The Guardian*, 12, 21–23.

Whitten-Woodring, J., & James, P. (2012). Fourth estate or mouthpiece? A formal model of media, protest, and government repression. *Political Communication*, 29(2), 113–136.

Wilson, C., & Dunn, A. (2011). Digital media in the Egyptian revolution: Descriptive analysis from the Tahrir Data Sets. *International Journal of Communication, 5*, 1248–1272.

Wines, M. (2011, December 26). A village in revolt could be a harbinger. *The New York Times*, p. A4.

Wolfsfeld, G., Segev, E., & Sheafer, T. (2013). Social media and the Arab Spring: Politics comes first. *The International Journal of Press/Politics, 18*(2), 115–137.

Wong, C. H., & Geng, O. (2014, October 13). Book ban rumors boost authors in China. *The Wall Street Journal.* Retrieved from https://blogs.wsj.com/chinarealtime/2014/10/13/rumors-of-book-ban-boosts-authors-in-china/

Woodhouse, A. (2015, 05 June). As YouTube celebrates 10th anniversary, Hong Kong leads the way in smartphone viewership. *South China Morning Post.* Retrieved from http://www.scmp.com/tech/enterprises/article/1816330/youtube-celebrates-10th-anniversary-hong-kong-leads-way-smartphone

Wu, D. (2011). Internet, it is not the Garden of Eden for rumors. Retrieved from http://news.xinhuanet.com/comments/2011-08/25/c_121911071.htm

Wu, J. B., Hom, P. W., Tetrick, L. E., Shore, L. M., Jia, L., Li, C., & Song, L. J. (2006). The norm of reciprocity: Scale development and validation in the Chinese context. *Management and Organization Review, 2*(3), 377–402.

Xiang, M. (2011, September 8). 73.1% of interviewees agree that there are a lot of rumors in society. *China Youth Daily*, p. 7.

Xiao, Q. (2011). The battle for the Chinese Internet. *Journal of Democracy, 22*(2), 47–61.

Xiao, Y. (2014). Moral hazard. *Nieman Report, 68*(1), 34–35.

Xie, L., & Zhao, L. (2007). The power of mobile messaging (短信的力量). *China Newsweek (中国新闻周刊), 326*(20), 16–17.

Xie, Y. (2017). It's whom you know that counts. *Science, 355*(6329), 1022–1023.

Xin, K. K., & Pearce, J. L. (1996). Guanxi: Connections as substitutes for formal institutional support. *Academy of Management Journal, 39*(6), 1641–1658.

Xin, Y., & Wen, Y. (2012). The year of the "war on rumor." Retrieved from http://www.rfa.org/english/news/china/internet-12262012131144.html

Xin, Y., & Yang, F. (2013). China's rumor crackdown has "no basis" in law. Retrieved from http://www.rfa.org/english/news/china/rumor-09052013105613.html

Xinhua. (2014). China waging war on online porn, rumors. *China Daily.* Retrieved from http://www.chinadaily.com.cn/china/2014-04/18/content_17446045.htm

Xiong, C. (2011). Catch the evil backstage manipulator of "online rumors." Retrieved from http://views.ce.cn/view/ent/201106/07/t20110607_22464196.shtml

Yan, Y. (1996). *The flow of gifts: Reciprocity and social networks in a Chinese village.* Stanford, CA: Stanford University Press.

Yan, Y. (2009). *The individualization of Chinese society.* Oxford: Berg.

Yang, G. (2000). Achieving emotions in collective action: Emotional processes and movement mobilization in the 1989 Chinese Student Movement. *The Sociological Quarterly, 41*(4), 593–614.

Yang, G. (2009). *The power of the Internet in China: Citizen activism online.* New York: Columbia University Press.

Yang, G. (2011). Technology and its contents: Issues in the study of the Chinese Internet. *The Journal of Asian Studies, 70*, 1043–1050.

Yang, G., & Jiang, M. (2015). The networked practice of online political satire in China: Between ritual and resistance. *International Communication Gazette*, 77(3), 215–231.

Yang, M. M.-h. (1994). *Gifts, favors, and banquets: The art of social relationships in China*. Ithaca: Cornell University Press.

Yang, Y. (2008, December 2). The outbreak of the biggest taxi strike in Guangzhou regardless of preferential measures from the city government. *Lianhezaobao*. Retrieved from http://www.zaobao.com/special/china/cnpol/pages1/cnpol081202.shtml

Yin, R. K. (2009). *Case study research: Design and methods* (4th ed.). London: Sage.

Yiyin. (2011). Where does the odd thought that "to believe in the rumor, rather than government's words" come from? Retrieved from http://opinion.people.com.cn/GB/13900781.html

Youmans, W. L., & York, J. C. (2012). Social media and the activist toolkit: User agreements, corporate interests, and the information infrastructure of modern social movements. *Journal of Communication*, 62(2), 315–329.

YouTube. (2011). Dalian people said "PX, get out of our city!" Retrieved from www.youtube.com/watch?v=skathwniA08

Yu, J. (2008). A review of anger-venting mass incident. *South Wind View*, 15, 20–22.

Yu, L. (2011). Dalian PX protest—More bitter than sweet. Retrieved from http://blog.english.caixin.cn/article/386/

Yu, S. (2010, February 25). Half of the entire province has been awash in rumor within two hours. *Orient Morning Post*, pp. A20–21. Retrieved from http://www.shangbw.com/rexian/201002/25-56374.html

Yu, Z. (2010). Five people arrested for spreading rumor on earthquake in Shanxi by internet and mobile phone. Retrieved from http://boxun.com/news/gb/china/2010/02/201002261539.shtml

Yzer, M. C., & Southwell, B. G. (2008). New communication technologies, old questions. *American Behavioral Scientist*, 52(1), 8–20.

Zaharna, R. S. (1995). Understanding cultural preferences of Arab communication patterns. *Public Relations Review*, 21(3), 241–255.

Zald, M. N., & McCarthy, J. D. (1979). *The dynamics of social movements: Resource mobilization, social control, and tactics*. Cambridge, MA: Winthrop.

Zamponi, L. (2012). "Why don't Italians Occupy?" Hypotheses on a failed mobilisation. *Social Movement Studies*, 11(3–4), 416–426.

Zayani, M. (2015). *Networked publics and digital contention: The politics of everyday life in Tunisia*. Oxford: Oxford University Press.

Zdravomyslova, E. (1996). Opportunities and framing in the transition to democracy: The case of Russia. In D. McAdam, J. D. McCarthy, & M. N. Zald (Eds.), *Comparative perspectives on social movements: Political opportunities, mobilizing structures, and cultural framings* (pp. 122–140). Cambridge: Cambridge University Press.

Zeng, F. (2015). Diffusion effects of Chinese environmental contentions: Cases of Not In My Back Yard conflict. *Journal of Northwest Normal University (Social Sciences Edition)*, 52(3), 110–115.

Zeng, J., Chan, C. h., & Fu, K. w. (2017). How social media construct "truth" around crisis events: Weibo's rumor management strategies after the 2015 Tianjin blasts. *Policy & Internet*, 9(3), 297–320.

Zeng, Z. (2013). Wukan: The whole story. *The China Nonprofit Review*, 5(1), 17–101.

Zhang, J., Zhu, Y., & Huang, L. (2008). Reporters and common folks in Weng'an. *Asian Weekly*, 22(27), http://www.duping.net/XHC/show.php?bbs=10&post=862362.

Zhang, T. (2008, May 14). In Wenchuan earthquake, why science fails to predict? *Lianhezaobao·Opinion*. Retrieved from http://yqshcf.blog.163.com/blog/static/23577500200841564736693/

Zhang, Z. (2010, November 3). A crime in any other country as well. *China Daily*, p. 9.

Zhao, D. (1998). Ecologies of social movements: Student mobilization during the 1989 pro-democracy movement in Beijing. *American Journal of Sociology*, *103*(6), 1493–1529.

Zhao, D. (2010). Theorizing the role of culture in social movements: Illustrated by protests and contentions in modern China. *Social Movement Studies*, *9*(1), 33–50.

Zhao, Y. (1998). *Media, market, and democracy in China: Between the party line and the bottom line.* Urbana: University of Illinois Press.

Zhao, Y. (2009). *Communication in China: Political economy, power, and conflict.* Lanham, MD: Rowman & Littlefield.

Zheng, Y. (2008). *Technological empowerment: The internet, state, and society in China.* Stanford, CA: Stanford University Press.

Zhu, H. (2007, May 30). Xiamen calls an abrupt halt to the PX project to deal with the public crisis. *Southern Weekend*, p. A1.

Zolberg, A. R. (1972). Moments of madness. *Politics & Society*, *2*(2), 183–207.

Zuckerman, E. (2015). Cute cats to the rescue? Participatory media and political expression. In D. Allen & J. S. Light (Eds.), *From voice to influence: Understanding citizenship in a digital age* (pp. 131–154). Chicago: University of Chicago Press.

Žižek, S. (2011). Good manners in the age of WikiLeaks. *London Review of Books*, *33*(2), 9–10.

INDEX